•••••••••••••

DEATH CITY

By the time the fourth and fifth bodies were discovered, Gainesville was beginning to resemble an
overgrown ghost town. Hundreds had already left
campus early for the Labor Day weekend, and
those who stayed behind were on the verge of
panic. Area bars and restaurants were nearly
empty as frightened students huddled together in
their tiny apartments, in dormitories, or in the
motel rooms they had rented as "safe havens"
until the killer was caught. Meanwhile, they slept
with knives, baseball bats, or even machetes by
their sides.

"They were crazy times," recalled Special Agent
Strope. "There were bodies here, bodies there. It
felt like the whole world was coming to an end."

KILLER ON CAMPUS

JAMES FOX AND JACK LEVIN

AVON BOOKS ◆ NEW YORK

KILLER ON CAMPUS is a journalistic account of an actual murder investigation and conviction for the 1990 murders of Sonja Larson, Christina Powell, Christa Leigh Hoyt, Tracy Inez Paules, and Manuel Taboada in Gainesville, Florida. The events recounted in this book are true, although some of the names have been changed. The scenes and dialogue have been reconstructed based on tape-recorded formal interviews, police department records, and published news stories. Quoted court testimony has been taken verbatim from trial transcripts.

AVON BOOKS
A division of
The Hearst Corporation
1350 Avenue of the Americas
New York, New York 10019

Copyright © 1996 by James Fox and Jack Levin
Cover photo by Silver Image
Published by arrangement with the authors
Library of Congress Catalog Card Number: 95-95100
ISBN: 0-380-76525-X

First Avon Books Printing: May 1996

AVON TRADEMARK REG. U.S. PAT. OFF. AND IN OTHER COUNTRIES, MARCA REGISTRADA, HECHO EN U.S.A.

Printed in the U.S.A.

RA   10   9   8   7   6   5   4   3   2   1

•••••••••••••••

Contents

1

▼

A Most Livable City

Gainesville, population 85,000, is a picturesque college town, situated in northcentral Florida off Interstate 75. One of its most attractive features is location: by driving a few hours, you can reach Tampa, Orlando, Jacksonville, Tallahassee, or beaches on either the Atlantic Ocean or the Gulf of Mexico.

In this traditionally sleepy and peaceful community, residents have long been more concerned about Gator football than about crime. More than half of the townsfolk are connected, as students, alumni, or employees, to Gainesville's centerpiece—the pastoral, sprawling, historic campus of the University of Florida—or to the much less obtrusive Santa Fe Community College in the northwest area of the city.

People in town were justifiably proud when Gainesville was selected in 1990 by the editors of *Money* magazine as one of the most livable cities in the United States. Actually, Gainesville was ranked thirteenth—an unlucky distinction to those who are superstitious—up from fifty-third in the previous year's ranking. Many residents believed it should have received a place at the very top of the list. And maybe it would have if street

crime hadn't become such a serious problem in recent
years.

Allan Lee Strope was a newcomer to Gainesville. The
forty-four-year-old former vice cop, with thinning dark
hair, matching mustache, and slightly rounded face, was
the spitting image of Lieutenant Norman Buntz of the
old, but classic, television series *Hill Street Blues*. Lee,
as he prefers to be called, looked so similar to the TV
detective that once, while on an undercover assignment,
a drug pusher approached him with a vague sense of
recognition. "Hey, you're a cop," the pusher said. As
Strope braced himself for trouble, the man added,
"Yeah, I seen you on *Hill Street Blues*."

For Strope, moving to Gainesville, Florida, was supposed to be a refuge from his troubled past. He had
grown up with an alcoholic father he hardly knew. His
dad had spent much of Lee's childhood in jail for a
variety of crimes, including passing bad checks and un-
armed robbery. As an adult, Lee himself had spent far
too many years chasing down criminals, mainly drug
dealers on the ugly streets of Bay City, Michigan.

In moving to the Sunshine State, Strope was anxious
to escape more than just working the vice squad. He
yearned to get away from his painful memories of that
devastating Christmas season, 1979, when his wife unexpectedly left him for good.

Arriving home from work at 1 A.M., Strope saw his
five kids peering out the window. The whole house was
lit up like a Christmas tree; all the lights were on. The
alarmed father rushed inside to see what was wrong.
"Mom's gone," the children told him tearfully. "She
said to tell you she wouldn't be back."

Shortly after the breakup of his marriage, Lee met
Cindy, a sympathetic and attractive young woman who
worked a civilian job in the Bay City Police Department
and had just left her own soured relationship. In 1981,
after a fast and torrid romance, the loving couple moved
with Lee's kids to Casper, Wyoming, where they were

married, and Strope took a job with the Casper Police "dope squad."

In 1984, the Stropes packed their bags and moved cross-country to Pinellas Park, Florida, situated on the west bank of Tampa Bay. Working for the Pinellas Park Police, Lee started and ran the narcotics and vice unit.

Strope had accumulated ten years' experience working in narcotics, and he was growing weary and frustrated. Once in a while, he had taken on homicide cases and had found them more satisfying. "With dope, you never get anywhere," complained Strope. "You make an arrest, and no one goes to jail for very long. But with homicide, you can put the guy away and he never comes out."

In 1988, the right kind of job for Lee opened up in the Gainesville field office of the Florida Department of Law Enforcement (FDLE), Florida's statewide law enforcement agency. His new assignment was homicide.

For Detective Strope, Gainesville bore little resemblance to Bay City, where he was born and raised and had spent most of his adult life. The weather was warm year-round, the pace of life slower, and the crime problem not nearly as vicious. The dope dens in Michigan were replaced by the frat houses at the University of Florida. And the pep rally before the annual Gator–Seminole football clash was a welcome relief from the dreadful race riots that Strope had witnessed up north. For a city vice cop, it was like a breath of fresh air.

The change of scenery did wonders for Lee Strope's personal life as well. He and his wife, Cindy, purchased a comfortable single-family home in town and settled in quickly. Lee's kids seemed to like living in Gainesville and got along well with their friends in the neighborhood.

His new "beat" was pretty tame, even for homicide, consisting mainly of domestic killings that were usually a cinch to solve. As a case agent, his investigations were quick and fairly straightforward. These were typically homicides committed in the heat of the moment by a desperate lover or an estranged spouse. Lee could usually find a clear-cut motivation in jealousy or vengeance, a lengthy history of escalating violence, and plenty of physical evidence to implicate the killer. There would be a heated argument, an exchange of insults and allegations, a violent confrontation. Then a spouse would pull out a gun and shoot the other; or a man would stab his girlfriend to death. And when the police arrived on the scene, the perpetrator would confess. Sometimes he would even call the police himself. Case closed.

In the summer of 1990, Gainesville was caught in a heat wave that didn't want to quit. Air conditioners in apartments and houses all over town worked overtime just to make life tolerable. The bars and lounges on Thirteenth Street and Archer Road overflowed with local residents who were simply looking to cool off a bit before they returned to their sweltering apartments.

Like other residents of Gainesville, Strope was prepared for the yearly influx of tens of thousands of undergraduates in August just before the start of the 1990 fall semester. It was an August that would seriously challenge *Money* magazine's "most livable" classification.

2

"Murder U"

The University of Florida in Gainesville (UF) has long enjoyed the reputation as a great place to go to college. In addition to its strong and expanding academic programs, particularly in preprofessional areas such as journalism and engineering, the UF campus offers a social life that is second to none. Rowdy frat parties, big-time college football, and unbelievable weather except for the much-too-humid months of July and August. If you're an eighteen-year-old, away from home for the first time, what more could you ask for?

But college life at UF is in fact much more than the delightful two thousand-acre, tree-lined campus, with its intriguing blend of old Gothic architecture and modern twentieth-century concrete. The city of Gainesville is a welcoming host to the tens of thousands of students who converge on this student paradise every fall. From the somewhat tattered downtown business district one mile east of campus to the sprawling new malls and shopping centers in the outskirts of town, students have a wide range of options. A variety of bookstores, just about every fast-food chain imaginable, and a plethora of bars all compete for the steady flow of dollars that college students have at their disposal.

The bar scene is especially lively in Gainesville, as one would expect of a major college town. Some enterprising drinking establishments promote ''eight-for-one'' happy hours. Others offer lavish buffets of hot wings and nachos to stimulate sales of beer and margueritas. By far the most imaginative local come-on, the ''bladder-buster'' promo, makes all drinks at the bar free until the first person seeks relief in the restroom. As one bartender explained, ''We all wait to see which wins out, the peer pressure or the pee pressure.''

With all that there is to offer, no wonder UF enrollments boomed during the 1980s while other universities around the country were starving for students. But opening week of school in 1990 radically changed the college's image. The ''Home of the Gators'' soon became known as ''Murder U.''

For the students at UF, the week preceding Labor Day is a time of carefree celebration, party hopping, and drinking before hitting the books. From all parts of the state, young men and women come to Gainesville, eager to make new friends and establish relationships that will last at least until graduation. They come with their cars, trucks, and U-Hauls loaded with clothing and furniture. Sometimes they even bring books.

Eighteen-year-old Scott Henratty was busily preparing for the beginning of his school year at Santa Fe Community College, a few miles up I-75. Accompanied by Bryan Oulton, his roommate and old high school pal, Scott had a few hours to kill before his five o'clock haircut appointment. The two buddies decided to drop over to see Sonja Larson, a long-time mutual friend from their hometown of Pompano Beach who was entering her freshman year at UF.

Eighteen-year-old Sonja was quite attractive, bright, and multitalented. At Ely High School, she had distinguished herself in an advanced academic program in science and preengineering. In addition to her studies,

Sonja also had found ample time to serve as student-manager for the girls' basketball and volleyball teams. Planning to pursue a degree in early childhood education, she was so eager to get started with college that she moved to Gainesville early to enroll in second-session summer-term classes. During this time, she lived in the Weaver Hall dorm on campus.

UF can accommodate only about thirty percent of its more than thirty-four thousand students in on-campus dormitories, leaving most undergraduates to locate suitable housing somewhere in the surrounding community. As a result, Gainesville is dotted with apartment complexes bearing such names as Hawaiian Village, Gatorwood, Casablanca East, and the like. Sonja was one of the unlucky ones who was unable to secure on-campus housing for the fall even after living in university housing during the summer term. But she was thrilled nonetheless to find a comfortable and affordable three-bedroom apartment to share with two other girls.

Henratty and Oulton knew that Sonja had found an apartment at the Williamsburg Village apartment complex on Southwest Sixteenth Street, right next to the Veteran's Medical Center and just a short walk from the UF campus. The two young men decided to stop by to see how Sonja's new place was shaping up. They would have called first, but her phone line wasn't working as yet.

Just as they were about to turn into the rows of white wooden duplexes and townhouses in Williamsburg, Henratty recognized Sonja's car, a silver Honda CRX, approaching ahead, moving slowly on the access road leading to Sixteenth Street. Larson was with her new roommate, 17-year-old Christina Powell, a freshman from Jacksonville, Florida.

Powell felt lucky to be going to the UF, especially since none of her six older brothers and sisters ever attended college. She had a great sense of humor and enjoyed a well-rounded life, which included playing catcher on the girl's softball team. Dimpled and pretty, with shoulder-length dark hair, Christi was always pop-ular with the boys in high school and had plenty of friends. She hoped that her freshmen year would bring her lots of new friends as well, and she was about to meet two new guys.

Henratty rolled down his window and yelled, "Hey, Sonja. *Qué pasa?*"

"I'm just goin' out to do some shopping," Powell replied with a cheerful smile. "Scott and Bryan, this is my roommate, Christi. These are my friends from high school."

"How about we all go out for a few drinks and maybe something to eat?" suggested Henratty.

"OK. Where to?"

"How about Chili's over on Archer Road."

Henratty felt good to see a familiar face in these un-familiar surroundings and invited Sonja and Christina to come by their apartment later on that evening. The girls had a lot to do in getting their own place ready but promised they would try to come over if they could.

Two days later, Saturday, August 25, Henratty had a morning orientation session at Santa Fe, which lasted barely more than an hour. Afterward, he dropped over to see how Sonja was doing, but no one answered his knock. Walking around to the side of the apartment, Henratty saw his friend's car parked outside and he be-came concerned. He stopped by again later that night at about 10:30, but just as before, no one seemed to be home.

Apparently, others had grown concerned as well. Christina Powell's sister, Barbara Milcum, and her hus-band had stopped by at 5 P.M. on Saturday in order to deliver some used furniture. Surprised that Christi had failed to meet them as arranged, they posted a blue note on the door, just beneath the brass apartment number 113 on the front door. The Milcums returned several times that evening to try and locate Christina, each time adding to their posted message and begging her to call home ASAP:

Christi,

*We decided to come back one more time. It is now
9:45. Mom said for you to call her when ya get
home tonight no matter how late it is!!!*

Seeing a stream of messages on the apartment door,
Henratty scribbled his own note announcing his visit:

Sonya,

This is Scott and crew.
It is 10:20. We're going to a party.
Come by our house after 2 P.M.

By Sunday, August 26, Frank and Patricia Powell of
Jacksonville could wait no longer to hear from their in-
explicably absent daughter. They tried to keep in mind
that Christina was likely busy out buying food and
household supplies for her new apartment as well as
making friends. But she had not called for days even
though she had promised to do so, and she clearly had
not been home either. It was not at all like their daughter
to be so unreliable; something had to be wrong. So the
worried parents hopped in their car and drove west on
I-10, then south down Routes 301 and 24, the seventy-
five miles to Gainesville.

When they arrived at Christi's apartment, all they
found was the sequence of messages left for the missing
girls. They added their own plea on top of those that
had been accumulating over the weekend. On the back
of a scrap of paper, they wrote:

Christi,

It is now 11:35 A.M. Sunday.
Wait here until we come back.

                         Mom and Dad

By midafternoon, the Powells grew weary in their efforts to remain calm and patient. Not knowing what else
to do, they contacted the apartment manager and asked

for help in investigating Christi's whereabouts. Given the suspicious circumstances, Phillip Rock, maintenance worker for Williamsburg Village, in turn called the Gainesville Police.

"We gotta wait here for the police before we enter an apartment. It's the rules, you know," said Rock.

At about 3:00 in the afternoon, before going off duty, Gainesville Police Officer Ray Barber, a ten-year veteran of the force, responded to the call for assistance. He immediately located the maintenance man and, together with Christina Powell's parents, tried to enter apartment 113.

The girls' unit occupied the top two floors of the three-story building. The kitchen entrance was from a back porch up a flight of wooden stairs at the rear of the building. A second entrance was located on the top floor through an interior hallway.

"None of these keys seem to work," complained Rock after trying his entire set of master keys to gain access through the kitchen. The heavy door appeared to be recently damaged, as if someone had tried to break through it. Hoping not to alarm the Powells unnecessarily, Barber said nothing about the fresh marks on the door.

Rock looked over to the worried father and said, "If we have to break in, you're responsible for the damage."

"Of course," Powell replied impatiently. "Just do it!"

Officer Barber took a stick and broke a small windowpane. Reaching inside, he found that the door was locked with a double-sided dead bolt. Rather than force open the rear outside door, he decided that it would be better to break down the interior door which led from the third floor hallway to the upstairs bedrooms.

Standing back to get a running start, Rock rammed his right shoulder against the door, collapsing it, frame and all, into Sonya Larson's bedroom. Catching his balance, Rock got a quick glimpse of the horror inside. Rock was visibly shaken and sickened by what he saw and dashed out to let the police take over.

"What's going on in there?" pleaded Frank Powell.

"I'm sorry, Mr. Powell, but you're going to have to wait outside," Barber replied.

"Why? What happened to my daughter? If she's in there, I've gotta go in. My daughter needs me."

"I'm sorry, sir. I can't let you in. There's nothing that you can do. Please wait outside."

Officer Barber found Larson's body lying in a pool of blood on the waterbed, her arms raised high over her head and her legs spread apart and dangling over the side of the bed. Her body was pulled halfway off the mattress, almost as if the killer had purposely tried to display her vagina to whomever discovered the body.

Larson was completely naked, except for a blood-stained multicolored T-shirt that was raised above her breasts and around her neck. A huge hole in her left thigh looked as though a chunk of flesh had been removed. It would later be determined, however, that the skin in that area had shrunk due to postmortem deterioration, leaving the bone exposed. Both her breasts were punctured from multiple stab wounds, including five tightly clustered cuts to the right nipple and a large gash on the side of the left breast. The inside of her right arm was covered with eleven bloody knife wounds. All her wounds had hemorrhaged, having been inflicted before death mercifully set in.

Larson's body had already begun the early process of decomposition, with her skin having turned a grayish green color, her face bloated, and her stomach distended. The entire scene looked almost surreal in its utter savagery.

Using his portable telephone, Officer Barber immediately called for backup before further exploring the crime scene. Under no condition would he permit the Powells to enter the townhouse turned slaughterhouse. Whether their daughter Christina was also inside remained to be seen, but it was not for her anxious parents to see.

Rock waited with the Powells while Barber continued

his search. The officer stepped slowly around Larson's bedroom, careful not to disturb anything. The room was cluttered with half-unpacked boxes and shopping bags, various household items, and pieces of clothing strewn about. But possibly the disheveled room would hold some vitally important evidence, even something as minuscule as the killer's hairs, that might help the police in solving the crime.

After checking the rest of the upstairs, Officer Barber moved apprehensively down to the lower floor of the apartment. The killer was probably long gone, given the length of time that the notes from friends and relatives had remained posted outside the apartment, not to mention the apparent condition of Larson's corpse. Still, even a seasoned veteran would wonder what other horrors he might encounter as he continued his search of the premises. Barber kept his gun out and ready just in case.

It did not take long for the other shoe to drop. Reaching the bottom floor, Barber immediately spotted the body of another woman—later to be identified as Christina Powell—lying on the beige carpet in the living room. Barber was shocked by the cruel ritualism that was reflected in the aftermath of this murder. It was strikingly different from the frenzied scene he had discovered on the top floor.

Powell's body lay flat on her back, spread-eagled and broadside in front of the living room couch. The contents of her brown leather purse were spilled onto the floor just above her head, suggesting that robbery may have been part of the motive for the crimes. In fact, no folding money was found anywhere in the apartment, and the rings regularly worn both by Larson and by Powell were missing from their fingers. Strangely, a six-by-nine-inch snapshot of a young man and woman together, likely from the pocketbook, had been cut in half, with the female portion missing.

A variety of personal and household items were strewn about, including a hammer and a framed picture that looked like it was about to be mounted on the wall.

A spiral notebook rested just above her head. There were crumpled paper towels everywhere that the intruder appeared to have used to clean himself. A white cotton bra, sliced apart at the shoulder straps, lay next to Powell's body. The brassiere appeared to have been pulled off forcefully. Her mustard-colored T-shirt also lay next to her corpse and appeared to have been torn off. By contrast, her panties, although stained with semen, had been neatly folded and placed near her left foot.

Tape marks were found on Powell's mouth, wrists, and ankles, leaving the impression that she would have suffered tremendously while bound and gagged, waiting for death. Blond and brown hairs were found stuck on the glue residue from the tape, perhaps left there by the killer—or killers.

Although initially hidden from view, Powell had died as a result of five deep stab wounds to her back, all within an area of not much more than five to six square inches. One of the wounds was so deep that it passed through her chest and exited below her right breast. Each knife wound was angled at one end and squared off at the other, indicating that a single-edge cutting instrument had been used to kill the young woman.

The most bizarre discovery of all involved sexual ritual. Between Powell's legs rested a towel and an empty bottle of blue Dawn dishwashing liquid. The killer seemed to have cleaned her with a soapy douche before raping her and perhaps afterward as well. Equally bizarre, Powell's nipples had been amputated with surgical skill. Yellow circles of discolored tissue, two and a half inches in diameter on the left breast and slightly larger on the right, were visible where her nipples had been.

The breast mutilation was particularly odd and perplexing. Had the killer butchered Powell in order to increase his victim's pain and suffering? The total lack of hemorrhaging around her injuries indicated, however, that the nipples had been cut and excised after Powell's death.

Another possibility was that this barbaric act had been performed for sheer shock value—as if the crime wasn't shocking enough already. Because the nipples themselves were nowhere to be found, however, it seemed most likely instead that the killer had saved them for his own gruesome collection.

If so, this wouldn't be a first in the annals of true crime. Like a ballplayer who keeps the baseball from his first major league home run, sexual sadists often collect memorabilia or souvenirs—diaries, clothing, photos, even body parts—to remind them of their most cherished moments with their victims. The Gainesville case clearly had a strong element of souvenir hunting and sexual sadism. The frenzied crime scene upstairs in Larson's bedroom might have been interpreted as the act of a jealous boyfriend gone berserk—a one-time fit of passion and rage. However, the downstairs ritualistic murder was an ominous harbinger of worse crimes yet to come. Only a sexual sadist would save and cherish his victim's nipples and rape her while she was bound and gagged. This was likely a man driven by sexual fantasy involving rape, mutilation, and perhaps even necrophilia.

The police speculated about the psychological significance of the macabre memento that the murderer had carried away from the crime scene. For a man who otherwise may have led an unremarkable life, his surgical souvenirs would likely represent a source of pride—a symbol of his conquest over the two young women. More important, the nipples could serve as tangible reminders of the "good times" with his victims. With the aid of his erotic trophies, he could extend the pleasure through reminiscing, daydreaming, fantasizing, and even masturbating.

The most disconcerting speculation was that these crimes would very likely be repeated sometime, somewhere. A sex slayer tends to have incredibly rich, vivid, detailed, and elaborate fantasies that drive him to kill and kill again. Through murder and mayhem, he literally chases his dreams. With each successive victim, he attempts to perfect the act, striving to make real-life experiences as good as his fantasies. But as the crimes "improve" and become more vicious, the killer's mental script becomes more demanding. Not only is his behavior inspired by fantasy, his fantasy is inspired by the crimes he has committed. As a result, the killer's fantasies and murders grow increasingly brutal and grotesque. The Gainesville police had a real problem on their hands—as they would soon learn.

Of course, they would have preferred to think that this was an isolated case and that the culprit would soon turn out to be a disgruntled boyfriend who had been rejected and went berserk. But that theory soon dissolved in the face of new and even more chilling events.

3

With Surgical Skill

Lieutenant John Henry Nobles, chief of detectives for the Alachua County Sheriff's Office (ASO), was concerned that his records clerk had not shown up for work. It was already past midnight, early Monday morning, August 27, and it was certainly not like eighteen-year-old Christa Leigh Hoyt to be late, even for the twelve to eight graveyard shift, as it's frequently called.

Hoyt, a petite young woman with a pretty face, brown hair, and blue eyes, was as dependable as anyone could be. As an honors student, majoring in chemistry, she worked extremely hard in her classes at Santa Fe Community College and was scheduled to graduate in September. Aspiring toward a career in law enforcement, especially criminalistics, Christa took her part-time job in the records department as seriously as her schoolwork. Ever since joining the sheriff's Explorers program as a teenager, Christa had a clear sense of what she wanted to do with her life. In addition to her self-reliance and determination, her friendly manner earned her the nickname Glowworm.

Ten months earlier, Christa had moved out of her family home in Archer, a few miles away from Gainesville, anxious to be out on her own at last. Despite her self-assured, independent air, she had a special, childlike fondness for teddy bears. According to her stepsister, "When she went to bed she would keep them with her. She slept in the middle of them all."

Lieutenant Nobles asked a clerk in the Communications Dispatch Center to try reaching Christa by phone, but she only got a recording. "Christa, if you're there, pick up the telephone. This is Gail in CDC. Hello. Hello, Christa. It's 1:36 in the morning and you need to be at work. Hello."

Lieutenant Nobles then told Deputy Sheriff Keith M. O'Hara to take a ride over in his cruiser to 3533 Southwest Twenty-fourth Avenue in order to check to see if Hoyt was sick or if something else was wrong.

Because of the poor lighting in the apartment complex, Deputy O'Hara had a difficult time finding Christa's unit. After almost fifteen minutes of searching through the darkened grounds, he finally located apartment M and knocked loudly on the front door. Thinking that Christa may have overslept—an easy thing to do for those working the late shift—he pounded harder and harder on the wooden door. The only response he got was from the apartment manager, Elbert Hoover, who had been awakened by the noise and came outside to investigate.

"What's going on here?" said Hoover, sounding somewhat annoyed.

"My name is Officer O'Hara of the Alachua County Sheriff's Office. I'm checking on a Ms. Christa Hoyt who resides in apartment M. Can you tell me where I might find the resident manager?"

"That's me," Hoover replied. "I can let you into her apartment if you want."

Suddenly, Hoover noticed something strange on the side of Hoyt's apartment. The wooden gate in front of the storage area just didn't look right. Inside a narrow corridor leading toward Hoyt's glass slider, the chain-link fence separating Hoyt's patio from her neighbors had been pulled down.

"Wait here for a minute. I'll check it out," said the

deputy as he considered the possibility that an intruder might still be on the premises.

O'Hara climbed over the broken fence to the sliding door leading into Hoyt's bedroom. The blinds were drawn, but the left side was raised slightly, enough to take a peek inside. Down on his hands and knees, the deputy shined his flashlight inside the bedroom.

Scanning the room, the light caught a pair of feet wearing tennis socks and sneakers and resting on the floor next to the bed. Deputy O'Hara moved the beam slowly upward until it revealed the form of a woman's naked body with legs spread apart, sitting motionless and slumped forward on the edge of the bed. Raising the light further still, O'Hara feared he would find the face of his colleague Christa Hoyt. He did not see her face—the body was headless. O'Hara radioed back to dispatch for a supervisor.

Martin Snook, a nineteen-year veteran investigator, arrived at Hoyt's apartment at about 3 A.M. to oversee the grim task of probing and chronicling the murder. He began the slow and difficult task of processing the crime scene. Every inch of the one-bedroom apartment had to be photographed, and every article of clothing and jewelry had to be cataloged as evidence. Almost anything, no matter how trivial it now seemed, could be an important key to solving the homicide.

Although the crime scene was to be videotaped by Deputy Al Rawls, Snook had to record with extreme precision every detail about the apartment. Walking through the front door into the living room, Snook first noticed a racket for racquetball and a can of balls. Christa had played her last match with long-time friend Paul Schwartz a few hours before her death. A blanket and pillow rested on the floor in front of the TV. Next to that was a set of keys, including two from the ASO. It looked to Detective Snook that Hoyt had come in from playing racquetball and had lain on the floor to watch some television for a while.

Even with his years of experience in working gruesome crime scenes, the detective was truly shaken by what he saw next as he peered down the narrow hallway into the bedroom. Crista Hoyt's head had been displayed on the top shelf of a bookcase. Her head was sandwiched between the left edge of the bookshelf and a small wooden jewelry box.

In a macabre scene, Hoyt's severed head had been trimmed neatly at the neck and carefully placed on a bookshelf for all to see. Other than two small scratches near her left eye, she barely had a mark on her. The tranquil expression on her face masked the extreme horror of her last moments of life.

Hoyt's lifeless, decapitated body was slumped over on the waterbed, naked except for her white socks and sneakers. Her trunk was sliced open from her breast bone to her pubic bone, and her internal organs had swollen outside of her abdomen, showing her gas-filled intestines, greenish-colored abdominal lining, and colon. The decomposition was already setting in, accelerated by the heat from the waterbed.

Hoyt's back was marbleized as a result of lividity. The victim's body had been lying flat, causing her blood to settle at its lowest point, in the area of the back. As a result, it was evident to Detective Snook that the killer would then have had to wait for some time—perhaps hours—before posing his victim's body upright.

A single two-inch knife wound entered her back and exited just below her breast. A subsequent autopsy would determine that the seven-and-a-half-inch-deep cut passed from her back, between her ribs, through her aorta, lung, and heart before terminating in the soft tissue of her left breast. As with Christina Powell, Hoyt's nipples had been carefully excised, leaving behind near perfect circles of about two and a half inches in diameter. The nipples were found hidden within the bedsheets.

Snook observed various articles of clothing and personal items scattered about the corpse. A torn T-shirt was rolled into a ball on the bed, her black shorts lay on the floor. Her bra and panties were also found, both apparently damaged from cutting or tearing. A used tampon was found on the bed against the wall. Hoyt's pocketbook had been emptied out onto the bed, leaving in plain view a fresh sanitary napkin, checkbook, lipstick, and birth control pill case.

A pink-flowered pillowcase, apparently taken from the bed, was stashed in the corner on the floor near the bookshelf. Inside the case, Snook found three framed photographs of Christa Hoyt—presumably taken from the headboard over the bed. Snook figured that the killer had fled the scene in haste, perhaps forgetting to take with him his souvenir bag of photos as well as the nipples left in the bed.

The glass sliding door leading to the back patio area was closed but damaged. There were several pry marks on the edge of the door where it butts up against the frame and several pry marks on the frame itself. A piece of the locking mechanism was knocked off, likely happening when the intruder broke his way into the room.

Some striking similarities to the Larson/Powell murders could not be ignored. All three victims were murdered with a knife; the lab would later determine that the knife wounds were produced by the same kind of instrument—a military Marine Corps knife called a Ka-Bar. Powell and Hoyt were both bound with tape; a lab comparison of the width of tape marks and the residue would later indicate a match. Both apartments were broken into using a sharp instrument; subsequent lab analysis would conclude that the same tool was in fact used. Both Powell and Hoyt were raped and both victims had their nipples mutilated in the same way.

It was also impossible to ignore the fact that a serial killer was on the loose in Gainesville and wreaking havoc on young, attractive coeds.

4

▼

Calling in the FDLE

Although not a member of the Gainesville Police Department (GPD) nor the ASO that had jurisdiction over the murders, Lee Strope had been kept informed about the gruesome details. At dawn, Monday morning, while most local residents were reading about the Williamsburg killings in the *Gainesville Sun*, Strope was already on the phone discussing the latest episode, the discovery of Christa Hoyt's body just a few hours earlier. He was shocked to learn that a sadistic killer had apparently struck again and that the third victim had been brutalized so viciously. He was also saddened to find out that Hoyt had law enforcement ties, having worked part-time for the ASO.

Strope had mixed feelings about the possibility that he might be asked to assist local and county law enforcement agencies in solving the case. On the one hand, he was intrigued, like everyone else, about the modus operandi involved in the three bizarre and gruesome slayings. At the same time, however, Lee was a bit relieved that the responsibility for cracking this perplexing case wouldn't fall on his shoulders. Anyway, it reminded him too much of the senseless crimes that he thought he had left behind in Bay City.

After breakfast, Strope attended a briefing at GPD on Northwest Sixth Street to discuss the murders of the three college students, Christina Powell, Sonja Larson, and Christa Hoyt. FDLE Bureau Chief Robert Smith, Assistant Bureau Chief Jack Wise, Special Agent Supervisor J. O. Jackson, and Special Agent John Burton also were present. It was decided at the time that Strope and other FDLE agents would assist the GPD and the ASO in carrying out the investigation of the two crime scenes.

As "luck" would have it, Lee Strope was selected as case agent, making him the focal point of the investigation into the three student murders. He was honored and flattered to have been assigned an important breaking case. But at that point, he could not have imagined the enormity of the task that lay ahead. He could not have foreseen that this would be the case of a lifetime. With A. L. Strope as case agent, the Gainesville murders were assigned the FDLE case number: GA-90-01-003.

5

Instant Terror on Campus

"We don't want to create panic," said Lieutenant Sadie Darnell, age thirty-eight, spokeswoman for the GPD, "but people need to be cautious about who they let into their apartments and who they let into their cars."[1]

Regardless of Darnell's desire not to inspire panic and her quiet demeanor, once the press released word of the latest horror, Gainesville became rife with fear.

Authorities believed the killings were somehow connected, said Gainesville's Police Chief Wayland Clifton in a statement of what was already painfully obvious to worried students and their parents. At the first crime scene, one of the victims was found nude and another was partially nude, police reported in a press conference.

"We're looking at a number of leads, a lot of evidence, but we can't say we have a definite suspect in mind," Clifton said with a heavy southern drawl.

Reporters pressed hard for details of the crimes. But Clifton sternly refused to give any information as to the condition of the third victim's body or to disclose how the three young women had been slain.

---

[1]Ron Word, "Three Young Women Found Slain Near Florida University," Associated Press, August 27, 1990.

The slayings prompted a flood of anxious telephone calls to police and the university, where classes began Monday. "We're receiving calls from all over, particularly from out-of-state parents," said Darnell. UF spokeswoman Linda Gray said the University also was inundated with anxious phone calls.

John Lombardi, newly installed UF president, had more than faculty grievances and student politics on his first-year agenda. He spent the first morning of the fall semester responding to the concerns of apprehensive family members and terrified students. By the end of the day, the university had already set up a free phone bank for the purpose of helping students to keep in touch with their alarmed parents.

Thousands of UF students made calls to their parents, jamming the long-distance lines for hours on end. The alumni office set up an emergency hot line and the university established a phone bank at a local shopping center, where students could call home. University officials kept in touch with one another by means of cellular phones, which they wore on their frequent travels around campus.

Local leaders sought to reduce the growing fears of students that the killer might strike again. The university promised to provide emergency on-campus housing in dormitory lobbies, lounges, recreation rooms, and even the gym to any student who wanted it. Church members offered to open their private homes as well. Police Chief Clifton promised, "In the next few days, in the next few evenings, you will see more police coverage than in any city you've ever lived in."[2]

Some students remained unconvinced. A twenty-one-year-old junior reminded a *New York Times* reporter that the image of a protected ivory tower campus has become little more than a myth, at least in Gainesville. "I used to live in New York City," Marti Upton told the reporter. "And I've had much more crime happen to me here than in New York."[3]

---

[2]Peter Applebome, *New York Times*, August 29, 1990, p. 6.
[3]*Ibid.*, p. 6.

6

▼

Bad Things Come in Threes

Tracy Inez Paules and Manuel "Manny" Taboada, both age twenty-three, had been close friends ever since high school. Tracy really was the all-American girl, having been selected by her classmates at American High School in Hialeah as both class president and homecoming queen. As a top student, finishing fifteenth in her graduating class, Tracy was chosen class salutatorian for commencement exercises. She was also deeply involved in extracurricular activities, including cheerleading, soccer, and softball.

Paules was popular among her peers in high school and at UF, where she majored in political science with definite plans to attend law school. With her stunning good looks, vivacious personality, and athleticism, she was often the center of attention within her large circle of friends.

Manny was no slouch either. In high school he played varsity football. In college he redirected his energies and attention to preparing for a career in architecture, a strength at UF, but he also set a little time aside to pursue a spot on the UF rowing team. Manny maintained a muscular physique by working out on a regular basis.

For her senior year, Tracy decided to accept Manny's

invitation for her to move into his place. His roommate had recently moved out, and there was a vacant bedroom available. This would be a good way to cut down on living expenses. After all, Tracy was saving up for law school, having worked hard all summer temping in a number of Miami law firms near her home. Moving in together was the smart thing to do; two could study as cheaply as one.

The friends shared a fairly typical two-bedroom apartment in a fairly typical Gainesville apartment complex known as Gatorwood. The buildings were indeed constructed of wood, and a wooden gator sign out front told passersby on busy Archer Road that this was "The Place to Be."

Given its recent history of burglaries and break-ins, about one per month during the past few years, the Gatorwood's slogan might more appropriately have read "The Place to B&E." Because of its proximity to a main thoroughfare, its wooded surroundings on three sides, and its lack of security, the complex offered easy egress for small-time thieves planning to make a quick getaway with stolen stereos and TVs.

By late August 1990, however, burglary was the last thing on the minds of nervous residents of Gatorwood and other apartment complexes in and around Gainesville. A vicious killer was on the loose, and everyone who hadn't left town was painfully aware of the danger. It seemed like open season on young, attractive coeds.

On Sunday evening, August 26, Lisa Buyer, long-time friend of Tracy and Manny, was understandably upset about the slayings but felt unable to help from her home hundreds of miles away in Fort Lauderdale, where she had a job in advertising. When first hearing on the late news about the Larson/Powell murders, Lisa called Tracy to see how she was holding up amidst the fear that she imagined would be sweeping through town. Although it was late, just before midnight, certain calls were too important to wait until morning. Besides, she imagined, Tracy was probably still awake anyway.

"I can't believe what happened up there," said Lisa.

"What are you talking about?" replied Tracy.

"The murders!"

"What murders?"

Lisa was surprised to learn that Tracy was totally unaware of the tragedy that had befallen two UF students just blocks away. Tracy had spent the weekend in Coco Beach and Merritt Island with her boyfriend, Kris Pascarella, and the couple had listened to nothing other than music on cassette while driving back to Gainesville. Tracy and Lisa spent an hour on the phone agonizing over the horrible event at Williamsburg Village.

Lisa was worried about Tracy. She would have felt a lot better if Manny were home. As big and strong as he was, he would be able to fight or scare off anyone who might try to break into their apartment. But Manny was working late, bartending at Bennigan's. Before hanging up, Lisa begged Tracy to lock the doors and be careful and told her that she'd call again the next day.

On Monday morning, August 27, Lisa was still uneasy thinking about the double murder at Williamsburg. She tried to phone Tracy, but no one answered. All day long Lisa grew increasingly alarmed at not being able to reach her pal. She called Tom Caroll, a mutual friend of theirs, but he hadn't heard from Tracy or Manny since early in the weekend.

Caroll wasn't able to do much over the phone to make Lisa feel any better, except to offer a variety of theories that might account for Tracy's and Manny's seeming disappearance.

"They're probably so busy with starting class and buying books that they probably didn't have time to call back," said Caroll, trying unsuccessfully to alleviate Buyer's distress. "Maybe they just haven't even checked the answering machine."

But for Lisa's sake, if not his own, Tom called over to Bennigan's to inquire as to whether Manny was at work. He was not even though he was scheduled to be.

Both Lisa and Tom had left numerous messages on Tracy and Manny's answering machine and hadn't heard from either for almost two days. By Tuesday morning, it was time to be more aggressive. They hadn't heard from Tracy or Manny, but they had heard of news reports of a third murder in Gainesville.

Lisa called Tom at 6:30 A.M.

"I'm sorry to wake you, Tom, but I'm really worried big time," admitted Lisa. "Would you mind taking a ride over to Tracy's and see what's going on?"

"What's that going to accomplish, Lisa?"

"I don't know, but if you won't go, I'm gonna have to drive all the way up there myself. I can't just sit here and wait to hear from them anymore. Something's wrong. I know it."

Caroll had an apartment in Rockwood Villas, not far from Gatorwood, and agreed to drive over to see if there was any sign of their missing friends. Their cars were there, but no one seemed to be home when he knocked on the door of apartment 1203.

Caroll found a pay phone and reported back to Lisa, who was nervously waiting to hear from him. No news was not good news as far as she was concerned. They agreed that, given the circumstances, it would not be at all inappropriate to ask the Gatorwood management office to get someone to check the inside of the apartment.

About twenty minutes later, Chris Smith, maintenance man who lived within the complex, met Tom Caroll outside of building 12. Smith knocked loudly on the apartment door and got the same result as Tom. No answer, not even a sound.

Smith turned to Carroll and said apologetically, "I'll bet you already tried knockin', huh?"

"Uh huh," he mumbled with a nod.

"All right then," the maintenance man said a bit apprehensively and removed a master key from his pocket.

Opening the door slowly, Smith and Caroll immediately saw Tracy's body lying prone on the beige carpet, twelve feet from the entrance to the apartment. Sickened by their discovery, both men hurried back into the hallway. Smith called the police to report a homicide, and Caroll called Lisa to report the tragic news.

In his four-and-one-half years with the ASO, Deputy

Dan Alexander had never encountered anything quite like what he would see that day. But then, that would be true for just about everyone on the force. Nothing in the police academy ever prepared them for dealing with the kinds of atrocities that had hit Gainesville in late August.

At about eight in the morning, Deputy Alexander was driving his cruiser down Archer Road on his way home, tired after having worked the midnight shift. He heard a call over the police radio that the body of a young woman had been found in the Gatorwood complex. Since he was literally right in front of Gatorwood when the broadcast came over the radio, he made a quick turn into the entrance of the complex to respond to the emergency.

Alexander met up with the maintenance man, Chris Smith, in front of building 12, located in the corner of the complex next to a small pond. Smith led him to apartment 1203, and then Alexander was on his own. As he entered, the deputy saw on the hallway floor in front of him the nude body of a young female. He also saw a trail of blood leading from the back right-hand bedroom to her body. It appeared to Alexander that the intruder had likely killed Paules in her bedroom and then had dragged her into the hall in order to shock whomever came through the door. Her body was displayed with a towel tucked beneath her buttocks.

A subsequent autopsy found that she had died from three stab wounds to her back that had penetrated her left lung. She had also been raped in her anus. Her pubic and anal area was coated with a soapy film that matched a bottle of dishwasher liquid recovered from the kitchen.

Following the trail of dried blood into the victim's bedroom, Alexander noted that Paules's bedsheets were yanked off in the direction of the bedroom door, further suggesting that she had been pulled from the bed and into the hallway. Her arms were also raised above her head as though dragged across the carpeted floor. Her suitcase, the one she had used for the presemester weekend getaway with her boyfriend, appeared to have been rifled through, and the items in her purse had been dumped out onto the bed.

Alexander moved cautiously through the two-bedroom apartment to make certain that the assailant wasn't hiding somewhere behind a door or in a closet. Entering the back left bedroom, he encountered the body of Manny Taboada. The victim was lying on the bed in a large pool of blood, wearing his undershorts and socks. His red T-shirt was saturated with blood of an even deeper shade of red. His arms and his face were also covered with blood, and his internal organs had swelled through a large open knife wound in his stomach.

Taboada had suffered multiple stab wounds. From the blood splatter on the wall above the headboard and the defensive wounds on his trunk and arms, Deputy Alexander could tell that Manny had put up quite a struggle. He died with his eyes open wide.

Both victims were dead, and the assailant had long since fled the scene. Alexander realized that there was nothing more he could do except to guard the premises until the detectives arrived to process the crime scene.

Lee Strope was on his way to the GPD when he received word that two more bodies had been found. He immediately drove toward Archer Road and the third crime scene. Strope arrived at Gatorwood and met with Special Agents Steve Leary and Allen Miller, who were there to begin processing the crime scene. Their task was to examine the murder scene, looking for fingerprints, shoe prints, blood spatters and stains, hairs, fibers, tool marks, anything out of the ordinary that might help solve the crime.

The FDLE had recently joined the effort to identify the madman who was terrorizing the city of Gainesville. With FDLE's involvement, the investigation would benefit from the special skills of its personnel and top-notch crime labs. FDLE crime scene analysts received over four hundred hours of intensive training in criminalistics and crime scene investigation techniques. Now they would be put to the test.

The typical serial killer transports his victims to a re-

mote dump site or makeshift grave. Finding a body does
not provide very much in the way of physical evidence,
particularly if the body is exposed to the elements and
to insects. Most of the physical evidence associated with
the murder is located in the killer's car or apartment.
Without a suspect, however, detectives don't have much
to ship to the lab.

In many respects, therefore, the Gainesville investigators were fortunate, more fortunate than in most other
serial murder cases. At least they had a crime scene to
investigate. Still, Agents Leary and Miller had a big job
ahead of them. They examined Paules's feet, ankles, and
legs. They photographed and scraped the tape residue
from her limbs. Since she had been dragged from the
bedroom into the hall, they also dusted for full or partial
fingerprints on her body. They collected everything that
could have any evidentiary value: blood, paper towels
that the killer appeared to have used to clean himself,
the towel left between Paules's legs, and a half-full bottle of Lilac dishwashing liquid from the kitchen.

One of the first items that they noted was a broken
lock on the sliding door, determined to be the point of
entry used by the perpetrator. This was the same type
of break-in found at the other two murder scenes. The
drapes covering the window in Taboada's bedroom had
been closed shut with two-inch duct tape, the same type
of tape used to bind Paules. The killer had, uncharac-
teristically, forgotten to remove the tape from the drapes.

Perhaps he had left abruptly for some yet unknown
reason, imagined Strope, as he looked around at the dev-
astation. The crime scene in the Gatorwood apartment
reminded him of the drug-related shootings he had left
in Michigan—only this was a lot worse.

7

"Decapigator"

When Patrick Sessions picked up his copy of the morning newspaper, he read the front-page headline and wondered: Could the murders of the students in Gainesville possibly be linked to the disappearance of his daughter Tiffany some twenty months earlier? Tiffany was a UF student who disappeared mysteriously near her Gainesville apartment on the afternoon of February 9, 1989. The twenty-year-old junior, majoring in business, vanished without so much as a clue while jogging along a secluded road southwest of the university, near I-75. Leaving her apartment complex, Casablanca East, the blond coed wore a red sweatsuit and carried a Walkman radio. She had left her keys and wallet behind, informing her roommate that she would shortly return.

Detective Strope had been case agent for the Sessions investigation, one of his first major assignments after arriving in Gainesville. This was also one of his most thoroughly investigated, but frustrating cases.

"It was like she was snatched off the face of the earth by aliens looking for human specimens," Strope recalled. "She simply walked into the woods and never came out. She vanished without a clue."

Tiffany's father, Patrick, lent more than a hand to the

investigation, orchestrating an exhaustive search for his missing daughter. He publicized her disappearance widely, hired a private detective, met with state officials including the governor, and rented a helicopter to survey the area. He printed 400,000 fliers displaying his daughter's likeness and set up a toll-free hot line, urging callers to phone in their tips. Despite his best efforts, however, Tiffany Sessions never returned.[4]

Tiffany Sessions's puzzling disappearance had a chilling effect on the usually carefree campus life in Gainesville. Yet the impact on students of the 1989 abduction paled in comparison with the terror that enveloped the community in August 1990.

By the time the fourth and fifth bodies were discovered, Gainesville was beginning to resemble an overgrown ghost town. Hundreds of students had already left campus early for the Labor Day weekend, and those who stayed behind were on the verge of panic, hardly venturing out of their apartments and dorms for any reason without a companion. Especially after dark, local police and state troopers patrolled the streets in unprecedented numbers. At both UF and Santa Fe Community College, student leaders initiated escort services for students walking across campus at night. The understated headline in the *Gainesville Sun* read, "Killings Numb City's Sense of Well-Being."

Area bars and restaurants were nearly empty as frightened students who had not left town huddled together in their tiny apartments, in dormitories, or in the motel rooms they had rented as "safe havens" until the killer was caught. Meanwhile, they slept with knives, baseball bats, or even machetes by their sides.

Compounding the intense public anxiety was the discovery, just days after the student murders, of two bodies in nearby Melrose, a rural village fifteen miles east of Gainesville known for its picturesque lakes and tree-lined streets, its historic homes and charming inns. A

---

[4]Craig Dezern, *Orlando Sentinel Tribune*, "No Clues After 20 Months in Tiffany Sessions Case," August 28, 1990, p. A8.

middle-aged Melrose man, the owner of a local restaurant, and his female companion, who was a teacher in the area, were found shot to death in their lakeside home.

Police quickly moved to quell unfounded suspicions by ruling out any connection between the bodies in Melrose and the campus killing spree. Yet some hysterical residents of Gainesville didn't buy it; they were more persuaded by the fact that seven brutal murders had occurred in less than a week. They reasoned that this was no mere coincidence, that the same monster must be responsible for all of the killings.

"They were crazy times," recalled Special Agent Strope. "There were bodies here, bodies there. Then I heard over the radio that a plane had crashed at the Gainesville Airport. It felt like the whole world was coming to an end."

Local shopkeepers were inundated with requests for various kinds of handguns, shotguns, stun guns, and canisters of chemical mace. Customers stood in line to buy weapons—some twenty deep to purchase guns at M & C Army Surplus Store on West University Avenue. Those who already owned guns stocked up on ammunition.

Some stores ran out of deadbolt locks and door chains; others became totally consumed with trying in vain to meet the incredible demand for protection. Locksmith Mark Floyd told Sharon Mcbreen of the *Orlando Sentinel* that he had worked thirty-six hours straight installing locks and changing keys. "Yesterday, it was just students," Floyd told the *Sentinel* reporter. "Now, its all over town. People are not going to sleep until they get their homes locked up."[5]

Apprehensive parents rushed to Gainesville from cities and towns across Florida in order, first, to assess the danger and then to rescue their youngsters if necessary. For many, the decision was easy—to pack their chil-

⁵Sharon Mcbreen, "Armed Against the Unknown," *Orlando Sentinel*, August 29, 1990, p. A14.

dren's bags and drive home. For others, however, the decision was to stay but be prepared to fight back. Jim and Kathy Davis told a reporter from the Gannett News Service that they had driven from their home in Sarasota to buy a gun for their daughter Stephanie, who was attending school in Gainesville. "I don't want my step-daughter to be confronted by a psychopath and be unable to defend herself," Jim Davis explained.[6]

Students were especially jolted by the apparently random nature of the murders. An eighteen-year-old sophomore at UF was typical in her reaction. "If it's a domestic situation, I'm safe. If it's drug related, I can count myself out," she declared. "But with this, you wonder who's next. It's hysteria here."[7]

Many male students had not felt personally endangered, at least after the first three murder victims were discovered. After all, it appeared that the killer was going after coeds, and that seemed to rule out the men. But when Manny Taboada was killed at Gatorwood, that false sense of security vanished instantly, leaving all students feeling vulnerable.

In Gainesville, university officials, seeking to allay student anxiety, held an afternoon meeting on Tuesday, August 28 at the campus center. The university's director of counseling, Jan Archer, asked students to hold the hand of the person seated next to them as a symbolic gesture of their shared obligation to care for one another. "We are trying to provide the counseling services that are needed," he said. "But more than that, we're going to have to help one another."[8]

Student government president Michael Browne similarly urged his fellow students at UF to think about the safety of their friends in town as well as their own personal safety. "If you're fortunate enough to have a car,"

---

[6]Keith Goldschmidt, "Fearful Gainesville Arms Itself Against Killer Stalking Town," Gannett News Service, August 29, 1990.
[7]Peter Applebome, "Panic on a Florida Campus After 5 Are Slain," *New York Times*, August 29, 1990, p. 1A.
[8]*Ibid.*, p. 6

he said, "now's the time to be generous-minded."[9] To students who hadn't left campus for home, the university student government attempted to distribute more than sixteen hundred metal safety whistles.

UF suspended class attendance requirements and normal registration procedures for at least ten days, giving students a chance to leave Gainesville and still decide whether to return to classes later without penalty. At a Tuesday afternoon press conference on the campus, Mayor Courtland Collier exhorted the citizens of Gainesville to unify in response to the grisly killings. "This isn't New York where there are a lot of crazy people," he declared. "We have just one."[10]

The student government at UF distributed fliers around campus containing the following message:[11]

It is important for all members of the community to stick together in this time of tragedy.

BE SURE TO:

Always walk with a friend or two everywhere you go.

Do not open your door to any strangers. This includes repairmen and policemen.

Always ask for identification and call their office to verify their identity.

Call home and tell your family and friends that you are safe and that you are taking safety precautions.

Check on your neighbors and friends regularly to make sure that they are safe and secure.

[9]Peter Eisner, "Fla. Serial Killer on Loose," *Newsday*, August 29, 1990, p. A14.

[10]Mike Reynolds, "Police Believe Gainesville Killer Still in Town," Reuters, August 29, 1990.

[11]Norma Wagner, "University Struggles to Function as Fear Pervades Gainesville," *Saint Petersburg Times*, August 29, 1990, p. 7A.

Lock all of your doors and windows at all times.

Use the "buddy system" at all times.

At an afternoon press conference, several days after the discovery of the murders, campus leaders including the president of Santa Fe Community College and Lombardi attempted to allay the mounting fears of students who were concerned enough about their personal safety to consider leaving town while the killer remained on the loose. Lombardi announced that fewer than one hundred students had notified UF they would not be returning because of the murders. He was "cautiously optimistic" that the killer would soon be apprehended but would continue to provide increased security and additional campus housing "so long as the police investigation continues."

In a valiant attempt to dispel fear, student government president Michael Browne welcomed students back to campus. "To tell you the truth," he said, "with all the police officers here, this is probably the safest college campus in the country right now."[12]

Two hundred students gathered on campus in the heat of the noonday sun to pray for the victims of the brutal killing spree. Some even offered prayers for the unknown killer, who was conjectured to be a lost soul, a tragic figure.

And then the media arrived in droves, not just the regional and state reporters, but journalists and TV correspondents from all over the world. The circus atmosphere created by the overwhelming presence of the press from everywhere imaginable infuriated many residents of Gainesville, who identified closely with their community and felt exploited, invaded, or at best unfairly stigmatized by the incredible amount of media publicity. Until now, Gainesville had enjoyed a reputation for being a livable, decent community. The town

---

[12]Patrick May, "Police Narrow Pool of Suspects," *Miami Herald*, September 1990, p. 1A.

had even regarded itself as an educational Mecca of sorts and a center of excellence in intercollegiate athletics.

Local concern over negative publicity may, to some extent, have been justified. When multiple murder strikes a small city or town like Gainesville, it becomes forever associated in the minds of millions of Americans with the heinous acts that occurred there. The good will and charity of its citizens are quickly overshadowed by the act of a single madman. Residents of Edmond, Oklahoma, for example, would like their town to be known for popular Olympic gymnast Shannon Miller or for the 1988 PGA Championship; to their dismay, however, Edmond is better known by many people for the 1986 post office massacre in which a letter carrier slaughtered fourteen co-workers.

In addition, it is particularly difficult for members of a small community to move beyond the local stigma brought on by a vicious murder. Townspeople tend to identify closely with the geographic unit in which they live. In Gainesville, therefore, everyone felt victimized, even if they were not college students, even if they weren't personally at risk.

By the time Phil Donahue came to town in early September, the citizens of Gainesville were downright indignant and inhospitable, believing that the presence of even one more national exposure via tabloid television would only add to their woes. Concerned about the bad publicity, the president of UF, John Lombardi, turned down an invitation to appear live on Donahue's show. Lombardi also said no to Sally Jessy Raphael and Joan Rivers; both gave up doing a show on the murders when it became impossible to line up guests. He had earlier agreed to do *Larry King Live* by satellite, but that was just after the bodies had been discovered and prior to the onslaught of reporters. Not wanting to add to the media hype, the university president released a statement explaining his reticence: "It's America, and if they want to do their shows, that's fine. But we're not going to condone it. We're not going to turn the University into a sound stage."[13]

Donahue was simply too much for some of the citizens of Gainesville to tolerate. Just as President Lombardi said no to the invitation, so did the chief of police. Local residents urged a boycott of the show. And while the program was on location and on the air, someone managed to get behind the set and cut the camera cables, causing TV sets to black out in homes across the country, at least for a few moments. Also during the show, angry townspeople drove around the makeshift, open-air stage next to the courthouse, beeping their horns repeatedly in order to disrupt the program.

While residents were defensive about the black mark that the killings had cast on their hometown, hundreds of Donahue fans packed the courtyard from which the show was aired. After all, this would almost certainly be the only occasion that would bring a major talk show host to town.

The white-haired talk show legend himself was keenly aware of his precarious position in the eyes of the townspeople. As soon as he stepped into the arena, he apologized for being there. "First of all, we do not want to be here and I'm sure you feel the same," Donahue said. "There is something unbecoming about the theatrical setting we find ourselves in today."[14]

There were other responses in the aftermath of the murders besides locking doors, buying guns, or even protesting the media. Some people in Gainesville laughed; in fact, they nervously laughed it off—the fear, the anxiety, the concern. Psychologists have long noted the value of humor as a tension-release mechanism, particularly in the face of fear. People who deal with murder on a regular basis—cops and crime writers—know this

---

[13]Jeff Brazil, "The Show Does Not Have to Go On, Gainesville Says," *Orlando Sentinel,* September 8, 1990, p. A1.
[14]*Ibid.*

defense mechanism all too well. Hang around with homicide detectives, and you're likely to hear a steady stream of jokes about murder and mayhem. Rather than callousness, making light of murder actually lightens the emotional burden.

UF sociology professor Ben Gorman understood this function of humor when he gave his students an odd classroom assignment in the wake of the murders. He developed a contest in which he challenged students to create the most imaginative nickname for the unknown killer. The winning entry was "Decapigator."

8

The Ghost of Bundy

News of the five Gainesville murders spread quickly to campuses in other Florida cities, igniting widespread anxiety, if not hysteria, around the state. So as not to contribute to the burgeoning level of fear, theaters in Tampa and Jacksonville Beach canceled their scheduled one-week showings of *Henry: Portrait of a Serial Killer,* a riveting semidocumentary about Texas death row inmate Henry Lee Lucas. Also because of the Gainesville murders, a television station in Miami dropped from its lineup the rerun of a popular miniseries, *The Deliberate Stranger*, about the life of serial killer Ted Bundy, starring Hollywood star Mark Harmon.

In Tallahassee, a few hours away from the Gainesville murder sites, the twenty-eight thousand students at Florida State University, eager to comprehend the tragedy, spoke in hushed tones about the ghost of Ted Bundy, whose gruesome Chi–Omega killing spree in 1978 was legendary. Now they were forced to relive the horrific crimes perpetrated on their own campus more than twelve years earlier, when Bundy bludgeoned to death two students as they slept peacefully in their campus sorority house. The rampaging serial killer had already taken the lives of dozens of other women across the country before he wound up in Tallahassee, on his way to Florida's electric chair.

Florida State students now speculated anew that the ghost of Bundy had returned to haunt them. Fearing the worst, students in Tallahassee began teaming up with friends when they left their apartments, locking their doors and windows, using paid escorts, and keeping closely in touch with terrified parents. Just as in Gainesville, campus police officers seemed to be everywhere, as they were called out in force to provide an appearance of security and order.

Although Bundy's sorority house of horrors was what you would expect of a massacre, a literal bloodbath perpetrated by a frenzied killer gone berserk, the work of the Gainesville killer was chilling in its orderliness. Information leaked through the press about the skillful decapitation, careful mutilation of the bodies, and evidence that the perpetrator had cleaned his victims' genitals. Reports circulated that the victims' bodies had been bound, sexually mutilated, raped, and then positioned by the killer as if they were on exhibit in a museum.

Many students in Gainesville felt that the police were far too closemouthed about releasing details of the murders. After all, how could citizens protect themselves if they didn't know what to protect themselves from? In their defense, the police argued that they would be remiss if they didn't restrict public access to the investigation. Releasing details would only complicate the work of the investigators by aiding the real killer to cover his tracks and to encourage prank phone calls and false leads. The police already were receiving hundreds of leads from concerned citizens across the state as well as another five hundred calls a day from reporters in other cities.

Not all of the news was accurate. Rumors almost always thrive in the absence of information from official sources, and in Gainesville, for the first few weeks after the murders, a news void fueled false rumors containing even more frightening and exaggerated versions of the crimes.

The rumor mill churned out item after item of half-truth and innuendo. It was whispered that the five victims had attended a party together only hours before the killings began; that the murders were somehow connected to a showing of the recently released film *The Exorcist III*, in which a series of gory slayings was depicted, including a decapitation; or that the killings had earmarks of satanic ritual. By some accounts, the decapitated head of Christa Hoyt had been set on a phonograph turntable so that the officers who first opened the door to her apartment would see it swiveling on the bookshelf. It was also hinted that a mirror had been placed near her head so that it could be observed through the window. In another version of this story, the mirror was placed behind her head so that whoever first discovered the display would witness his or her own reaction in the reflection. In yet another version, her head was reportedly found on a kitchen counter. It was conjectured, furthermore, that the serial killer might be a medical student, perhaps even a surgeon; after all, the killer seemed to possess more than a passing knowledge of human anatomy as well as surgical skill. There was also speculation that the police knew of more bodies—perhaps as many as eight in total—but were covering up to avoid mass hysteria, or that the authorities had telephone conversations with the killer, who warned them of more bodies to come, or that one of the victims actually survived and was being held under heavy guard at a local hospital.

The most intricate and imaginative rumor was published in the student newspaper, the *Independent Florida Alligator*, under the headline "Killer May Be Bundy Imitator." The paper claimed to have the killer's number when it theorized:

Ted Bundy was born Nov. 24 and executed Jan. 24 at the age of 42. The five Gainesville slayings, which the police said may have begun Aug. 24, have centered in an apartment-laden area around Archer Road, which is also

State Road 24. The second murder was on
Southwest 24th Avenue.

Most of the information spread by word of mouth on
the streets of Gainesville was misinformation. Although
grossly inaccurate, these rumors were symptomatic of
the tremendous anxiety shared by the members of a
community desperate to define a terrifying situation.

9

Why Here?

Henry Lee Lucas, John Wayne Gacy, Gary Heidnick, Wayne Williams, Robert Berdella, Kenneth Bianchi, Angelo Buono, Alton Coleman, Leonard Lake—all serial killers who in recent years have stalked the highways and neighborhoods of America, looking for victims. Although almost anyone is at some risk, however small, serial killers tend to prey on the most vulnerable targets—prostitutes, children, hitchhikers, runaways, as well as elderly hospital patients Part of the vulnerability concerns the ease with which these groups can be abducted or overtaken. Children and the elderly are defenseless because of physical stature or disability; hitchhikers and prostitutes become vulnerable as soon as they enter the killer's car or van; hospital patients are vulnerable in their total dependency on their caretakers.

But as the Gainesville murders painfully demonstrated, college students can also be the target of choice for sexual sadists and vicious slashers. Places like Williamsburg Village and Gatorwood are thought to be safe, far away from the violence and crime of the big city. But this perception may in fact be part of the problem. Many serial killers are inventive and cleverly take advantage of the naïveté of young college students.

In 1972–1973, serial killer Edmund Emil Kemper had a field day victimizing coeds at Fresno State College and the University of California at Santa Cruz, after offering them rides home from school in his car. A few years earlier, John Norman Collins similarly abducted a half-dozen coeds at Eastern Michigan University in Ypsilanti, dumping their mutilated remains in remote areas around the county. And, of course, Theodore Bundy exploited the naïveté of students on a number of college campuses, from Seattle to Tallahassee, using his charm and winning smile as bait.

Many of the college students in Gainesville during late August 1990 were away from home and on their own for the very first time. Exploring their newfound freedom, many wide-eyed students cruised a seemingly steady stream of open-house parties that cropped up all over the place. Everyone was out and about meeting new people, opening their doors to total strangers who instead were viewed as "friends in the making." There was lots of noise everywhere, enough perhaps to drown out screams of terror. And, of course, there seemed to be little need to lock the doors anyhow; this was Gainesville, Florida, not New York City.

Larson, Powell, Hoyt, Paules, and Taboada did not die because of their carelessness, and it would be wrong to "blame the victim" for the horrible crimes committed against these innocent young people. Yet for a cunning sadist bent on destruction, a locale like Gainesville could seem very attractive, a veritable playground for murder.

Elliott Leyton of St. John's University in Newfoundland, Canada, and the author of *Hunting Humans: The Rise of the Modern Multiple Murderer*, suggested that college students might be frequent targets of serial killers as part of a class war. According to Leyton, serial killers have unfulfilled social ambitions, and they take their frustrations out on members of a particular social group. "University women are classic victims," Leyton said, "because they represent to the killers the quintessence of the upper middle class that they are unable to achieve."[15]

In this age of resentment, as the gap between the haves and have-nots continues to widen, college students are increasingly being victimized by all sorts of violence. They are more and more being seen as the recipients of opportunities denied to other members of society. On December 6, 1989, for example, twenty-three-year-old Marc Lapine, having been denied admission to the Engineering School at the University of Montreal, opened fire in a classroom on campus, killing fourteen female students. Lapine blamed them for taking his seat in the class. In a less severe case occurring during the same year, twenty-six Brown University undergraduates were assaulted with needles by a neighborhood gang whose members saw the local students as the unwelcome enemy.

Despite the vulnerability of college students and the growing resentment directed at them, communities invariably rush to support a campus that has been struck by a serial killer. In Gainesville, to be sure, the public reaction and law enforcement response to the killings were as strong as could be. Had five prostitutes been murdered instead, even in the same vicious manner, few townsfolk would have displayed the same degree of concern. Very few people would have felt motivated, for example, to assist scared prostitutes or even to call the police tip line with information. And certainly, 150 cops would not have been assigned to the case nor would millions have been spent in trying to catch the killer.

---

[15]Mary Nemeth with Frank Adams, "The Florida Ripper," *Maclean's*, September 10, 1990, p. 38.

10

Three Heads
Are Better Than One

Even before the bodies of Tracy Paules and Manny Taboada had been discovered, the police recognized the need to respond with full force to the breaking crisis. Almost immediately, a large combined task force of investigators, comprised of members of the GPD, the ASO, and the FDLE was assembled.

The Gainesville task force was a joint effort of all three agencies. The Williamsburg Village murder site was located within the local police jurisdiction, whereas the Hoyt and Paules/Taboada homicides fell within the jurisdiction of the ASO. Because of its vast experience in homicide investigation as well as its technical expertise in forensics, the state law enforcement agency contributed the overwhelming majority of personnel and other resources.

Typical of most multiagency law enforcement efforts, politics played a major role in the daily operation of the Gainesville task force. The leadership was a bit top heavy, because each agency wanted to share in making decisions and claiming credit. The three officers-in-charge (OICs) were Captain R. B. Ward of the Gainesville Police (and later Deputy Chief Ron Perkins when Ward was on leave, battling cancer), Captain Andy Hamilton representing the ASO, and FDLE Special Agent Supervisor J. O. Jackson. The OICs and Agent Strope met several times a day, huddled together in a corner office on the second floor of the Gainesville Police Station, in order to review reports and discuss fresh leads.

Situated on the ground floor of the building, the investigative teams of detectives worked out of a large common area called the all-purpose room that functioned like a serial homicide think tank. Lee Strope had pasted on the wall photographs of the victims as they appeared in life along with a computer-generated banner that read Stay Focused. Surrounded by dozens of overflowing file cabinets and phone banks, the investigators grew together like a family and came to regard their room like a second home. This was where most of the action took place.

At its peak, the task force included over 150 investigators, many of whom participated in assignment teams. Team 1, headed by FDLE Special Agent Bob Kinsey, devoted all of its energies to following up leads pertaining to the Williamsburg Village homicides. Team 2, led by ASO Sergeant Jim Eckert, and Team 3, directed by FDLE Agent John Burton, had responsibility for the Hoyt murder and the Gatorwood assault, respectively. In addition, Special Agent Dennis Norred of the FDLE was in charge of team 4, which tracked down information regarding promising suspects. And there were many.

In some homicide investigations, detectives thirst for tips and leads from anyone who may have seen something suspicious. Any piece of information, no matter how small or seemingly trivial, may turn out to be a critical piece of evidence.

In Gainesville, the problem was at the other extreme—information overload. Because of the high-profile nature of the student murders, the task force was inundated with tips from an anxious public—a citizenry that was both afraid that the killer might still be on the loose and eager to make sure that the culprit was brought to justice. Still others called the task force with the hope that they might someday be able to boast of their role in cracking the case.

Although many of the phone tips would eventually prove useful, the vast majority were nothing more than busy work for an overburdened team of investigators. One person called with a "hot tip" that her brother-in-law owned knives; another reported on his neighbor who seemed a bit too interested in following the investigation through the media. Even psychics called to offer their special gift in pursuit of the killer.

The arduous task of managing the information flow fell on the shoulders of W.H. "Bear" Bryan of the ASO. Each tip was assigned a priority ranking, from 1 for critical leads needing immediate investigation to 3 for what represented little more than something that could easily have been filed in the nearest wastebasket.

"The priority 3's were mostly a waste of time," Strope complained. "But even these were followed up on. Afraid of losing the next election, the prosecutor wanted us to cross every *t* and dot every *i*—at any cost."

The high-priority leads were assigned to one of the teams of investigators, depending on the subject matter. Once the leads were followed, investigation reports were prepared and entered into a computer local-area network in the basement of the building. In the "head shed," an analytic squad of four experienced investigators, led by Special Agent Bill Davis, sleuthed their computer screens, looking for patterns and critical facts that would otherwise be missed.

The overload at the top of the task force among the OICs was far from ideal. "More than one leader in that kind of an operation would be a problem," noted Steven Egger, author of *Serial Murder: An Elusive Phenomenon*.[16]

Actually, the organization of the task force resembled a football team but with three head coaches. With no

---

[16]Keith Goldschmidt, Gannett News Service, November 1, 1991.

one person calling the plays, there was at times excessive confusion and inefficiency. Strope's role was like that of the captain of the team. He spent much of his time coordinating communication between the "coaches" upstairs in the OIC office and the "players" on the "field" downstairs.

The OICs held frequent meetings with the entire task force in order to review and discuss new leads that came in as well as the results of the investigation of old leads. In the first few days after the murders, meetings were held twice daily to go over the enormous volume of information that was surfacing at the time. Eventually, the frequency of meetings was cut down to one per day and then finally to one every few days. After several weeks into the case, the phone tips and leads began to arrive at a much slower pace, and investigators spent more of their day on the street tracking down leads and interviewing witnesses.

As far as Lee Strope was concerned, the fewer meetings the better. Although he understood the vital importance of sharing information within the task force and coordinating activities, there was just too much talking (and waiting to meet to talk) and not enough doing for his taste. "In the 1950s, this case might have been solved already," complained Strope. "While it's true that computers weren't around back then—and they're useful of course—detectives didn't have to put up with the bureaucracy and politics that can stymie an investigation."

Most homicides are easy to solve. In fact, two-thirds of all murders, most involving people who know one another well, are cleared within fourteen hours of the crime. Serial murders are different, precisely because the perpetrators are typically strangers to their victims.

Despite the tremendous difficulty in trying to identify an apparently cunning serial killer, Strope and the massive Gainesville task force quickly rounded up a number of good suspects. At the top of the list stood the name of Edward Lewis Humphrey, an eighteen-year-old UF freshman, who was known around town for his erratic and belligerent behavior. As luck would have it, Humphrey had been arrested on charges of beating his seventy-nine-year-old grandmother as well as assaulting several women on the street while in plain view. Because of his slightly pudgy body and youthfulness, the task force members nicknamed their prime suspect the Pillsbury Dough Boy.

11

The Pillsbury Dough Boy

It isn't necessary to delve deeply into the background of Edward Lewis Humphrey in order to find a period in his life when he was just another student. In high school, he certainly didn't look like a monster, and he clearly didn't act like a crazy person. In fact, during his first year at Melbourne High School, Ed's keen intellect, physical fitness, and boyish good looks—the sandy blond hair, clear blue eyes, and ready smile—made him a popular and successful student. He had made the football team, was elected to the student council, and joined the Spanish club; yet he still found time to maintain a B+ average. Everybody seemed to agree that Ed was headed for an outstanding college career—perhaps like his father, George, who had attended Harvard's School of Business or like his older brother, George Jr., who was an honor student at UF.

By his senior year of high school, however, the joy in Ed Humphrey's life had disappeared completely as he slipped deeper and deeper into an abyss of depression and despair. Perhaps it was his parents' acrimonious divorce or the mononucleosis he had contracted, which so often left him totally drained of energy or motivation. Maybe there was a biological basis for his extreme moodiness, the manic outbursts, his ravings and rantings, the incoherent tantrums. Whatever its origin, however, Ed's demeanor changed very much for the worse whenever he was off the lithium that his doctor had prescribed. On medication, Ed was at least manageable; without it, he became a raving lunatic, a loose cannon.

In February 1988, Ed Humphrey became intensely depressed about his suddenly poor grades and the low scores he had received on his PSAT. His father had left the state of Florida, and his mother had moved into his grandmother's home in Indiatlantic. After dropping out of high school in an apparent attempt to end it all, Ed overdosed on Tylenol and then spent time in Holmes Regional Medical Center in Melbourne.

George Jr. could not help but recognize that his brother's mental health had deteriorated badly and that he could use some help keeping out of trouble. George was leaving the area to begin his first year at the University of Florida Law School. So he asked Ed to move with him to Gainesville, where they shared an apartment.

Despite his older brother's good intentions, Ed's misfortunes continued. In April, as the two boys and George's girlfriend were on their way to spend the day at a nearby beach, Ed suddenly opened the door and jumped to the pavement from the backseat of his brother's speeding car, doing close to seventy miles per hour. After receiving treatment in a psychiatric ward and then returning to Indiatlantic to complete his high school degree, he rammed the late-model Buick he was driving into a utility pole. His face smashed into the windshield, leaving him with scars on his forehead and on both cheeks. To repair his badly fractured leg, doctors implanted a steel rod from his hip to his knee. He was in a wheelchair for weeks and then walked with a noticeable limp.

During the summer of 1990, Ed Humphrey's mental health took another turn for the worse as his behavior became even more erratic and frightening. He was seen in public on numerous occasions acting in an inappropriate fashion—mumbling and laughing to himself, being loud, threatening strangers, and yelling obscenities. He seemed to talk incessantly and incoherently about wanting to join the Marines, about the Eighty-second Airborne, about "recon," about going to Iraq or Saudi Arabia, about killing Arabs, about cutting people with knives.

Even Ed's appearance changed to match his mood swings. More often than not, he now aimlessly wandered the streets looking like a homeless vagrant who lacked either the resources or the good sense to care for himself. It wasn't just his pronounced facial scars and limp; Humphrey had also put on some weight, became excessively heavy around the middle, dressed in torn and tattered clothing, and sometimes looked filthy. When he wasn't in trouble with the police, it seemed that he was unnerving the people he encountered in public places or at least making a nuisance of himself. Wherever Ed went, he was always at the center of attention, but in the most negative sense.

Ed Humphrey's presence had become well known to authorities in Gainesville. He had completed a summer session at UF, but not without incident. And when he returned to visit with his mother and grandmother, Ed's self-control seemed to slip a couple of notches and his anger grew.

On the afternoon of August 1, 1990, the Indiatlantic Police were dispatched to a local residence in order to quell what appeared to be a domestic dispute between Humphrey and his grandmother. Arriving on the scene, Deputy Doug Hammock was informed that Ed had not taken his medication. The deputy then spotted a knife on the front seat of Ed's gray '79 Cadillac and placed it in the trunk of Humphrey's car. There was little more he could do at the time.

Five days later, Ed Humphrey drove his Cadillac to Patrick Air Force Base, where he gained entry by convincing the north gate sentry that he had previously served as a counselor there and that his purpose now was merely to visit the Education Center on base. Shortly afterward, military security reported that Humphrey had created a disturbance: he was angry and upset, he was making a scene, he was shouting and screaming, he blurted out his intention to swim to Iran in order to kill people. Looking under the driver's seat of Ed's car, officers discovered and confiscated two concealed weapons: a Ka-Bar marine knife with a seven-inch blade and a six-inch buck stainless-steel knife.

Wherever he went, Ed Humphrey caused trouble. His attempts to visit a ''girlfriend'' he had met on a previous visit out West were no more successful than his efforts at home. On the evening of August 10, the Kit Carson County Sheriff's Office in Burlington, Colorado, received a report of a strange young man who was acting in a suspicious manner at a local convenience store in the town of Straton. Arriving on the scene, Town Marshal Vern Drescher found Ed Humphrey who had locked his keys in his Cadillac and was ''acting mental.'' Drescher assisted Humphrey to get into his car and last saw him drive west out of town on Interstate 70.

Hours later, however, Ed Humphrey was back in trouble. According to police reports, he pulled into a gas station in Ordway, Colorado, to fill his tank but was unable to pay the bill. He was on his way to Montana to visit his girlfriend, Humphrey claimed, when hitchhikers stole all of his cash.

His tale of woe failed to convince the gas-station attendant who immediately called the police. When the officers showed up, Ed was arrested and his automobile impounded. During a twenty-four-hour period in the county jail, he became violent and could not be subdued without medication. He was evaluated by two psychiatrists, who reportedly found no signs of psychopathology. His grandmother rushed by plane to Denver, where she was met by two deputies who had accompanied Ed to the airport. Grandmother and grandson were escorted onto a plane to Florida.

On August 17, back home in Gainesville, Humphrey was reportedly involved in an incident during a routine transaction at the First Union Bank. When a teller asked him to produce identification, Ed was observed to become verbally abusive, stating, "No one would dare cross me. . . . I've got knives that would cut you open in a flash. . . . I know how to use them. . . . I've been trained on military missions. . . . You think I'm kidding, don't you?"

On the evening of Saturday, August 18, wearing a pale-blue T-shirt, dirty white sweatpants, and old high-top sneakers, a passenger identified as Ed Humphrey was seen boarding a crowded Greyhound bus from the terminal in Gainesville to Orlando. Unable to find a seat toward the front, the young man shouted to other riders, "I paid for a fucking bus seat and I want a fucking bus seat now!" Still agitated, the man finally located an empty seat in the third row from the rear of the bus. Once seated, he immediately began listening to loud hard-rock music through a portable headset. When the driver asked him to "turn it down," the man responded angrily, "Fuck you, I paid my fare."

During the trip, the man identified as Ed Humphrey spoke excitedly with several of the other passengers. Holding a pocket knife with a four-inch blade, he told them that he could hear the Devil talking to him through the music and that he was upset because the American military was not bombing "the worthless people of Iraq." During a stop in Ocala, he created a scene at the terminal snack bar when he yelled at the woman behind the counter, "Bitch, wait on me," and then pulled out his knife in a threatening gesture. Back on board, he bragged to other passengers that he had "told that old bitch off."

During the early morning hours of August 23, Ed Humphrey was seen driving his black Cadillac to the Lil' Champ food store on the corner of Northwest Twenty-fourth Street and Thirty-ninth Avenue in Gainesville. Ed went into the store to use the rest room and then bought a few items including an issue of *Hustler* magazine. He looked filthy and intoxicated. His arms and legs were covered with what appeared to be mosquito bites, his legs and knees were full of dirt, and he had apparently urinated in his blue pants. One clerk

later told investigators that she could smell the odor of
alcohol on the man who resembled Humphrey. While
waiting at the checkout counter, he had talked to her
about being in the military service and about going to
war in the Middle East. Then, he had suddenly left.

The next day was Friday, August 24—just before the
Gainesville murder spree was discovered. Humphrey
drove to a small shop at the Oaks Mall in Gainesville,
where he purchased an inexpensive gold chain. While
inside the store, he asked the clerks whether they knew
the Eighty-second Airborne and told them that he was
"going to Iran" to kill people. One clerk on duty at the
time of Ed's visit described Humphrey as "an emotion-
less zombie" whose eyes were "dead," "cold," and
"evil."

Humphrey then walked over to the Oaks Mall movie
theater, where he watched *Darkman*, a newly-released
movie about a scientist who was badly disfigured by an
explosion in his laboratory and who then decided to seek
revenge by killing those who had wronged him. Ed sat
by himself next to a wall about halfway down from the
screen. He was wearing a baseball cap, knee-length
shorts, and a white T-shirt. As he watched the movie,
Ed chewed tobacco that he occasionally spit on the floor
next to his seat. Whenever a violent scene appeared on
the screen, Humphrey uttered the words "Heavy artillery, heavy artillery" or "Go, go get 'em." He would
respond, when asked to quiet down by annoyed patrons
seated near him, "Eighty-second Airborne, Eighty-
second Airborne."

Around midnight on August 30, a couple of days after
the murders had stopped, a man identified as Ed Humphrey entered a Texaco gas station on West University
Avenue in Gainesville. According to a clerk on duty,
Humphrey wore a bandage around his right hand and
acted very strangely. He rambled on nonstop for ten
minutes about having a friend who "was a coward for
the way he attacked the girls." Ed talked incoherently
about fighting with knives and about being tough enough
to handle himself against his violent friend. Before leav-

ing, he turned to the clerk and asked rhetorically about the murders in Gainesville, "Do you believe what is going on here?"

Only hours later, Ed Humphrey was arrested for assaulting his seventy-nine-year-old grandmother in her sprawling Indialantic home. According to police reports, Humphrey walked into the living room of the house, where he found Elna Hlavaty seated in a chair. He first told his grandmother that she was on the verge of death and headed for hell. He then demanded that she get on her knees and find a contact lens that he had lost somewhere on the living room floor. Elna pleaded with her grandson that it was too dark in the room to locate the missing lens, but he would have none of her excuses. Without warning, Ed lifted his grandmother out of her chair and began choking her with both hands. He then struck her several times across the face as she fell to the floor. The right side of Hlavaty's face was already swollen as she was transported to Holmes Regional Medical Center in Melbourne for emergency treatment.

12

The Two Faces of Ed

On the afternoon of August 30, 1990, FDLE Special Agents Wally Gossett and Dom Pape walked into the Brevard County Detention Center in Melbourne. They were there to interrogate Ed Humphrey, who was incarcerated on the premises for having assaulted his grandmother. Gossett and Pape were less interested in Ed's family feud than in his possible involvement with the student murders. Not only had he recently been assaultive, but he had been seen around Gainesville babbling irrationally about murder and mayhem.

Guards escorted the chained and handcuffed young man with the scarred face and pronounced limp from his jail cell to the small detention room, where the two investigators were waiting. Humphrey's eyes were heavy, and his head was bent. Dressed in his prison-issue red uniform, he looked as if he hadn't shaved or combed his hair in days, and he appeared to be in a daze.

Taking a seat across the table from the two investigators, Humphrey slumped down in his chair. He then tried to explain in a barely audible voice that he just wanted "to relax and take it easy.

"I want to be free," he muttered. "I don't want to be in here anymore."

Agents Gossett and Pape were appropriately sympathetic but also professional. They introduced themselves to Humphrey and immediately advised him of his constitutional rights. Ed indicated that he understood but was willing to sign a waiver. And then he talked.

At first, Humphrey spoke mainly about his background—his volatile family life, the places he had lived growing up as his family moved around the country, and his grades in school. Ed was an Eagle Boy Scout. He had been on the student council at Melbourne High School, and had so far accumulated twelve college credits. He told the investigators that his birth date was October 5, 1971. His parents couldn't get along and had separated.

Turning to the Gainesville murders, Ed claimed to be fearful of the serial killer on the loose. "I was leaving Gainesville," he explained, "because there's some psychopath running loose and he's not taking any prisoners . . . I don't want to be part of it."

Seeking to direct the conversation, Gossett asked Ed to speculate as to what kind of guy might have killed the five college students.

"I'll tell you exactly who he is," Ed responded. "What I think he is, from what I have read, that if you see this dude, don't mess with him, man. Probably like a Ninja. Probably really thin. Probably like me, you know. Probably similar to me."

When asked to do so by Pape, Humphrey described the killer as someone with "blond hair, blue eyes, just like me. He's a clone of me, except that he is very thin."

Many of Gossett and Pape's probing questions elicited inconsistent and incoherent rambling from Ed concerning his religious beliefs, personal philosophy, and the details of his life that were apparently unrelated to the murders in Gainesville. The suspect referred to himself variously in the conversation as "God," "the almighty," "the Messiah." And then, at one point, he suggested that the killer had somehow violated Ed's personal oath.

When Pape asked him to describe that oath, Humphrey reached into his scouting background for an answer and rambled on. "A Scout is trustworthy and loyal, helpful, friendly, courteous, kind, obedient, cheerful, and reverent," Humphrey responded.

"On my honor, I'll do my best to do my duty, to God and my country and obey the Scout law and to keep myself at all times physically strong, mentally awake, morally straight," Ed continued without hesitation.

"And I pledge allegiance to the flag of the United States of America and to the republic for which it stands, one nation under God indivisible, under God things, other things like Death from above, Eighty-second Airborne Division Infantry."

In a disjointed and convoluted discourse, Ed repeatedly disclaimed any personal knowledge of or involvement in the crimes. He emphatically told his interrogators that he had never killed anyone in his life, that he had no desire to kill anyone, and that the perpetrator "probably doesn't have any scars on his face at all." He speculated incorrectly that the killer hadn't "messed around" with his victims before he took their lives and that he had entered the victims' apartments through a window. He even asserted that the victims were still alive, although perhaps only in a spiritual sense.

But Humphrey also gave his interrogators grounds for suspecting his complicity in the brutal murders. He expressed intensely angry feelings, complaining bitterly about the way other people had rejected him, how they had stared at his disfigured face, especially during recent months.

He told Gossett, "The stuff is really hitting the fan. . . . It seems like wherever I go. In the last three months, maybe two and a half months. God, hell man, I'm getting like knocked down. Slammed . . . I walk into a store, somebody goes like this. You know, they look at you . . . You know, it's just like you want to run, man."

Early in the interview, Humphrey began to give his interrogators vague clues as to his deteriorated psychological state at the time of the murders. The scars on his cheeks and forehead were put there by "the beast," he said. Then, in explaining his anger toward those in Gainesville who had rejected him, Ed suddenly exclaimed, "I wasn't myself. I'll be honest. I wasn't Ed."

At this juncture, the interrogation began to focus more on the apparent split in Humphrey's personality. Was he simply saying that his mood had changed, that his depression had worsened after arriving in Gainesville? Or was he trying to suggest something much more profound psychologically—that he actually possessed separate and distinct selves, like in *Sybil* or *Three Faces of Eve?* More to the point, could Humphrey be a Dr. Jekyll and Mr. Hyde character who had a decent, law-abiding side to him but who possessed an evil side as well?

Ed repeatedly asserted that killing wasn't right. But when asked to speculate about the killer's thinking, he also spoke in the first person: "I'm the Grim Reaper. You fuck with me and you're going to die. And that's the way it is. Don't ask me why, that's the way it is. But if you want to fuck with me, then you're going to fuck with death, and if you want to die, that's just the way it's going to be."

Gosset and Pape were intrigued by Ed's seemingly dual personality. It wouldn't be the first time that a serial killer claimed to be a victim of multiple personality. Ken Bianchi, one of the two notorious Hillside Stranglers who together brutally murdered ten young women in the Los Angeles area, attempted an insanity defense centering on the theory that he suffered from a multiple-personality disorder. In his own defense, Ken claimed to have been an abused child who escaped, at least psychologically, from cruel parental treatment by developing a fantasy world of pleasure and kindness. At the same time, his angry and hateful feelings toward his abusive parents were stored in a reservoir that he suppressed.

In later life, Ken's two selves—the loving and the hateful—split into their own personalities, which competed for control. The angry "person" took turns with various alter egos for dominance over Ken's body.

Through hypnosis, a second personality surfaced, that of "Steve," a hostile, crude, impatient, and sadistic character who proudly claimed responsibility for the slayings for which Ken Bianchi had been charged. "Killing a broad doesn't make any difference to me," bragged Steve.

Everything now made sense to the psychiatrists—at least on the defense team. Fortunately for the prosecution, however, it was later shown that Ken Bianchi had malingered in order to escape legal responsibility for the murders: not only had he faked being hypnotized, but he had lied about being abused as a child and had faked multiple personality as well. The only thing real about Ken Bianchi was the fact that he was a cold-blooded killer.

Could Ed Humphrey actually be like Kenneth Bianchi—either a victim of a severe psychiatric disorder or a liar who was eager to place the blame elsewhere? During the course of the interview, Humphrey gave Gossett and Pape more and more reason to believe that he might actually possess two personalities: one, a law-abiding and decent character named Ed, and the other, a violent and protective character named John. At one point, Ed's voice seemed to be completely absorbed by his alter ego; the most damaging testimony about Humphrey came not from Ed, but from "John."

Pape asked "John" to tell him who had killed the five college students, and Humphrey responded.

"I did," John said.

Pape asked again, "You did?"

"Yeah."

"How did you kill them?"

"With no pain."

"Huh, with no pain?" Pape asked incredulously.

"No pain."

"Did you use any type of instrument or weapon?"

"Just a knife," John answered.

Gossett then took over the questioning.

"Did you know who they were before you killed them?" he asked.

"Oh, of course," John replied.

"How did you know them?"

"Because they really hurt Ed," John said.

"How did you get in? Gossett asked.

"Me?"

Gossett was more precise this time: "Yeah. How did John get in?"

"Like a ninja," John replied.

Continuing the same line of questioning, Pape asked, "Like a ninja? How would a ninja get in?"

"Dressed in black."

"Dressed in black?"

"No, nothing showing but black."

Gossett tried for more details. "Ninja mask?" he asked.

"Not even. See the eyes there? Nothing," Humphrey said, pointing to his face.

John's "confession" gave the task force a prime suspect—exactly what it seemed to need in order to appease an anxious and impatient public. Ed Humphrey was a manic-depressive, all right. Maybe his testimony lacked credibility. After all, the Gainesville murders seemed, at least in many respects, to have required a degree of sophistication and planning that only a clearheaded, straight-thinking killer would possess.

But a theory of multiple personality very nicely explained the discrepancies. Ed was indeed confused, disorganized, and mentally ill, but his alter ego John—the real killer—was, in sharp contrast, a cunning and crafty sadist, a person who by virtue of temperament and motivation might easily pull off a well-organized series of murders.

Ed's testimony was filled with inaccuracies and irrelevancies. But when John spoke, everything made sense. John was familiar with details of the crimes that might have been known only to the killer. He called the serial murderer a ninja and alluded to the fact that he had worn dark clothing, which investigators knew to be true based on crime scene evidence. John confessed to being present at two of the apartment complexes in which the murders had occurred. He talked almost obsessively and in great detail about the knives he had owned. He suggested plausibly enough that the killer had disposed of his weapons somewhere in the woods behind the apartment buildings. It appeared more and more that the Pillsbury Dough Boy was really two people: he was a troubled young man, but he was also the perfect suspect.

13

The Perfect Suspect

Less than a day after discovering the fourth and fifth bodies at Gatorwood, investigators already had a prime suspect in Edward Lewis Humphrey, a former resident of the complex. The hostile, angry young man often acted in a strange, erratic, even violent, manner. But did he have what it would take psychologically to rape, stab, and dismember his victims? To engage each one of them in an intimate life-and-death struggle? Or to rip, with callous disregard for their humanity, the last vestiges of life from their young bodies?

Even more to the point, the killer had remained in hiding, probably in the woods, until he was ready to strike. He was able to enter and exit each crime scene without being detected. He had skillfully brought with him to each murder site whatever weapons and materials he would need to bind, gag, subdue, and then slay his targets. He had even cleaned the bodies of the victims and had thought to take away the weapons after each murder. The Pillsbury Dough Boy had the physical strength, but could someone so confused and disorganized commit a series of crimes presumably requiring such careful forethought and planning?

Hardly, thought Agent Strope. *Ed can barely walk without tripping over himself.*

A psychological profiling team from the FBI Training Academy in Quantico, Virginia, was on the scene almost from the beginning of the investigation. This may have been an unusually early—perhaps premature—involvement, but the case was so extraordinary in its scope and impact that the federal agents felt compelled to assist without delay.

The FBI's team of profilers is world renowned as being the very best at performing its craft. Based on features of a crime scene, autopsy findings, and police investigative reports, FBI profilers will attempt to construct a portrait of a sexually sadistic offender, speculating as to the important psychological and demographic characteristics that might lead to his apprehension.

Even knowing the FBI's good reputation, not all the task force members were thrilled about what they perceived to be an intrusion of the FBI profilers into their case. A number of them expressed the view that "any investigator worth his salt does profiling every day as part of his routine work."

Profiling is itself more of an art than a science, sometimes revealing significant clues as to the predilections of a sex murderer but also sometimes yielding a mistaken or even misleading conclusion. In the Boston Strangler case, for example, a profiling team shed more heat than light on the identity of the killer of thirteen women ranging in age from nineteen to eighty-five, murdered in and around Boston from 1962 through 1964. Members of the team—experts trained in psychiatry, medicine, criminology, and anthropology—speculated that there were actually two Boston Stranglers—one who preyed on the older victims and another who preyed on the younger victims. The portrait painted by the profiling team suggested that the strangler of young victims would possibly be a homosexual, whereas the other strangler would turn out to have been raised by a domineering but sexually seductive mother whom he detested, to live alone, and to be sexually impotent.

The man who was later apprehended as the Boston Strangler was nothing like either of the team's profiles. Albert DeSalvo had chosen his targets not by age, but on a random basis, depending simply on who happened to answer the door of an apartment when he knocked. DeSalvo was neither homosexual nor impotent. In fact, he demanded sex with his wife five or six times a day. Nor did he hate his mother—instead, he respected and admired her—but he thoroughly despised his father for the brutal manner in which he had treated his mother.

The case of the Boston Strangler suggests that psychological profiling may not always lead to helpful or even valid conclusions. Yet there are also some examples of crimes in which profiling has worked in astounding, almost miraculous, fashion to identify a suspect. The so-called Mad Bomber had terrorized the New York City area from 1940 to 1956 with his homemade bombs and taunting letters to local newspaper reporters. An expert profiler, psychiatrist James Brussel conjectured that the Mad Bomber would turn out to be a conservative, foreign-born, middle-aged man who lived by himself. The psychiatrist also predicted that the Mad Bomber wore a double-breasted suit, which he buttoned all of the way up. When arrested for the bombings, George Metesky fit the profile exactly, even wearing the buttoned double-breasted suit that Brussel had foreseen.

At the core of its profiling strategy, the FBI distinguishes between *organized nonsocial* and *disorganized asocial killers*. Based on its study of thirty-six homicidal men, twenty-five serial and eleven nonserial killers, the organized type typically is intelligent, is socially and sexually competent, is of high birth order, is a skilled worker, lives with a partner, is mobile, drives a late-model car, and follows his crime in the media, whereas the disorganized killer generally is unintelligent, is socially and sexually inadequate, is of low birth order, is an unskilled worker, lives alone, is nonmobile, drives an old car or no car at all, and has minimal interest in the news reports of his crimes.

According to the FBI analysis, these types tend to differ in terms of crime scene characteristics. Specifically, the organized killer uses restraints on his victims, hides or transports the body, removes the weapon from the scene, molests the victim prior to death, and is methodical in the style of killing. In contrast, the disorganized killer tends not to use restraints, leaves the body in full view, leaves a weapon at the scene, molests the victim after death, and is spontaneous in his manner of killing. The task of profiling involves, therefore, drawing inferences from the crime scene to the behavioral characteristics of the killer.

On August 29, the day after the Gatorwood crime scene was found, Special Agents John Douglas and Jim Wright of the FBI's Behavioral Science Unit flew into Gainesville from their headquarters in Quantico. That afternoon, they met with members of the task force to be briefed about the preliminary results of their investigation. The profilers from Quantico then reviewed whatever crime scene materials were available.

Douglas and Wright's report suggested that the ''primary motivation of the offender was to manipulate, dominate, and control his victims.'' The profilers speculated that in killing and mutilating the five young people in Gainesville the offender had demonstrated his intense anger and had attempted to humiliate his victims. Afterward, he had displayed his victims' bodies for the shock value. His primary targets were the females, and he had murdered Manny Taboada in order to get to Tracy Paules.

Douglas and Wright identified a number of commonalities among the crime scenes. At every site, the perpetrator had used tape to bind or gag the females and had used a knife as his weapon. Moreover, every crime scene abutted a wooded or otherwise secure area to which the offender could easily flee without being detected.

Douglas and Wright's psychological profile looked

very much like Edward Humphrey. According to the profile, the killer would be a white male—probably in his late teens to mid-twenties—who exhibited evidence of "youthfulness, drug/alcohol abuse, or mental illness." *Humphrey was an eighteen-year-old manic depressive with a history of mental illness and erratic behavior*

The offender would either have lived, worked, or regularly visited the area in which the crimes occurred, suggested the profile. *At the time of the murders, Humphrey was living in Gainesville and had, for a time, resided in the Gatorwood apartment complex.*

At the time he committed the murders, the killer would have paid less attention to his personal appearance and hygiene, according to the FBI agents. *Eyewitnesses told investigators that Humphrey recently looked dirty and, on occasion, had a putrid odor.*

The profile theorized that the killer would be a loner. *Humphrey had few friends and was often seen in public places by himself.*

Douglas and Wright speculated that the perpetrator would live alone or with someone on whom he depended financially. *Until recently, Humphrey resided with his grandmother in Indiatlantic and then moved to an apartment in Gainesville, also financed by her.*

He would have a dominant female in his life and an absent or ineffective father, according to the profilers. *Humphrey was very much dependent on his grandmother, especially after his parents divorced and his father had left the area.*

He would possibly have a criminal record, said the FBI experts. *Humphrey was under arrest for assaulting his grandmother. The police had been called at least twelve times since April 1989 to pacify him after he created disturbances with his grandmother or mother. He also had been accused of attacking two women in Vero Beach on October 6, 1988.*

Douglas and Wright noted that the killer had the physical prowess to gain entry, subdue his male victim, and move the bodies of his female victims. *Humphrey was six feet two, more than two hundred pounds, and a former football player.*

He likely would have a visible physical defect such as a speech impediment or severe acne, predicted the FBI team. *Humphrey's face was severely scarred.*

The profile hypothesized that the assailant would recently have experienced a change in his behavior or attitudes, noticed by other people. *Many people observed that Humphrey's behavior had recently become more bizarre and unpredictable.*

Immediately following the murders, he would have undergone enough anxiety to be noticed by other people, indicated Agents Douglas and Wright. *Humphrey was witnessed vomiting, wearing urine-stained clothes, and acting in a particularly bizarre manner (for example, eating grits with his fingers).*

The Gainesville killing spree stopped as quickly as it had begun—five murders during a terrifying weekend in August and then nothing. It was likely, Strope reasoned, that the killer may have struck somewhere else before. Lee questioned, given the extreme inhumanity reflected at the crime scenes, whether the Gainesville killer was a rookie. The task force hoped to locate similar crimes in other counties or other states that he may have committed before arriving in town.

To help in this regard, the task force completed five VICAP forms, one for each of the student homicides. Housed at the FBI's Behavioral Science Unit in Quantico, the Violent Criminal Apprehension Program (VICAP) is a computerized system for collecting and comparing information pertaining to unsolved homicides around the country. It is designed to flag similarities in unsolved murders that might otherwise be obscured by distance in time or place. The purpose of VICAP is to assist local police in linking up with agencies in other jurisdictions that may have experienced related crimes.

Although an excellent idea in theory, VICAP has encountered some practical limitations since its inception in 1985. For one thing, many local police departments simply haven't cooperated in filling out VICAP questionnaires in relation to their unsolved homicides. As Strope noted, "lots of little departments don't give a damn about VICAP."

More important, recognizing patterns within a series of crimes is not an easy task, even with the aid of a high-speed computer. Further, when a pattern does emerge, there is still no guarantee that the perpetrator will ever be identified.

Still, the Gainesville task force dutifully completed the long and complex VICAP forms, describing in fine detail all that was known about the victims and the crime scenes, hoping that the FBI's computer might help to identify other murders that the killer had committed elsewhere.

For a time, the police had a number of interesting suspects. They investigated a thirty-year-old fast-food cook who surrendered to authorities in Polk County, Florida, on August 29, the day after the last two bodies were discovered in Gainesville. This suspect faced charges he had broken into a Lakeland woman's house where he threatened her with a butcher knife. Members of the Gainesville task force had taken the suspect's fingerprints, footprints, blood, and hair samples and had inspected his home. The search of his residence unearthed a number of curious items, including women's panties, knives, a hangman's noose, pornography, and satanic books. However, the detectives were never able to connect him to the crime scenes through lab tests or eyewitness reports.

Another promising suspect early in the investigation was a fifty-eight-year-old car salesman who was wanted by the FBI for the stabbing death of a fifty-two-year-old brunette woman he had previously dated. Her mutilated body was found in a wooded area of Warren County, Ohio, on August 10, three days after he had disappeared from sight. Task force members had initially placed the suspect in the Gainesville area, where he was considered responsible for the theft of several automobiles just a week before the bodies of the five students were discovered. But he was later dropped from the list of suspects when his presence in Florida could not be confirmed and physical evidence failed to implicate him.

Other intriguing "suspects of the week" included a Fort Walton Beach mortician who reportedly had sexual intercourse with corpses in the morgue and a part-time anatomy and physiology instructor at Santa Fe Community College who may have come in contact with Christa Hoyt at school. The task force left no stone, or good suspect, unturned.

Investigators from the Gainesville task force also hunted for suspects in other parts of the Southeast. In Dothan, Alabama, a small town some thirty-six miles north of the Florida border, a twenty-three-year-old nurse was found raped and then stabbed to death by an unknown assailant. Like the victims in Gainesville, the victim had brown hair and was murdered in her townhouse apartment. In the Gainesville multiple murders, however, the killer was extremely proficient with a knife. By contrast, the Dothan, Alabama, assailant seemed to have little skill with his weapon. The stab wounds to his victim's body were fatal but imprecise. In the end, task force members concluded that the two cases were not similar enough to be linked.

Gainesville investigators looking for similar unsolved cases also flew to Shreveport, Louisiana, where they checked into a gruesome triple murder that had occurred some months earlier. On November 6, 1989, a fifty-four-year-old man, his twenty-four-year-old daughter, and his eight-year-old grandson all died of multiple stab wounds after being attacked in their home. Some investigators downplayed the possibility that the Shreveport slaughter was related to the murders in Gainesville. There were simply too many important dissimilarities to be the work of the same killer.

For months, even as lead after lead became dead ends for other possible offenders, the Pillsbury Dough Boy remained in the public spotlight as the task force's number one suspect. Newspapers around the state of Florida ran front-page stories about his background, his questioning by police investigators, and charges against him related to the assault of his elderly grandmother. As early as September 2, the *Gainesville Sun* reported in a headline story entitled "From Good Student to Unstable Young Man" that "18-year-old Edward Lewis Humphrey is still the top suspect in the murders of five college students in Gainesville." The *Miami Herald* reported that the task force had "retrieved 'promising' evidence" when they searched Humphrey's Gainesville apartment, his 1978 Cadillac, and his grandmother's white two-story Colonial home 180 miles away. Using a metal detector, police officers searched a creek alongside the apartment complex in which Humphrey had resided. They painstakingly picked through the garbage in the apartment's dumpster. Investigators also obtained hair and blood samples from Humphrey while he was incarcerated in Brevard County Jail.

According to the *Herald,* a jail guard testified that Humphrey had referred to himself as "John" and that he had been evicted by his three roommates from his Gatorwood apartment after a physical altercation. The *Florida Times-Union* in Jacksonville reported that Humphrey earlier claimed to know the person responsible for the deaths of Christina Powell and Sonja Larson. The *Tampa Tribune* suggested that, for a short time, Ed had lived in a dorm at UF where, at the same time, two of the victims had resided. The *Tribune* wrote in addition that an unnamed acquaintance of Humphrey was also a suspect in the slayings.[17]

In the meantime, Humphrey remained in custody in lieu of one million dollars bond. Whatever remained of Ed's good reputation in the community had dissolved into a nationally publicized image of evil and insanity. No longer was he regarded merely as the strange young man from Indiatlantic who often made a nuisance of himself but was essentially harmless. Now he was trans-

---

[17]Details of newspaper coverage found in Lisa Getter, "Gainesville Police: Task Force Retrieved 'Promising' Evidence," *Miami Herald,* September 9, 1990, p. 5B.

formed into a disfigured, psychotic monster—a modern-
day version of Jack the Ripper, who quite possibly had
preyed upon five young people, snuffing out their lives
in hideous fashion.

By the time Humphrey's Melbourne trial on charges
of aggravated battery began in October, his grandmother
had already recanted her original allegations of Ed's
abusive treatment. At his bond reduction hearing earlier,
she had watched as her grandson, shackled and clad in
his jailhouse red uniform, was led into the courtroom by
two deputies. Otherwise disoriented and teary eyed, he
smiled only once as Hlavaty blew him a kiss from across
the room. The side of her face still badly bruised, she
testified that her grandson was capable of controlling his
violent behavior, that he wouldn't harm anyone—unless,
of course, he was provoked by them.[18]

Hlavaty suddenly had no memory of the events surrounding her injuries, claiming instead that she probably
had taken a fall while helping Ed search for his contact
lens. In court, however, Dr. Jere Fitts, an emergency
room doctor who was on duty at Holmes Regional Medical Center on the evening that Hlavaty was brought in,
disputed her explanation.

"She had multiple contusions on the right side of her
face and jaw, she had fractures, nasal contusion and
abrasion, a loose tooth and possibly a fracture in the area
that holds the teeth in," Fitts testified. "She would have
had to have received at least more than three or four
blows."[19]

Deputy Douglas Hammock added that on the evening
of the alleged assault Hlavaty's blue-and-white dress
was soaked with blood, that blood from a wound on her
head dripped into her face, and that she had a bruise
above her right eye.

The deputy also said that he was with Ed Humphrey

[18]Lisa Getter, Phil Long, and Tom Dubocq, "Police Take Hair Samples, from Slaying Suspect," *Miami Herald*, September 7, 1990, p. 1A.
[19]Cynthia Barnett, "Judge Keeps Data from Jury," *Gainesville Sun*,
October 10, 1990, p. 9A.

as he sat in the back of a cruiser on the night of the confrontation with his grandmother. "I hit her. I hit her. I hit her. I'm sorry," Humphrey had said, his hands and arms covered with blood. In a self-destructive outburst, he rammed his head into the Plexiglas shield separating the front and back seats of the patrol car and then writhed in pain.

Elna Hlavaty had asked the authorities to drop the charges against her grandson but to no avail. Ed Humphrey was convicted and received a twenty-two-month sentence for assault, the maximum sentence possible to impose under Florida law.

14

The *Press*ure on the Task Force

The local and national press had a field day covering the fact, rumor, and speculation surrounding the vicious Gainesville student murders. Fueled by the fears of Gainesville residents as well as by the morbid curiosity of millions of Americans from Sarasota to Seattle, reporters from as far away as Italy even came to Gainesville looking for a story.

Although Chief Clifton obliged the media by holding daily press conferences, he was reluctant to give details. Of course, that didn't stop reporters from digging behind the scenes, looking for a scoop. It would be no exaggeration to say that media competition for a new angle was fierce, if not cutthroat. Reporters attempted to cultivate their own personal inside sources within the investigation. Some of the less scrupulous scribes even offered detectives on the case cash, expensive gifts, and even sex for their cooperation, with, of course, a guarantee of anonymity. At the extreme, some tabloids offered huge sums of money—"enough to retire on," as one investigator put it—for a few choice crime scene photographs.

Any desire to keep some of the grisly details away from public consumption evaporated within days of the murders. The *Saint Petersburg Times* reported early on that pieces of flesh from the first three victims were missing. Although close to the truth, it left plenty of room for imagination and wild speculation. The *Orlando Sentinel* stretched the limits of tasteful reporting to the extreme, however. As early as August 28, the *Sentinel* reported accurately that two of the victims had their nipples removed and also revealed that Hoyt had been decapitated and her head placed on a shelf. At least one cat was out of the bag.

One consequence of restricted access to information was that the families of the victims were themselves ill informed about whatever progress was being made in the case. They often learned about new developments just like everyone else in Florida—by reading about them in off-the-record newspaper accounts.

The five victims were dead and buried, yet their families suffered repeated emotional blows each time new information leaked out in the press. The families and friends of the victims were constantly bombarded with details of the crimes, some factual and some fictional. They often heard the details not from the task force or through official channels, but from reporters who wanted a reaction to their latest scoop.

The emotional problems of surviving victims—the families and friends of Sonja, Christina, Christa, Tracy, and Manny—were intensified because of the intrusion of the mass media. In high-profile cases, like the Gainesville slayings, members of the media often try to get close to families of the victims, hoping to obtain quotes from them. Some of the families did their best to avoid all contact with the press and television reporters. Others nominated spokespersons to serve as go-betweens to deal with publicity.

Understandably, surviving victims generally want to know everything regarding the death of their loved ones and the efforts by the criminal justice system to bring the perpetrator to justice. Because of the newsworthiness of serial murder investigations, however, police and prosecutors tend to be especially cautious about sharing information with victims' families. Officials fear that confidential material will surface in the newspapers. As a consequence, law enforcement authorities become especially guarded about discussing high-profile cases, even with surviving victims, out of concern that the families will succumb to pressure from the media and reveal important details.

The Gainesville task force tried to maintain tight control over what information about the crimes could be released to the Larsons, Powells, Hoyts, Pauleses, and Taboadas. Aware that reporters from around the country were constantly trying to interview the grieving parents, the police were cautious not to jeopardize the investigation.

The families, in a sense, were seen as a liability. The task force brought each of the families to visit its headquarters in January 1991. The primary purpose was not to brief the families, but to pump them for additional information about the victims that may have been missed previously—where they had been, whom they were friends with, whom they spoke to, and so on. The loved ones of the victims got answers to very few of their own questions about what happened and why. Some of the families begged to see the crime scene photographs; without seeing the truth for themselves, their imaginations were allowed to run wild. The request was denied.

Whether or not intentional, some information pertaining to a multiple murder and its investigation is bound to reach story-hungry reporters. When such information is released, or leaked, to the press, the relatives often learn secondhand about developments in the case from reading the newspaper. It was a major source of discomfort and aggravation to the surviving victims of Gainesville that they were not the first to be told of whatever information was released to the public. Although many of the relatives understood that certain facts of the case had to remain confidential, they felt that family members had a right to know first, before the general public did.

The attempt by the Gainesville task force to restrict news releases was an important strategic move. Oftentimes, "suspects" will come forward to turn themselves in for crimes they did not commit either out of a misplaced sense of guilt or simply for the publicity. Recognizing this, homicide investigators routinely hold back certain key information about a crime so that they can quiz so-called compulsive confessors concerning their claims of criminal responsibility. Much more important, investigators try to control the release of information so that they can capitalize when a real suspect happens to slip during an interrogation by mentioning some detail of a crime that had not been made public.

For this reason, the leaks in the Gainesville investigation became extremely detrimental. When a possible suspect mentioned some specific detail of the crimes, the task force had to figure out whether he had revealed the information before or after the newspaper had published it. For example, prime suspect Edward Humphrey had made a number of statements to people around town, suggesting that he had special knowledge of the murders. The critical question was whether he had merely picked up the information from reading local newspapers. Because the media was so much out of their control, investigators were forced to maintain a detailed log of news coverage—both electronic and print—with which to compare suspect statements.

Another major impediment for the police was the speed with which the press learned of each new suspect. Agent Strope knew that time was of the essence whenever a new suspect surfaced. Asking eyewitnesses whether they recognized a particular suspect would be useless once his photo was printed in the newspaper. Thus, the task force only had about forty-eight hours to canvas the neighborhoods surrounding the murder sites with a photo lineup containing the mug shot of the latest potential killer. Strope knew that within two days the papers would have learned the suspect's identity and would have plastered his driver's license photo across the front page of the morning edition.

Overall, the relationship between the task force and the press was far from positive. Reporters constantly

complained about the task force's unwillingness to release or confirm certain information. In turn, investigators complained about the exploitation of anonymous
inside sources—members of the task force who were
apparently leaking or selling confidential records. The
OICs brought in a security expert to check the phones
in the all-purpose room for bugs and even threatened to
seek out the "traitors" with lie detectors. At the same
time, the press wrote harsh editorials criticizing the task
force for mismanagement and incompetence. From the
point of view of Lee Strope and his colleagues, the press
simply underestimated the complexities involved in
bringing to justice a cunning serial killer.

15

Pubes and Tubes

Agent Strope and most others on the task force fully expected that with Ed Humphrey in the picture, the case was now a "slam dunk." They had a good suspect in custody even though it was for an unrelated assault on his grandmother. Ed said all the right things, looked guilty as sin, and even fit the FBI psychological profile. All they had left to do was to analyze physical evidence linking Ed Humphrey to the crime scenes, and the case would be closed. Turn out the lights, it's time to go home.

As the days and weeks passed, the FDLE lab technicians in Jacksonville worked tirelessly, analyzing a large volume of physical evidence collected at the three crime scenes, including blood, semen, hairs, clothing, shoe prints, and tool marks. Some of their work involved trying to identify the nature of certain evidence. For example, what kind of shoe or sneaker had made the bloody imprint found on the phone in Tracy Paules's bedroom? And what exactly was the blue soapy substance that coated the three pubic hairs found on the blanket at Hoyt's apartment? Other lab tests involved classifying physical evidence. For example, each bloodstain had to be blood typed. The most critical lab work, however, involved comparing evidence found at different murder sites as well as matching crime scene evidence to samples taken from various suspects, including the Pillsbury Dough Boy. There was so much to do, but the Jacksonville lab was state-of-the-art and well staffed for the job.

Meanwhile, Lee Strope had obtained several search warrants in an attempt to gather evidence that might further implicate the Dough Boy. Humphrey's apartment, his car, and his grandmother's home in Indiatlantic were turned upside down by detectives looking for the murder weapon, bloody gloves, even the missing nipples.

At Grandma Hlavaty's home, where Ed stayed from time to time, investigators came upon a knife stored in a milk jug. But it had no obvious signs of blood or tissue on it and was extremely rusted, as if it had remained undisturbed for a prolonged period of time. In addition, the dimensions of the knife's blade simply didn't fit any of the victims' wounds. Investigators also discovered a Ka-Bar knife hidden behind the hot-water heater at Humphrey's campus address in the Hawaiian Village complex; but covered with dust, it looked like it had been there for years. Also at Ed's Gainesville apartment, investigators found several gloves, any one of which might have been worn by the murderer to hide his identity. Yet all of these gloves were of the one-size-fits-all variety; none had distinguishing features that might have been used to identify it as being at any of the crime scenes. And nowhere did they find any body parts.

What started out looking like an open-and-shut case turned decidedly more difficult following the series of disappointing searches. Indeed, the paucity of hard evidence against Ed Humphrey tended to support his outraged family's contention regarding his innocence. There was no weapon recovered, few if any reliable eyewitness accounts, only a suspect so confused and cantankerous that he could hardly get himself out of the rain, let alone figure out how to kill five people and get away with it.

* * *

Bureau Chief Steve Platt, director of the Jacksonville crime lab, kept the task force well informed on all forensic developments. Numerous latent prints had been lifted from scene 1 (Larson/Powell) and scene 3 (Paules/ Taboada) but not as many from scene 2 (Hoyt). There had been some unidentified latent prints on the blinds at scene 2, a palm print on the sliding glass door at 3, and at the doorway at 1. The unidentified prints that were in good shape were run through the Automated Fingerprint Identification System, but no matches were found.

Fabric and glove prints were also taken from crime scene 3. There were potentially two types of glove prints. One was similar to cotton work-type gloves with definite weave/rib marks. The other was a textured, non-slip type with little gripping knobs on the fingertips, like latex gloves. Both types of prints were potentially on Paules's left leg. At scene 1, there was evidence of the fabric-type glove in the purses and on the billfolds. There was no indication of those types of prints at 2.

A shoe print was found at scene 3 on the phone by Paules's bed. A similar tread print was found at scene 2 outside, about forty to fifty feet from the apartment. The prints came from Reebok BB4600 high-tops, and at all three scenes, the markings looked like the shoes had not been worn much. At scenes 1 and 2, the shoe size could have been 9 to 9½, but the size wasn't clear in the scene 3 shoe print.

Platt noted that the tool marks on the points of entry were the same at all three crime scenes. They were identified as being caused by a six-inch Stanley Handyman screwdriver with a five-sixteenths-inch blade. Platt indicated that the Stanley tool, also marketed as the Workman, was a rather common item. After examining the entry marks at scenes 2 and 3, the lab concluded that the tool should be easily identifiable once found.

Strope was interested in all of the details of Platt's reports, and he dutifully took notes. But after having struck out on the searches of Humphrey's residences and vehicle, he was frustrated in thinking that none of the findings pertaining to glove and sneaker prints or tool marks did anything to implicate Ed.

Not every avenue was a dead end, however. Just about the only compelling physical evidence possibly to connect Humphrey to the crime scenes were five pubic hairs found at the first and second murder sites. Under a warrant for a body search, samples of head and pubic hairs had been pulled from Humphrey for the purpose of forensic comparison.

Hairs differ from person to person on a variety of dimensions, including coarseness, thickness, color, and dozens of other characteristics observable only through a microscope. In forensic use, the lab attempts to compare a head or pubic hair recovered at a crime scene—from bedsheets or the victim's body—with samples taken directly from a suspect. Unfortunately, hair comparisons cannot exactly place a suspect at the scene of a crime, but they can at least exclude him.

An exhaustive series of tests conducted by the FDLE lab using two alternative methods concluded that the hairs recovered from the crime scenes in Gainesville were very consistent with hair samples taken from Ed Humphrey. He could, therefore, not be excluded as a viable suspect.

On the other hand, hair evidence does not constitute the conclusive proof resulting from fingerprinting or even DNA. Indeed, many experts argue that hair comparison evidence is far from infallible, even if it is collected and analyzed in a competent manner.

Despite the limitations inherent in hair analysis, however, some FDLE lab experts were willing to stake their professional reputations on their conclusion that the crime scene hairs and Humphrey hairs were one in the same. Asked at a task force meeting whether the lab could be mistaken, Platt responded unequivocally, "It is highly unlikely that the hairs assigned to Humphrey would be from someone else." He added that only once in the entire career of his lab examiner had she found hair samples from two individuals that could not be distinguished.

Despite Platt's confidence, state attorney Len Register was reluctant to bring Humphrey forward to a grand jury and for good reason. Failure to win an indictment based on the hairs would be political suicide. A jury might possibly be swayed by the scientific testimony of hair specialists. Still, Register knew that in Florida the appeals court has been skeptical of hair testing, requiring for conviction a confluence of evidence in which hair analysis plays only a minimal if supporting role.

The murder conviction of Rodney Charles Horstman in Polk County, Florida, for example, was overturned on appeal because there was little besides hair evidence to implicate the defendant. Horstman had been seen on the night of the murder attempting on several occasions to make sexual advances toward a woman, who was found dead later that evening. The police recovered head and pubic hairs on the victim's underwear, on her body, and in her mouth that were "indistinguishable," according to court testimony of the lab expert, from that of the defendant's. Yet in overturning the guilty verdict, the court was quite firm: "The State emphasizes that its expert, Agent Malone, testified that the chances were almost nonexistent that the hairs found on the body originated from anyone other than Horstman. We do not share Mr. Malone's conviction in the infallibility of hair comparison evidence." The court also expressed concern that hairs could easily be planted on a victim by a third party in order to frame a defendant.

Thus, without corroboration, hair comparisons would not be sufficient to implicate Humphrey in the Gainesville slayings. Further tests could be run but not without serious problems. For example, Steve Platt indicated that his lab could test the hair evidence for traces of lithium, which Ed Humphrey had been prescribed for his illness. The testing process would have destroyed the crime scene hairs themselves, however, and the task force was not willing to sacrifice this valuable evidence.

Fortunately, investigators had other physical evidence on which to draw a conclusion about the identity of the perpetrator in Gainesville. He had also deposited semen at all three crime scenes—on Powell's panties, in Hoyt's vagina, and in Paules's rectum. In the search for physical evidence to tie Humphrey to the crime sites, hair comparisons quickly took a backseat to the analysis of DNA.

DNA (short for deoxyribonucleic acid) contains the genetic codes for inherited characteristics. There is, therefore, a unique DNA blueprint for everyone except identical twins that can be extracted from samples of human cells in saliva, skin, sweat, bone, and follicles of hair but especially in blood and semen. Therefore, DNA typing can be used not only to implicate a suspect, but also to exclude someone whose DNA does not match that found in crime scene evidence.

DNA molecules provide a genetic code consisting of an extremely lengthy sequence of four letters—A, T, C and G—representing the four nuclear types: adenine, thymine, cytosine, and guanine. The letters occur in pairs—A is always associated with T and C with G—and the pairs are arranged along a spiral-shaped structure known as the double helix.

A genetic code, or "genetic fingerprint," present in DNA can be determined from small amounts of bodily tissue or fluid. Enzymes are used to cut the DNA into fragments or segments of the genetic code. These segments are separated and sorted by a lab process to form a pattern that looks like a grocery store bar code used for scanning prices.

As with all types of forensic tests, the potential value of a DNA analysis depends on the condition of the physical evidence itself—the state in which it is found and the care with which it is handled. For example, the semen found in Tracy Paules's rectal swab was genetically compromised by fecal bacteria. Its value was similar to that of a partial or smudged fingerprint.

The first use of DNA testing in court proceedings was at a 1987 Orlando trial in which the defendant Tommy Lee Andrews was found guilty of rape based on a DNA match. Since then, DNA analysis has been used to convict or acquit thousands of suspects in cases around the country.

Even with its increasing use in court, however, DNA analysis has been rather controversial. The legal concerns reside not in the scientific theory itself, but both in the interpretation of results and in the quality of the testing process. In 1989, for example, a case against an accused child rapist was dismissed because sloppy DNA testing was used to implicate him at his trial.

The Gainesville task force didn't expect any serious legal challenges to using DNA for its case. Not only had the Florida courts been fairly receptive to this new technology, but the FDLE lab was reputed to be about as careful as could be in following strict testing protocols.

Monday, September 17, 1990, was a memorable day for Lee Strope—the day the "bomb" fell, or, as he put it, "the day that will live in infamy."

Bureau Chief Steve Platt came to the morning meeting with good news and bad news from their DNA testing. The good news was that the semen found at the three different crime scenes genetically matched one another. This ruled out the possibility that each victim had just had sex with her own boyfriend rather than with the same person—the killer. The bad news, however, seemed to let Edward Humphrey off the hook; his blood sample did not have the same genetic code as the semen found at the crime scenes.

Platt's announcement to task force members had pretty much the same shocking effect as would a goal-line fumble by the Gators in front of a hometown crowd. A few of the agents yelled "shit" and other expletives, and then the room was stone silent.

For almost three weeks, the investigators had assumed that Ed Humphrey was "their man" and that the case was all but wrapped up. But now it was back to the drawing board for Lee Strope and the task force. Who was the phantom semen "donor"? Had he operated alone or did he have a partner—perhaps Edward Humphrey—in carrying out his killing spree?

Some task force members were almost relieved that the DNA evidence failed to implicate Humphrey, because they had always suspected that he was the wrong man. Others still believed that Humphrey was involved, perhaps as one member of a killing team. Maybe Ed hadn't raped all the victims, they argued, but he could still have been at one or two of the crime scenes, assisting his partner in locating victims, restraining them, and committing the murders. The two-killer theory was appealing: it allowed investigators to expand their quest for another perpetrator without abandoning the premise that the Pillsbury Dough Boy was somehow involved in the murders.

Back on the trail for a killer with some other name than Humphrey, the task force systematically examined and excluded hundreds of potential subjects (a less threatening synonym for suspects)—boyfriends, ex-boyfriends, employers, and neighbors—who had known one or more of the victims and may have had an ax to grind. Many had perfectly airtight alibis—having been, for example, far away at the time of the murders. Others were cleared from consideration based on what the task force referred to as "pubes and tubes": their hair and blood type simply didn't match the crime scene evidence.

The lab tests of semen found at all three crime scenes had determined the murderer/rapist to be a type B secretor. He had the uncommon blood type B; as a secretor, moreover, his blood type was evident through glandular secretions into bodily fluids including his semen.

Overall, 9.6 percent of the population are B secretors (twelve percent have blood type B, and eighty percent of those are secretors). Since type B secretors are more common among blacks than whites (and a black male head hair was found on Larson's finger), the task force was especially interested in the fact that some of the victims had dated black men. Sonja Larson had a black boyfriend who attended the University of Tennessee and had had another black boyfriend before him. Christina Powell had had three or four black boyfriends. Paules had been dating a black attorney from Miami. The task force was able, however, to eliminate all former boy-friends from the list of potential suspects on the basis of lab tests and alibis.

Strope and his colleagues kept returning to the many similarities among the victims and crime scenes in order to generate new investigative leads. The task force collected phone records, cash and credit card receipts, and spoke to scores of friends and relatives in an attempt to chronicle the last few days and weeks of each victim's life. Contained in a ten-foot-long master time line of all five victims, the task force hoped to find commonalities in the activities of the murdered students. The police were looking for restaurants, stores, or other places where several of the victims had been, which might possibly identify a waiter or salesman who had had contact with them.

Each time a new subject surfaced through whatever means, the task force would then attempt to identify some point of contact between the subject and the victims. Why would he have targeted Powell or Hoyt or Paules?

Officer Gary Lockard reported learning, for example, that on Friday, August 24, around 4:30 P.M., Ed Humphrey had gone to building 11 at Gatorwood, his former residence, to try to reclaim his bicycle that he left behind. Manny Taboada and Tracy Paules, whose building was catercorner to Humphrey's destination, were outside in the parking lot at the time.

For three weeks, FDLE crime intelligence analyst Jack Dennard remained stationed in room 222 at the Super 8 Motel off of Archer Road. His assignment was hardly as dramatic or challenging as a motel stakeout. Rather, Dennard spent hour after hour, day after day, chain-smoking cigarettes, drinking Cokes from his own portable refrigerator, and watching videos on a VCR he brought from his home in Jacksonville. And the videos were hardly as interesting as *Darkman* or *Exorcist III*. Instead, his task was to review VHS tapes taken from the security camera at Vern's Quick Stop, a convenience store near Christa Hoyt's apartment.

Dennard examined each frame of videotape at the rate of two per second, waiting to see Hoyt enter the picture and then inspecting who else was in the store at the time. Even though the security film was later computer enhanced at a NASA lab to improve the resolution, it was still difficult for Dennard to recognize with certainty Hoyt or anyone else on the poorly defined images. After weeks of having his eyes glued to the screen, he found nothing of major significance resulting from the assignment.

Another common feature to the murders was that they all occurred in fairly isolated locations, in close proximity to densely wooded areas. Strope reasoned that if there were indeed two killers, as many in the task force were beginning to think, then the woods would have provided a perfect hideout for them to meet nightly in late August to get ready for their deadly missions and then to recon after the plans had been executed. Aided by dogs, trained search teams thoroughly scanned the woods near the murder scenes but uncovered nothing in the way of suspects or useful evidence.

16

The Two-Killer Theory

In the early morning hours of August 25, just about twenty-four hours after the slayings of Sonja Larson and Christina Powell, a man identified as Ed Humphrey was spotted peeking into an apartment at the Oak Forest complex, which abutted the wooded area near Southwest Thirteenth Street. The occupant, a young female student at UF, had stayed up late reading and was about to retire when she caught a glimpse of the strange young man on the balcony outside her second-floor window. Before he was able to dash off, she got a good enough look to recognize the intruder as being Ed Humphrey, a customer she had spoken with the previous afternoon at After Thoughts in the Oaks Mall, where she worked part-time.

Because it occurred only a day after the first set of murders, this sighting seemed significant to the task force. The time of the incident represents the only hole in an otherwise unbroken four-day sequence of daily attacks on students. Like the other crime scenes, this location was bordered by secluded, wooded areas. If the intruder hadn't been scared off, would this have become murder site 2? If so, Ed Humphrey looks more and more like a perpetrator.

Not that he could possibly have committed the murders on his own. It was clear now that Ed simply lacked the required emotional makeup to have pulled off such a complex series of crimes. Moreover, the task force was now aware that semen found at all three crime scenes belonged to the same person, and that person was not Edward Humphrey.

In another bizarre twist, the possibility was discussed among task force members that the semen might have been planted at the crime scenes by Humphrey in order to confuse the investigators and make himself look innocent. Perhaps the Pillsbury Dough Boy had gotten the idea from a film popular at the time of the killings called *Presumed Innocent*, in which a vengeful wife inserts semen into another woman's vagina with a syringe to make her own husband look guilty. The problem with this interpretation was that an individual like Ed Humphrey, who obviously lacked the ability to kill in methodical fashion, probably also lacked the adeptness required to carry out the clever and delicate task of planting semen.

A much more believable explanation was that Ed Humphrey was a member of a killing team—one of two like-minded friends or associates who had gotten together for the purpose of satisfying their sadistic desires by murdering college students.

If two killers were responsible for the Gainesville slayings, then this case was far from unique. Actually, some twenty-five to thirty percent of all serial killings are committed by teams—two or more buddies, lovers, friends, or cousins who go out on a Saturday night the way that other people might get together for a game of cards. The difference is that serial killers don't play poker; simply for the fun of it, they torture and slay their victims.

The Hillside Stranger who brutally tortured and murdered ten young women in Los Angeles actually turned out to be two cousins: Kenneth Bianchi and Angelo Buono. The Calaveras County killers—responsible for the torture and deaths of as many as twenty-five victims in the woods of northern California—were two buddies, Leonard Lake and Charlie Ng. The Sunset Strip Killer, named for the strip in Los Angeles where the victims were picked up and murdered, turned out to be a pair of lovers: Douglas Clark and Carol Bundy (no relation to Ted).

Another possibly germane characteristic of team killers is that one of them is usually subordinate to the other. Bianchi was much younger than and had great respect for his partner in murder. Bianchi would have followed his older cousin anywhere, even into acts of torture and sadism. Similarly, Leonard Lake admired the buddy with whom he hunted down his victims. According to Lake's wife, "Leonard was a different man when he was with Charlie."

Could Humphrey have been the subordinate member of a team of two killers? His family claimed that Ed didn't have the attention span to have executed the murders in the methodical fashion implied by the crime scenes. But according to people who knew him, Humphrey often would take on the personality and style of whomever he was with and follow the lead of whomever he admired. In addition, Ed was clearly enamored with the military lifestyle. He might have obeyed the orders of his "superior officer" to commit murder, whether this person was truly in the military or simply playing the military role. Humphrey may have been a "good soldier" who did whatever he was told. Perhaps the "John" he referred to in earlier interviews was more than a figment of Ed's wild imagination.

The two-killer theory would go a long way toward resolving several glaring inconsistencies in the Gainesville case. First, it would explain why the crime scenes were of a mixed type in terms of the psychological profile. At every murder site, there were indications of an organized killer—someone who carefully and craftfully orchestrated the murders—and of a disorganized killer—someone whose mental illness created a chaotic set of circumstances.

In addition, the two-killer theory would explain why

victims were attacked in such inconsistent fashion. Powell and Paules were both restrained with tape, had their shirts ripped off, were stabbed only enough to ensure death, were sexually assaulted, and were cleaned with soap or liquid detergent, whereas Larson and Taboada were stabbed repeatedly and excessively but little else. If two killers were present, then one person (the controlling, organized assailant) might have killed Powell and Paules, and the other member of the team (the more frenzied and disorganized attacker) might have overpowered Larson and Taboada.

Even the Christa Hoyt crime scene would seem to make more sense under the assumption that two killers collaborated. First, it appeared that it would have been extremely difficult for only one person to have decapitated Christa as cleanly as was done. It was more plausible that one person carefully rotated the head with both hands, while the other assailant used one hand to slice her throat and the other hand to maneuver away the flesh as he cut it.

Second, even the positioning of the young woman's head on the bookcase in the bedroom suggested the presence of two killers rather than one. The bookcase was apparently carried from the living room to the bedroom for the express purpose of being in full view of police officers when they opened the front door and glanced down the hallway. Given the size of the bookcase—not to mention its flimsy construction—it would have been quite awkward for one person to carry it alone, unless that person possessed considerable strength and agility. There were no scratch marks on the floor to indicate that it would have been dragged from room to room. More likely, the bookcase was carried by two individuals, each holding it at one end.

Finally, the two-killer theory helped to explain why Christa Hoyt's excised nipples and a pillowcase filled with a set of souvenir photographs of the victim were left behind. Especially considering the length of time that the killer spent in Hoyt's apartment after he committed the murder, it didn't make sense that he would have been so careless. Assuming two assailants, however, each one may have believed that the other was responsible for taking the souvenirs from the scene. In the process, both left them behind.

Throughout the fall of 1990, members of the task force hotly debated whether or not Ed Humphrey was still a viable suspect. Everyone agreed that there was another killer to be found—the one whose semen was left at the crime scenes. But the issue that remained to be resolved was whether or not Humphrey was there too. On one side of the room, some investigators felt that it was time for the task force to cut its losses, that is, to face the fact that they had made a mistake about Humphrey's complicity and to go in another more productive direction. Even stronger, some members were adamant in claiming that stubbornly keeping Humphrey in the picture was seriously retarding the investigation. On the other side of the room, there was resistance to eliminating Humphrey as a suspect. Not only had the lab matched his hairs to crime scene evidence, but experts confirmed their position regarding his possible involvement in the murders. On the afternoon of December 14, for example, a task force meeting was convened to hear from Dr. Harry McClaren, a forensic psychologist from Quincy, Florida, who had been hired to assess Humphrey's possible role in the crime spree. After reviewing the relevant psychological evidence, including a tape of Humphrey's interrogation, McClaren felt strongly that Humphrey was capable of committing the murders, although he could not have done it alone.

The unwillingness of many task force members to discard Ed, a source of continuing distress to the Hlavaty clan, can be understood in the context of a theory from psychology known as *cognitive dissonance*. According to this perspective, human beings have a powerful need to justify the decisions that they make, whether about selecting a new car or even an old suspect. It was very difficult for those detectives who had invested so much of their energy and time in following a certain path ultimately to consider it a total waste. As a result, those who worked most closely on investigating Humphrey would be the most resistant to dropping him as a suspect.

Even as late as June 1991, state attorney Len Register continued to cling to the two-killer theory. In an interview with the *Gainesville Sun*, he asserted, "The two-perpetrator theory is still an extremely viable one." He was, however, unable to answer the critical question as to how the two partners met or how they were able to maintain a relationship prior to the murders.[20]

This was indeed one of the most troubling questions surrounding the possibility that two perpetrators had slain the five students. In other serial murder cases, the evidence of a long-term and close relationship between killers is unequivocal and therefore never at issue. The Hillside Stranglers were two cousins who shared an apartment. They were often seen with one another by other people and never attempted to deny or conceal their association. Lake and Ng were similarly observed many times in public. In fact, they were apprehended together. And, of course, Clark and Bundy were lovers.

Thus, how could Humphrey have been so close to someone that they had killed in tandem but were never seen together in public? Where were the reliable eyewitnesses? Where was the credible evidence that they had even known one another at all prior to the crimes being committed? And, Ed had been seen in Indiatlantic on the night that Tracy Paules and Manny Taboada were slain. How did he manage to get all the way back to Gainesville—some two hundred miles away—and connect with his partner?

Strope was deeply troubled about a final major flaw in the two-killer theory. The Gainesville murders reflected some degree of care and planning in their execution. *Why would a killer with any brains, and certainly someone as cautious as this*, wondered Strope, *dare to have anything at all to do with a rambling idiot like Ed Humphrey?*

[20]Tom Lyons,"Evidence in Student Slayings Supports Second-Killer Theory," *Gainesville Sun*, June 5, 1991, p.1A.

17

The Big Break

In a tireless effort to find the missing DNA link—the Gainesville killer or possibly Humphrey's partner in crime—the task force expanded its forensics investigation. It collected and analyzed hundreds of blood and pubic hair samples from all sorts of subjects, no matter how tenuous their connection to the case.

Week by week, the lab came up empty on the "tubes and pubes" roundup. Months passed without a "hit," and frustrations in the task force began to mount. The families of the victims grew impatient for justice. And the media was increasingly critical of the investigation.

The pressure on Strope and the task force to solve the case came from all fronts, but none was more powerful than their own desire to find the villain. Lee Strope realized that it would be a long haul. He knew they would have to get lucky.

"In our garbage runs," Strope said, "we had investigators chasing around subjects to get a sample of saliva or blood. We checked hospitals, blood banks, any place that we could get a sample. We even tried to get saliva off of cigarette butts or straws from McDonald's. If you were a B secretor, we were hot on your trail."

Getting lucky required more than just transforming

the FDLE lab into a blood bank of sorts for the population of Gainesville and anyone who happened to have any connection whatsoever to the community. The task force reviewed and reassessed all their investigative leads, looking for some new avenues to explore.

From almost the beginning of the investigation into the Gainesville massacre, the task force had been alerted to a multiple murder in Shreveport, Louisiana, that occurred almost a year earlier. On November 6, 1989, the Shreveport police received a frantic call from Bob Coyles. He had walked over to visit his good neighbor, Tom Grissom, who lived on Beth Lane in the Southern Hills area of the city. Inside the red brick house, Coyles was shocked to discover a hideous scene of bloodshed and human carnage. Three butchered bodies—Tom Grissom, his daughter Julie, and his grandson Sean— littered the living room and bedroom floors.

The police theorized that pretty twenty-four-year-old Julie Grissom, found stabbed to death, had been the killer's primary victim. The hands of the Louisiana State University senior had been bound with duct tape, and her breast had been severely bitten. After his attack, the killer had posed the brunette's nude body on the bed in a sexually provocative pose, apparently for the purpose of shocking those who discovered it. He had draped her legs over the side of the bed and dropped her feet to the floor. Her hair had been fanned out behind her. Then the killer had placed a towel at his victim's feet and had cleaned her genital area with vinegar.

Both Tom Grissom and his eight-year-old grandson, Julie's nephew, had been jumped from behind and had suffered multiple stab wounds to their backs. Taking advantage of the element of surprise, the killer had apparently eliminated these two victims in order to get to Julie. With incredible fierceness, he had swiftly overpowered her father and then easily disposed of the young boy.

The possible link between the Gainesville slayings and the triple murder in Shreveport some nine months earlier was initially downplayed and for good reason. For one thing, the victims in Gainesville had been viciously mutilated, but not the Shreveport woman. Her father and nephew were likely secondary victims—simply in the wrong place at the wrong time—and had been slaughtered rather expeditiously—without ritual, ceremony, or postmortem positioning of the bodies.

In addition, the Gainesville and Shreveport attacks were as different as night and day literally. The Florida students were slain in the hours before or after midnight, whereas the Grissoms had been killed in the early evening, just after dark. Where was the "signature" often employed by investigators to link the crime scenes in different locations to a single serial killer?

A connection might have been made, however, on a statistical basis. In both cases, the primary victims were young white female college students with brown hair. It is extremely rare for college-aged females, let alone college students generally, to be stabbed to death by an unknown assailant. In fact, it happens on average only thirty times per year in the United States.

What is more, both crimes were multiple murders. In each one, the assailant had used two-inch duct tape to bind his female victims, had displayed the bodies of his female victims in a sexually provocative way, and had attempted to clean up afterward. In Shreveport, the victim's clothes were run through the wash cycle. In both incidents, the women were douched (in Shreveport, with vinegar; in Gainesville, with detergent).

It is true that the Gainesville murders were more brutal in terms of both body count and bloodshed than the earlier case in Louisiana. But this pattern is quite consistent with the general tendency for serial killers to increase their level of perversity and barbarism over time. In the Hillside Strangler case, for example, Bianchi and Buono's first victim was strangled to death and then dumped unceremoniously from a moving automobile. As their murder spree progressed, however, the killing cousins weren't satisfied with committing a simple murder. Instead, in subsequent slayings, they would first carry their victim to Angelo Buono's upholstery shop, where they tied her to a chair and tortured her in unspeakable ways before finally ending her life. For many serial killers, murder becomes easier the more often it is committed. More important, perhaps, brutality is like an addictive drug; serial killers need larger and larger doses in order to fuel their fantasies to maintain the "high" that they gain from their sadistic activities.

Many serial killers do indeed have a "signature," which they express in their preference for certain kinds of victims; crime scene locations; methods of torturing, murdering, and disposing of their victims; and so on. From the point of view of investigators who are eager to solve a case, the presence of a strict pattern may be seen as a foregone conclusion. Unfortunately, however, killers do not always act so consistently as authorities might expect, varying their operations and victim characteristics in response to the details of their fantasies as well as to the changing circumstances and opportunities they encounter from crime scene to crime scene. Sometimes they even change their plans in reaction to media publicity.

One other possibility occurred to task force investigators in attempting to explain differences between the Shreveport and Gainesville crime scenes. It was clear that Ed Humphrey had spent November 1989 in Gainesville; he was nowhere near Shreveport during the time that the massacre occurred. Perhaps the Shreveport killer had operated alone; he might have teamed up with the Pillsbury Dough Boy only after he got to Gainesville.

The task force hoped, therefore, that someone with ties to both Shreveport and Gainesville would emerge as a suspect. With this is mind, the investigators began comparing hospital and university records in both cities, looking for common names. Unfortunately, none was found.

The big break came on January 11, 1991, when the task force learned that tall and lanky Danny Harold Rolling had passed through town in late August 1990. The thirty-six-year-old drifter and career criminal had been picked up for armed robbery some thirty miles south in Ocala. The Gainesville task force had received a phone call from detectives in Ocala, informing them that a guy by the name of Rolling in custody there had apparently stolen a car from a Gainesville resident. Maybe the task force should look closely at Rolling as a possible suspect. The fact that the car thief had grown up in Shreveport, not far from the Grissoms' home, was enough for the task force to place him at the top of its list of suspects.

Rolling certainly didn't look like a serial killer, although he was deceptively strong and had often defied the law. He was a big friendly guy who liked to chat with strangers and dominate conversations. He spent many of his evenings in bars and lounges, drinking rum and Cokes and picking up women. So long as he concealed his prison record and unstable personality, Danny's dark brown hair and wild hazel eyes, his talented singing and guitar playing, and his charming ways were quite effective in drawing an audience. He never mentioned that he was on the run from the law after shooting his father in the head and then committing a series of armed robberies.

One of the more puzzling—really confusing—aspects of trying to connect Danny Rolling to the Gainesville homicides was the fact that he had typically committed armed robberies and burglaries rather than murders and that he had always used a gun, not a knife. In his hometown of Shreveport, Louisiana, he had been seen by neighbors angrily stabbing a one-inch board in the backyard with a huge knife. But in injuring his father and stealing from grocery stores in Alabama, Georgia, Mississippi, and Florida, he had carried a handgun.

Nevertheless, many of Danny's acquaintances who watched him grow up and observed his behavior over a period of time described him with terms like "emotionally unstable," "impulsive," and "childlike." He was a man who could hardly focus on a conversation or concentrate on a single idea for very long. When he talked, he rambled. When he was lucky enough to find a job, he was quickly fired. When he tried an armed robbery or a burglary, he was easily caught. Not unlike their musings about Edward Humphrey, many investigators on the task force now wondered out loud how a small-time crook who committed such ill-conceived and sloppily planned daytime stickups could also plan and execute a series of daring nighttime sexual murders.

What many observers failed to understand was that serial killers don't need the intelligence of brain surgeons to lure their victims and avoid detection. They may be manipulative and cunning, having some degree of criminal savor faire, but they are not necessarily smart. They may be crafty and deceptive—even masters of presentation of self—without having genius IQs.

How much intelligence would it take for Danny Rolling to stab, mutilate, decapitate, and then attempt to cover his tracks by cleaning up a little? If the killer had been so clever, he would probably have realized that his sperm could be used to trace him to the crime scenes.[21]

In the eyes of investigators, Danny Rolling's criminal history may not have quite fit the profile of a "sex-crazed" serial killer. The task force might have ignored him, therefore, but they couldn't ignore the fact that Rolling was from Shreveport. Strope thought about how dramatically the emergence of Danny Rolling had changed the scope of the entire investigative effort. "When R. B. Ward left at the end of October 1990 to go on sick leave, Humphrey was believed to be the sole perpetrator," said Strope. "When R. B. returned from his sick leave during the winter 1991, Danny Rolling was the prime suspect."

---

[21]Mitch Stacy, "Experts Say Rolling Only Loosely Fits the Mold of a 'Serial Killer,' " *Gainesville Sun*, August 27, 1991, p. 7A.

18

The Shreveport Connection

In January 1990, two months after the Grissom murders, as more and more suspects were eliminated and the case in Shreveport grew as cold as Louisiana's wet winter weather, the Shreveport Police Department had decided to turn to the FBI in an effort to develop a profile of the killer. On the morning of January 8, 1990, Officer D. W. Ashley met with FBI agents Al Brantley, Greg McCrary, and Steve Etter, all members of the Behavioral Science Unit at the FBI Academy in Quantico, Virginia.

After discussing the multiple murder of the Grissoms and analyzing the crime scene, the agents submitted their profile: the killer of the Grissom family would probably turn out to be a single white male in his late twenties to early thirties who has an athletic, muscular build and thinks of himself as a "macho man." Lacking any feelings of remorse, the killer probably didn't enjoy murdering a child but "took care of business" when the situation required it. He probably has a record for committing sexual offenses, assaults, and burglaries; has spent time in prison; and harbors an antiauthority attitude that makes it difficult for him to hold a job. He also has a reputation for being quick to anger and is confrontational. The efficiency and organization of the crime scene suggests that the killer may be a "hit man" who was hired by a spurned lover.

The FBI profile accomplished little more than to take up space on Detective Gary Foster's desk in the Shreveport Police Department. But one year later, as 1990 gave way to 1991, a serendipitous link—a crime fighter connection—between the police from two southern cities eight hundred miles apart began to look mutually advantageous. The Shreveport case produced Gainesville's leading suspect; and the Gainesville case did much the same for the yet unsuccessful Shreveport investigation.

In many respects, Danny Rolling fit the profile constructed from the Grissom crime scene. He was a divorced white male in his thirties, big and strong, who had a criminal record and had spent considerable time behind bars. He possessed a ferociously confrontational style and a very poor work history. Though Rolling had never been known as a hit man, he might have been willing, under the right circumstances, to exchange bloodshed for a few bucks. On the day of the murders, Danny was fired from his job at a restaurant, only a mile down the road from the Grissom home.

19

The Whole Tooth
and Nothing But the Tooth

By the close of 1990, the investigators in Gainesville turned their attention to the drifter from Shreveport who had a long history of criminal violence. Danny Rolling was looking more and more like he could be the missing link. The only thing absent was hard evidence.

At the time, Rolling was being held in the Marion County Jail on charges of armed robbery, car theft, and fleeing and eluding the authorities. Special agent Don Maines, who had closely followed the Shreveport connection for months, quickly learned from Rolling's military record that Danny had the right blood type—Type B. This prompted Maines to ask the prisoner for a sample of his blood—a request to which Rolling freely consented.

Rolling's blood sample was immediately sent to the Jacksonville lab, as had been done routinely with the blood specimens from countless other subjects. But the results of the blood tests were hardly routine. A preliminary enzyme test of Rolling's blood subtype—a first pass screening done prior to a more elaborate DNA exam, revealed that Rolling belonged to a small "elite" group—the .3 percent of the population who could have produced the semen found at the Gainesville crime scenes.

On January 11, 1991, Strope and the others in the task force got word of the preliminary lab tests on their newest prime suspect. Some quick calculations suggested that out of the population in and around Gainesville at the time of the murders, only about 600 would have had this particular blood subtype. Considering the small percentage of those who would have been in Shreveport at the time of the Grissom murders, Rolling was looking pretty good. But, of course, the task force had been disappointed so many times before when good leads seemed to fizzle overnight. Strope tried not to get too excited about this latest twist in the case.

State's Attorney Len Register added his own cautionary note to the mildly jubilant atmosphere. The blood test would likely not stand up in court. Rolling had given his consent while in custody, and, besides, he was on medication at the time. Any half decent defense attorney could challenge the admissibility of the evidence and would probably win. Register also noted that there wasn't even enough evidence, so-called probable cause, to convince a judge to issue a warrant for a new blood sample. The task force would just have to find some other means of obtaining physical evidence implicating Rolling, without his participation. They could only hope that Rolling would casually discard something with sufficient bodily fluid for a lab workup. Maines remained assigned to the jail and waited.

The prisoner happened to be having trouble with his teeth. In fact, on January 22, 1991, the jail dentist had extracted one of Danny's teeth and then packed the area with gauze. It was standard procedure, as a security measure, for Corrections Officer Sgt. Donna Borgione to observe the entire dental procedure. She watched as the dentist excised Rolling's upper-right molar, wrapped it and the bloody gauze packing in a red plastic bag and disposed of it in a nearby bin. Then, later, returning to the jail infirmary, Sgt. Borgione confiscated the discarded pulled tooth and gauge, which she handed over to the task force to be analyzed.

Results of the DNA analysis of Rolling's bloody tooth—the 101st DNA blood test conducted by investigators—were unequivocal. Bureau Chief Steve Platt came to the task force again with good news and bad news. This time, it was good news for the task force, and bad news for Danny Rolling. His positive match on DNA from all three crime scenes was enough to convince investigators that they were definitely on the right track: he was their man. It would also be enough to convince a grand jury months later to indict Danny Rolling for the murders of Sonja Larson, Christina Powell, Christa Hoyt, Tracy Paules, and Manny Taboada.

Just to make sure that the DNA evidence from the pulled tooth wouldn't be thrown out of court because it was seized improperly, investigators then obtained a warrant to procure another blood sample from Rolling. Actually, they got a lot more than blood. On Friday, February 8, Lee Strope went to the Marion County jail, to serve Danny Rolling with a search warrant. Strope confronted the prisoner, informing him, "Danny Harold Rolling, I have here a search warrant signed by the court to take from you certain evidence from your body."

Technician Gordon Thorp and Steve Platt proceeded to seize handwriting exemplars, photographs, three vials of blood, saliva samples, head and body hairs, along with full sets of hand-, finger-, and footprints. All of the evidence was then taken to the Jacksonville crime lab for analysis.

Strope then drove to the Ocala Police Department to serve a search warrant on their property room. Lee's mission was to gather a number of pieces of evidence that had been taken when Rolling was arrested for the Ocala robbery. He got a Walkman, a hand-drawn map, a yellow-handle screwdriver, a blue backpack, a blue fanny pack, a handwritten note regarding emergency notification, a light blue pocket comb, one gold pierced earring, and a black T-shirt.

But the suspect had still to face charges for the armed

robbery he had committed. On September 18, 1991, Danny Rolling went to court and received a life sentence as a habitual offender for his Winn-Dixie robbery in Ocala. Hearing the decision, he turned to the judge and said, ''God bless the people of Florida, and Lord help me.'' But his troubles had only begun.

On the same day, Edward Humphrey was released from prison.

20

Case Closed

Most serial killer experts from around the country who were polled by local newspapers concerning their assessment of Danny Rolling as the likely Gainesville student killer concluded that he wasn't the type. For example, Vermont psychologist John Philpin, who profiled the Gainesville murders for the *Miami Herald*, doubted that Rolling could have committed such grisly homicides because he lacked "a little flash of brilliance"—more a career criminal specializing in burglaries and robberies, not sex crimes.[22]

Actually, strict patterns of criminal behavior are more often found in the thinking of observers about serial killers than in the actions of serial killers themselves. Rolling's criminal activities could easily have been in a sense on two distinct and independent tracks. On the one hand, robbery was little more than a means to an end for him. He always had tremendous trouble finding any job that paid more than minimum wage and even more trouble keeping one. His criminal career as a robber, burglar, and car thief compensated for his poor work

[22] "Rolling Lacks 'Flash of Brilliance' to Be Serial Killer, Expert Says," *Tampa Tribune*, February 11, 1991, p. 3.

history, providing him with the support he felt he needed to spend time in bars, pick up women, and buy them gifts.

On the other hand, Danny could also have committed brutal murders for their own sake. The Gainesville killer had slashed, stabbed, and dismembered his victims apparently without regard for their humanity. Money was simply not the motive; instead, the perpetrator had tortured and killed to feel in charge, to control and dominate, to experience the thrill of causing his victims to suffer.

Like most people, of course, Danny Rolling's personality varied depending on his needs at a particular point in time as well as the demands of the situation. This aspect of Danny Rolling's character emerged while he spent time at a Gainesville campsite deep in the woods, from which he orchestrated the student murders. Even while he was in the midst of his killing spree, just after the decapitated body of Christa Hoyt had been discovered by police only a mile away, Rolling decided to rob the First Union Bank on Archer Road. What is more, only days after killing the last two college students in Gainesville, he then traveled to Tampa and began a week-long spree of burglaries and thefts. Wearing a ski mask, he robbed a Save 'n Pack grocery store and committed three home burglaries.

In making his getaway from the scene of the supermarket robbery in North Tampa, Danny pointed a gun at a deputy and said, "Lady, I don't want to shoot you." Then he jumped into his stolen Buick and made his getaway, almost running down two other officers who had blocked his path. Deputies fired nineteen shots at Rolling's automobile, causing it to career off a concrete wall and crash into a mobile home. In the confusion, Danny was able to run into a wooded area nearby and make his escape, at least temporarily.[23]

---

[23]"New Charge Ties Killings Suspect to Gainesville," *Gainesville Sun* February 9, 1991, p. 1B.

At the site of one of the house break-ins, Rolling stopped to make a phone call to his father in Shreveport. At another, he took a 1983 silver Ford Mustang. Then, on the same day, he drove the car to Ocala in order to rob a Winn-Dixie supermarket in that town. Wearing sunglasses and a fisherman's cap but shirtless, he placed a .38-caliber gun to the head of a grocery clerk and demanded that he give him all the money in the cash register. Only minutes later, Rolling was arrested as he tried to elude the local police and then wrecked his stolen Mustang.

There were also some similarities between Rolling's behavior at the murder sites and his modus operandi while committing burglaries and thefts. After arresting Danny in the Winn-Dixie robbery, the police found a canvas bag in his car containing a large screwdriver, a handgun, and a black T-shirt. The screwdriver and T-shirt were especially significant. Crime scene analysis indicated that the Gainesville killer had used a large screwdriver to break into his victims' apartments. Also, a bloodied piece of black fabric—probably from a T-shirt—had been found next to Manny Taboada's body. The police theorized that the intruder's T-shirt had been torn during his struggle with Taboada.

On August 30, just a few days after slaying Manny Taboada and Tracy Paules, Rolling entered a single-family home in a student housing complex through an open bedroom window and stole the keys to a tan Buick Regal parked outside. Before leaving the house, Danny first ate some oatmeal and watched television. He then casually strolled from the house and drove the stolen Buick out of Gainesville.

In Tampa, just as at the Gainesville murder sites, he broke into a residence by forcing a sliding glass door that opened onto a secluded backyard. At one burglarized apartment, he stopped long enough to eat a banana and, taking his sweet time, left the peel on a chair he had pulled into the dining area before finally making his exit. The entire time, the occupants were fast asleep upstairs. One can only imagine what Danny would have done to them had they awakened.[24]

Despite the apparent inconsistencies, it all began to fit into place for the task force. Rolling was in Gainesville at the time of the murders. He was strongly implicated in the similar multiple homicide in Shreveport. Burglary tools were found in his possession, including a screwdriver that the lab matched to the pry marks at each of the murder sites. And, of course, the DNA match placed Rolling at the scene of the crimes.

Although Rolling had been identified as the prime suspect in January 1991 when the first probe of his blood came back from the lab positive, it was not until the fall that the State's Attorney sought a grand jury indictment. It took months for the prosecution team to piece together a theory of Rolling's actions during August 1990—a theory about how and why he butchered the five young victims. It also took months to decide whether Rolling had acted alone, or whether someone else assisted him— presumably the one who had left unidentified pubic hairs at the crime scenes.

In November 1991, the grand jury indicted Danny Rolling on five counts of first degree murder, three counts of sexual battery, and three counts of armed burglary with assault. It would take months before the next major milestone. With Rolling safely in custody and an airtight case against him, it was little more than a formality, although symbolically an important one, when on Tuesday, June 9, 1992, Lee Strope and Ed Dix drove to Florida State Prison to serve Danny Rolling with a warrant for his arrest for the brutal Gainesville slayings.

---

[24]"Thefts May Tie Man to Slayings," *Palm Beach Post*, January 27, 1991, p. 18A.

21

I Have a Dream

Typical of large-scale manhunts, the task force received thousands of phone calls from citizens who thought they saw something or someone on the nights in question, who wished to volunteer their own pet theories on the murders, or even who wanted to tip off the police to their weird or strange-looking neighbors. The calls ranged from the mundane to the ultrabizarre, giving the task force members who handled the phones plenty of amusing stories to discuss over their box lunches.

On August 30, 1990, soon after the five murders had been discovered, an anonymous caller reported information about a possible suspect, a twenty-five-year-old bodybuilder who resided in Gainesville and was studying chemical engineering at the university. The tipster indicated further that this man had a fascination with Ted Bundy, so much so that he would save newspaper articles on the infamous serial killer, only he would paste his own photo over the likeness of Bundy. According to the caller, the subject constantly said that he wanted to be just like his hero and, pointing to the newspaper articles, stated, "One day this will be me." The informant also noted that his suspect kept a dead dog in the trunk of his car, which he would place in parking spaces that he wanted to reserve for himself.

Pernell Ellen Larson of Champlin, Minnesota, called the task force to report that she had overheard the prime suspect, Edward Humphrey, discuss the Gainesville student murders. Investigator Chris Johnson interviewed Ms. Larson about this potentially important lead but quickly determined it to be unfounded. The fifty-one-year-old woman told Johnson that she witnessed a group of twelve people standing in her own backyard in Minnesota, people she recognized from watching TV shows like *America's Most Wanted* and *Unsolved Mysteries*. She asked her uninvited guests to identify themselves, and one blurted out, "I'm Edward Humphrey." She then overhead her backyard gang conspiring to kill coeds in Gainesville. The woman also volunteered that she had inside knowledge linking the Gainesville killings to the Kennedy assassination and the death of actress Marilyn Monroe.

Among the most unusual calls into the task force were those from self-professed psychics as well as others who said they weren't psychics but had a vivid dream about the slayings. Not wishing to overlook any lead, no matter how silly it appeared, each of these "visions" had to be documented and investigated.

The earliest "sighting" came on August 27, the day after the bodies of Sonja Larson and Christina Powell were discovered. Phillip George Sapp called the Jacksonville Sheriff's Office, introduced himself as a psychic, and told Detective H. L. Scott of an experience he had had upon entering a local pawn shop. Sapp had gone to a pawn shop on Atlantic Boulevard in order to sell his watch. As the owner of the shop approached to assist him, Sapp had a sudden vision, a "flash," that the proprietor was the man who had raped, mutilated, and murdered the two girls in Gainesville, one of whom was from Jacksonville. Sapp went on to suggest that the pawn shop proprietor owned eavesdropping equipment that he used to locate his victims and that the man was assisted by two accomplices. The informant also advised the detective of his premonition that the culprit would strike again (he was at least right about that).

Detective Scott was initially suspicious of Sapp because of his knowledge of details of the crime and because he had once lived in Gainesville; however, he was quickly ruled out as a suspect.

Most detectives maintain a healthy degree of skepticism regarding parapsychology. They tend to consider "psychic reports" to be the veiled confessions of a guilty conscience rather than the inexplicable visions of a clairvoyant.

Self-described psychics are generally viewed as prime suspects first and star witnesses second, a lesson that Steven Linscott learned the hard way several years ago, in 1980, when he called the Oak Park, Illinois, police with a special insight. Linscott, a student at the Emmaus Bible College, had awakened in a cold sweat from a bad dream in which a blond man was seen beating a woman to death. Linscott had experienced this frightful vision just as twenty-four-year-old nurses' aid, Karen Ann Phillips, was actually being murdered several blocks away. As it happened, the Oak Park Police were very intrigued with Linscott's nightmare, so intrigued that they considered him their "best shot" for solving the case.

While the Bible student was flattered that the police were so attentive and interested in working with him, they were actually more interested in Linscott himself than in his nocturnal recollections. The cops considered him more likely a psychopathic participant in the murder than a telepathic spectator. Linscott began to get a bit suspicious when the police requested samples of his blood, saliva, and hair. But by then, the case against him was snowballing much too fast to be stopped.

The case against Linscott had many holes—most notable, his dream victim was black, but Phillips was white. Still, Steven Linscott was the only good suspect that the police had, and he was eventually convicted of murder by a jury of his peers. Even his appeals proved unsuccessful, that is, until 1992 when newly developed DNA testing techniques exonerated him and won his release from prison after twelve nightmarish years in custody.

Fortunately, no one in Gainesville got such a raw deal with the possible exception of Ed Humphrey, who many believed to be the victim of media hype and circumstance. At least in responding to psychics, the task force showed restraint, perhaps even disinterest.

On September 9, 1990, Special Agent Joe Nickmeyer received a call from a highway patrol officer who indicated that he was at the Exxon Station at Thirty-fourth and University Avenue, Gainesville, accompanied by a man who had information on the murders. Nickmeyer hurried over to meet them and was introduced to Roger Bentley, a psychic from Tampa. Bentley reported that he and several other psychics had convened a special meeting to discuss their visions concerning the student murders and to compare notes. Bentley turned over the minutes of their meeting to the investigator. Unfortunately, the information was of no use to the task force.

On October 1, 1990, Special Agent Wally Gossett received a call about a woman named Geanine Slagle, who was reported to have experienced a sudden vision concerning the Gainesville homicides. This was a lead that had to be pursued—Ms. Slagle worked as a chef in the governor's mansion.

While visiting a friend on the last weekend in September 1990, Ms. Slagle had started feeling odd, as if her mind was being invaded by a powerful force. Her voice, appearance, and personality had all suddenly changed, and she ordered her friend to get a piece of paper and pencil and to transcribe whatever she said. Slagle went on to describe the person responsible for the Gainesville slayings: he was a white male, forty to fifty years old, between six feet two inches to six feet four inches tall, with black hair, green eyes, glasses, and possibly a mustache. She further "saw" that he lived in or around Gainesville and taught criminology at UF. Slagle also reported that the killer had the name of Andrews or Anderson, although the names Amy and Steven also came to her during this peculiar experience.

On October 16, 1990, Special Agent Wayne Porter received a telephone call from Dennis Hooker, a retired psychologist from Stockport, Ohio, who had a psychic vision about the killer, or rather killers. Hooker saw a murder team comprised of two men, ages twenty-five and eighteen, one of whom was from Cincinnati and the other from the Cleveland area. One had stomach problems, and the name Alan was somehow involved.

Investigators also met with a Tampa dentist claiming to have psychic powers that could solve the crimes. During the interview between the dentist and Agent Telly Larrinaga of Tampa, however, things went from strange to outrageous. The dentist started relaying experiences from his own background involving a sexual identity crisis. Based on his own sexual problems, he believed that he could understand and, therefore, profile the personality of the Gainesville serial killer.

Paul Fransen may not have won the prize for most accurate vision, but he certainly was the most persistent psychic that the task force encountered. Beginning in October 1990, the Illinois psychic repeatedly contacted the task force to report a vision that he had had involving a home at 2116 Southwest Twenty-third Street, which appeared in his dream to be situated near a T-shaped intersection in a rural part of Gainesville. According to Fransen, the killer had either lived or had had contact with the residents at this address.

Given the high volume of better leads that detectives were sifting through at that stage of the investigation, the lead describing Fransen's dream was set aside for much later action. Nearly a year passed before Fransen called again, concerned that no one had followed up on his "hot tip" pertaining to the Twenty-third Street address. Finally, a few weeks later, while attempting to tie up loose ends in late August 1991, Special Agent Gary Akins drove to the address and interviewed the occupants. He showed Linda Acre and Larie Allen the photo lineup of Ed Humphrey, whom they recognized from newspaper coverage. The women had also heard the name Danny Rolling but only through from the media.

They denied, however, ever having any personal contact with either suspect. Ms. Acre allowed Akins to search through the house and the shed in the backyard, but he observed nothing at all unusual. Agent Akins wisely recommended the psychic's lead be classified as NFA, for no further action.

Fransen reported other psychic impressions that had come to him. He "saw" the killer wearing a police uniform and cleaning up one of the crime scenes. Fransen was relentless in his attempts to get his message across. He even tried to contact the friends and families of the murder victims, hoping to obtain clothing or other personal items belonging to the victims to enhance his psychic experiences. For example, Fransen wrote to Lilly Greazes, who was Sonja Larson's coach at Ely High School, asking for something that Larson had touched or worn.

It is difficult to ignore the fact that in the annals of true crime psychics have on occasion helped police to locate a missing body or an unknown perpetrator. Still, critics downplay these as isolated successes, suggesting that psychic visions are so vague and general that certain features may appear "accurate" by luck or sheer coincidence. The accuracy of one psychic vision in the Gainesville case is likely to impress, however, even the most skeptical observer.

On Friday, January 11, 1991, the task force got word from the crime lab in Jacksonville that the technicians had found a blood sample that on preliminary testing appeared to match the semen recovered at all three crime scenes. The blood belonged to a prisoner in the Marion County Jail by the name of Danny Harold Rolling.

Feeling exhilarated, Strope left the meeting with the OIC to relay the news to agents working the common room, stopping on the way to inform the head shed of the laboratory match. The name Rolling was of no particular significance to the agents who had been spending every day poring through investigative reports on their computer screens.

Agent Bill Davis typed a query into the database

searching for any reports containing the word/name *Rolling*. The search produced references to "rolling" cars and an incident when Ed Humphrey was "rolling his eyes" but also to one name that was very close to that of the latest good suspect.

Davis couldn't believe what he read on his screen. Shortly after the murders, Sharon Carroll, a psychic from Harrisburg, Pennsylvania, had called to report a vision that the Gainesville killer was a man with the name Rollings who worked as a maintenance man in the area of the campus. "I was sitting with my husband watching TV the night of the first murders," Carroll recalled. "And as soon as it came on TV, I said I know who did it."[25]

Investigators were able at the time to locate a janitor with a similar name who worked at a local hospital, but he was soon excluded based on physical evidence. No further action had been taken in response to this lead. Somewhat ironically, Special Agent Don Maines had concluded his report by saying, "This investigation will proceed, keeping in mind the 'tip' provided by Sharon Carroll. The degree of accuracy regarding the information cannot be evaluated at this time."

---

[25]Mitch Stacy, "Sightings, Psychic Pointed to Rolling as Killings Suspect," *Gainesville Sun,* November 19, 1992, p. 6A.

22

True Confessions

During his months awaiting trial, first at the Marion County Jail, then at correctional facilities in Tallahassee and Starke, Danny Rolling was hardly silent about the atrocities he had committed. Actually, he had a big mouth, and he used it quite often, especially in confessing (and perhaps bragging) to other inmates in the joint.

In 1992, Lee Strope and the task force turned their attention to meeting with prison inmates who had been incarcerated with Danny Rolling and were willing to snitch. They hoped to supplement the mounting physical evidence against the defendant with significant admissions concerning his activities in Gainesville.

Not every prison "confession" by Rolling to a fellow inmate could be confirmed by task force investigators. On February 27, 1992, Special Agents Don Maines and Dennis Fischer drove to Marion County for the purpose of contacting inmate Robert Lee James. During a previous interview with the inmate, James had made a statement about Danny Rolling that very much interested members of the task force. He claimed that while being incarcerated together in the Marion County Jail Rolling had confessed to having murdered two girls in Gainesville.

On this second visit, Maines and Fischer asked James whether he was willing to permit the case agent to give him a polygraph examination regarding the inmate's statements about Rolling. James agreed, and Lee Strope administered the test. Unfortunately, Strope concluded that there appeared to be deception in the responses given by James.

On Wednesday, June 24, 1992, Strope traveled to Palm Beach County Jail and interviewed Frederick Bowman, an inmate who claimed to know Danny Rolling from their months—from November 1991 through January 1992—incarcerated together in the federal holding facility in Tallahassee. While serving time in Tallahassee, Bowman held a job as "porter"—he provided books and bedding to inmates who were locked down. During this time, Bowman had many occasions to observe and to talk with the man suspected of killing five college students in Gainesville.

Bowman told Strope that Danny would get very agitated and repeatedly slam his fists into the concrete walls of his cell. When Bowman asked him why he was so upset, Rolling would answer, "I think I fucked up. I didn't cover my tracks."

On other occasions, Rolling revealed certain aspects of the Gainesville murders without ever making direct reference to them. He told Bowman "of cutting off a girl's head and leaving it in such a position on a bookshelf to send some sort of message to whoever would find it." He also said, "I didn't know they were so young. . . . The girls came on to me, then they teased me like they wanted me."

A few weeks later, on Thursday, July 9, 1992, Strope traveled to the Federal Correctional Institution in Tallahassee, where he interviewed William Gilford. At the time, Gilford told Lee that he had talked with his fellow inmate, Danny Rolling, while they were incarcerated together at the federal facility in January and February 1992. The two men were also jailed together in Tampa in 1991. In speaking with Strope, however, Gilford could not remember anything Rolling had revealed to him that might be relevant to the Gainesville case. The inmate claimed that he and Danny had simply never discussed the student murders.

Shortly after Strope's interview, however, the special agent received a call from Lieutenant Wells, who, while working his rounds at the Federal Correctional Institution, had had a conversation with Gilford. The inmate's memory had suddenly improved. Gilford now recalled getting angry with Danny Rolling and saying, "You should get the electric chair for what you did to those girls."

Rolling replied, "What I should do is kick my way through this wall, cut off your tongue, and shove it up your ass, like I did the girls in Gainesville." Gilford could provide no additional details about their encounter.

On Tuesday, July 14, 1992, Strope went to the Florida State Prison at Starke in order to interview inmates Russell W. Binstead and Robert "Bobby" Lewis, both of whom reportedly had become friends of Danny Rolling while in prison. After two frustrating years filled with hundreds of false leads, dead ends, as well as bureaucratic paper pushing, his perseverance paid off.

Strope first met with Binstead, a long term involuntary tenant of the Florida State Prison, having been convicted of a score of felonies.

STROPE: OK, the date is July 14, 1992. The place is Florida State Prison. Present in the room are myself, Agent Lee Strope, Agent French with the attorney general's office, inspector general's office, and inmate Russell W. Binstead. Before we get started, would you raise your right hand? Do you swear to tell the truth, the whole truth, and nothing but the truth, so help you God?

BINSTEAD: Yes, sir.

STROPE: You do? Would you answer it loud please?

BINSTEAD: Yes, sir, I do.

STROPE: OK, we're here talking to you about inmate Danny Rolling, and I'd like you to start from the beginning when you first met Danny when he first came to the institution. We've covered this lightly beforehand, but I'd like you to go ahead and put it on tape, realizing that you're sworn in and that I would like you to tell the truth and tell us everything you know about this conversation that you had with Danny Rolling.

BINSTEAD: All right. The first time I seen Danny Rolling I believe was on a Friday. I don't remember the exact date, but they'd brought him in from North Florida Reception Center. They put him in a cell on the second floor of W wing, where I was working as a runner. I just walked down at that point to see what he looked like. You know, I'd read so much about him and heard so much about him I wanted to see just what he looked like. You know, if he looked like the monster that they said he was. Uh, I asked him how he was doing, and he says, "I'm doing all right." I asked him if he needed anything. He says, uh, if I could get him a Bible. I said, "Fine, I'll get you a Bible, right." That day there, you know, was really the first date that was the extent of my conversation with him. The next day being a weekend was Saturday. The several officers, some of them in groups, some of them singly, walked down and was looking at him, talking to him, and saying things to him. What they were saying I don't know, but he become very upset and, uh, I was informed by one of the medical staff that he was in tears down there. So I walked out and, uh, to see what his problem was or just find out what was going on if nothing else. He told me that those officers had been in there messing with him, calling him, uh, animal, mutilator, what they was going to do to him, put him in the electric chair, and they had him in tears. He said at that point, he called me brother and said that he had been, uh, he was born

again and he was a Christian, that God had forgiven
him for everything that he had done, right. I said at
that point that God may have forgiven you but the
state of Florida and Gainesville, Florida, hasn't forgiven you, not for, uh, for what you did there. He says,
"I did that. I killed those people." He says, "But God
has forgiven me, says from here on out I got a new
life."

STROPE: Did he make any mention of drugs?

BINSTEAD: No, not at that point. This was, he made
mentions of drugs, but it was like weeks later before
we ever got into anything with drugs. He kinda went
off and he sang a couple of songs, uh, Christian songs,
pretty nice voice, you know. Uh, he, uh, we talked.
He said he was an artist. He said that he, uh, he wrote
songs. He drew, uh, I asked him if there was
something I could get him to help him to spend his
time. He said, uh, I could get him a pencil and some
paper, something to write with or draw with. I had
some art supplies, so I supplied with some paper and
some pencils and he went to work. He drew some
pictures, uh, signed them. He wrote a story. He, uh,
about some robberies or one specific robbery. Wait, it
was the robbery that he committed in Gainesville, uh,
he said, that he was addicted to crack and alcohol. He
says both of those make him into a different person.
He did say that when he committed all the crimes that
he committed in Gainesville (inaudible) he was under
the influence of crack cocaine.

STROPE: Why do you suppose he opened up to you?
Why do you suppose he talked to you?

BINSTEAD: There was nobody else to talk to. I mean he,
he couldn't go in, he trusted us. He trusted me. He
felt like I'd been locked up nineteen years, uh, I knew
what was going on around here, uh, all the staff, the
security staff, even some of the doctors, and all the
officers were all hostile toward him or very blunt with
him. You know, they wouldn't give him anything ex-

tra. You know, I used to feed him, gave him whatever he needed. You know, if he—he didn't have any soap, I'd go buy him some soap, you know. If he, uh, if he got hungry, I'd give him some food. You know, if he got bored, I would talk to him.

STROPE: Why do you think he trusted you?

BINSTEAD: He just said that he immediately, he said he immediately knew that I was a good guy and that he could trust me. He says I'd been locked up so long and says he felt like that they were down on me as they were on him, you know. He felt like if, uh, if I couldn't help him, nobody could. There was another man working with me, Robert Lewis, uh, he kinda fell into the same, the same mode there, you know, he trusted us both, and we both looked out for him, you know.

STROPE: Well, I'm sure the question will be asked at some time or another: What was your motive for talking with Danny?

BINSTEAD: My motive was to find out as much as I could about the, about the Gainesville murders. I knew, or I supposed that, uh, evidence in the case was scant, you know, I mean it was—it was slim. It was, it took them so long to charge the guy after the indictment I figured, uh, if they really had a concrete case on the guy, you know, (inaudible) immediately charged him and immediately started, started pushing, you know.

STROPE: Aside from curiosity about the truth, did you have another reason for it?

BINSTEAD: Yes, I did. When they first happened in August, I was—I was going to outside court. I was in the back of a sheriff's van when it come on the radio and at that point over the radio they'd found two bodies and I had a conversation with the officer driving the van. I said, "Now one day we'll end up with that guy (inaudible), you know.'' I said, ''I hope so anyway,'' and, uh, the guy says, ''Yeah, it's where he belongs, you know.'' And I said, ''I'll pull the switch on him myself if they ever put him in there (inaudible) they allowed me to do it, you know, cause all he did he killed some young girls. I have sisters, nieces, uh, everything I, most of the people I love in this world are—are women in my family, you know, just that the crimes, just totally turned me off.''

STROPE: Did you ever have any conversations with Danny about his defense? About what he had planned to do as far as how he's going to handle the defense?

BINSTEAD: Well, he, his first thing that he wanted to do, he wanted to escape. He wanted to cook up some kind of plot, uh, and escape. If that failed, he wanted an insanity defense. And I explained to him that the only time that you can present an—an insanity (inaudible) an insanity defense will be accepted is, uh, if you can prove that you don't know right from wrong. Other than that, insanity won't work. Uh, but that was his, he wanted to pursue an insanity defense.

STROPE: OK, several weeks ago I believe Danny Rolling attempted suicide. Could you tell me about that?

BINSTEAD: Yeah, but he was, he wouldn't go the doctors on a, one day, and, uh, they got fed up with him, told him he was discharged, uh, they no longer need to see him, and they were going to send him to another part of the prison, P wing, I believe it was.

STROPE: So let me interrupt. If he went to P wing, he'd be away from you and Robert.

BINSTEAD: Yes, he would.

STROPE: So he wanted to stay in W wing?

BINSTEAD: Yes, he did. He, uh, asked how he could do it. I said, ''There's only one way you can do it and that is to fake a suicide.'' At first he—he didn't want to. He says, "Man that goes against everything I (inaudible)." I said, "Well, hey, that's the only way you can stay here. That's the only way we can cook something up." He says, "Well, I'll do it." He says, uh, said, "Look, there's no place to tie a sheet." I said, "Just take a sheet, wrap it around your neck like a tourniquet, tighten a book real tight, and just lay down on it like it's choking off the blood to your head." I said, "As soon as they see that, they'll move you SOS. You'll be on suicide watch. You won't go anywhere." He immediately started wrapping the cord around his neck, tying the book.

STROPE: Where did he get the sheet? Did he tie, tear, or rip a sheet up or something?

BINSTEAD: He had a sheet in his cell. They had different levels. He was on a level of monitoring, that, uh, he was allowed all his property, his sheets, everything.

STROPE: Well, getting back to Gainesville, did Danny ever tell you where he stayed in Gainesville?

BINSTEAD: He—he had said that he had lived in a campsite. He didn't say where the campsite was. If he was, I wouldn't, I wouldn't know the area 'cause I don't know Gainesville. He said that he camped in the woods. He said he come out at night. He says that was how he was able to stay loose as long as he did, was staying in the woods and coming out at night. He said he was a night creature. He says he just didn't feel comfortable in the daytime.

STROPE: Did he make any mention of the case against him in Gainesville? What evidence the prosecutor may have against him?

BINSTEAD: He laughed at one time and said something about a pubic hair and, uh, that, you know, he said that they don't have a case, you know. I said, I told him that they got something. You were indicted, you've been charged, they got something, you know.

He said something about DNA and a pubic hair.

STROPE: What did he say about DNA?

BINSTEAD: He didn't really know too much DNA. I—I really don't know much about it myself. He just mentioned that's what they had for what it's worth.

STROPE: Did he mention that maybe he'd left some evidence behind?

BINSTEAD: Uh, no, he didn't. He—he may have mentioned it like, man I might have left that behind. You know he didn't come out and say anything like that. He said that was the evidence that, uh, the state had.

Strope asked Binstead a few more questions that yielded nothing much of significance. After probing the convict one more time concerning his motivation, however, Lee got Binstead to reveal the true and more self-serving purpose for cooperating.

STROPE: What do you personally hope to gain out of all this?

BINSTEAD: Personally I'd like to, uh, get some of this time cut off of me, you know, so I can stand a chance of seeing the street again. Uh, I'd personally like to see him go to the electric chair, other than that, I can't really say.

Strope was elated about the information he was able to pull from his inmate source. Not only had Danny Rolling apparently confessed his crimes to Binstead, but he also revealed his manipulative, conniving side.

Lee was keenly aware of the origin of the word *con*. He knew that convicts are not the most reliable sources of information, especially when they can personally benefit from ratting on their cellmates. The best strategy at that point was to ask similar questions of another of Rolling's confidants and compare answers.

Agent Strope next interviewed inmate Bobby Lewis,

Sonja Larson.
(Photo courtesy of the Florida Department of Law Enforcement)

Christina Powell.
(Photo courtesy of the Florida Department of Law Enforcement)

Christa Leigh Hoyt.
(Photo courtesy of the Florida Department of Law Enforcement)

Tracy Inez Paules.
(Photo courtesy of the Florida Department of Law Enforcement)

Manuel "Manny" Taboada.
(Photo courtesy of the Florida Department of Law Enforcement)

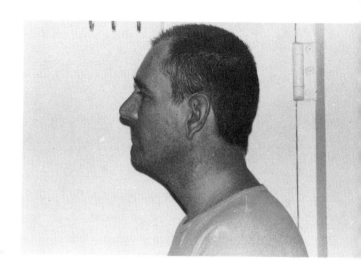

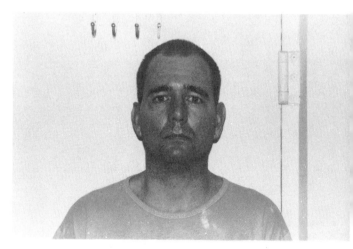

Two views of the Gainesville killer, Danny Harold Rolling.
(Photo courtesy of Allan Lee Strope)

An aerial view of the Gatorwood apartment complex showing an adjoining area of woods to which the killer made his escape.

(Photo courtesy of Allan Lee Strope)

Allan Lee Strope, case agent for the Gainesville homicides.

(Photo courtesy of Allan Lee Strope)

George and Ricky Paules place flowers at the Thirty-fourth Street wall painted in memory of the five slain students.

(Photo courtesy of Oscar Sosa, Gainesville Sun)

a lifer who had been a close friend of Rolling's from the day that the Gainesville suspect was transferred to the state penitentiary in Starke.

Lewis's prowess was already legendary among Florida State inmates. He was the one and only prisoner in Florida's history ever to escape from its death row—and live to tell about it. But he also saw himself as a victim of injustice.

The inmate told Strope his sad story. "Lewis said they've got him in here for killing a guy who said he was going to kill Lewis," recalled the case agent. "Bobby told me that he went to the FDLE, he went to the city, he went everywhere. He told them this guy is going to kill him, but the authorities wouldn't do anything about it. They said they couldn't do anything until the guy hurt somebody in Lewis's family. So, one day he was standing with his daughter, who had a big bag of candy in her hand. The phone rings, and Lewis talks to this bad guy. He says, 'See that candy your daughter's got? I'm going to give her more than candy.' Lewis figured that was more than he could take. He loaded his shotgun and got his buddy to accompany him. They went over the guy's house. And when he opened the door, Lewis blasted him. The guy who went with him testified against Lewis and never got a day. But Bobby Lewis is here for life. . . . The reason he's cooperating is he's hoping he'll at least get out of the building he's been in for eighteen years. He's eligible for parole in seven years, and he wants someone to go to the parole board and say, 'Hey, listen. Lewis helped in the Rolling case.' "

During their half-hour interview, Lewis confirmed a number of points that Binstead had raised earlier in the day. Lewis told Strope that Rolling admitted committing the Gainesville student murders and admitted faking a suicide attempt to avoid being transferred to another cell block. Lewis also noted that his prison pal revealed three specific details of the Gainesville crimes: that he had used gray duct tape, that he had excised the nipples from

Christa Hoyt's body, and that he had used a screwdriver to break into all three crime scenes.

Through Lewis, Rolling had given a "teaser," a few carefully chosen tidbits to convince the investigators that he was indeed the Gainesville killer. Also through Lewis, he hinted that he would have much more to say when the time was right.

"When I get through telling my story," Lewis recalled Rolling saying, "I'll be the most famous person in the United States." He would soon get the chance.

23

Speaking on Behalf of Danny

By the first of the year 1993, Danny Rolling was ready
to confess in an official, though indirect way. Detectives
Steve Kramig, Ed Dix, and LeGran Hewitt drove to the
Florida State Prison at Starke in order to hear Rolling
tell his side of the story. Rolling was accompanied not
only by his attorney, Johnny Kearns, but also by Bobby
Lewis, his friend and confidante from the joint. Rolling
was ready to talk, but Lewis would do most of the speaking. Bobby would serve as his buddy's mouthpiece, his
mediator, his go-between.

On two separate occasions, the investigators posed
questions to Rolling, and the sessions were videotaped.
Lewis would respond, however, either from his knowledge of earlier discussions with Danny or with Rolling
leaning over to whisper the answer into his ear. At times,
when critical matters of fact were in dispute, the interrogators looked directly at Rolling, asking for confir-
mation.

Bobby Lewis started off the interview by explaining
why Danny Rolling wasn't prepared to speak for himself, necessitating this most unusual arrangement:

LEWIS: The main problem is when me and him talk about what he has done, he gets very emotional. That's one of the reasons why he asked me to do this here. He has a lot of remorse and gets very emotional at times, dealing with them things. They're hard for him, they're very hard. And (turning to Danny Rolling) you've told me bluntly and honestly everything I guess you ever done that's wrong.

ROLLING: Yes.

LEWIS: And want to get it out and get right with his self. I offered to help him. He gets emotional with me too. It's kind of hard. Most of the things I don't understand he's tried to make me understand. I know what he tells me. I know he's being honest. That's why it's been hard for him, waiting for y'all to come forward, where he can get it out. Get it out of the way . . . And this guy has done everything he could to let y'all know—through me, in the best way he's able to deal with this here—what he wants to do . . .

ROLLING: Bobby is my mouthpiece. He is my confessor. I have confessed to him. He will speak to you. I'm free to to give you answers about any of the five murders in Gainesville . . .

It took a long time for Danny Rolling to convince the three detectives that Bobby Lewis, serving as his spokesperson, could accurately relate the details of the Gainesville murders. Hewitt, Dix, and Kramig were concerned that this odd manner of taking a confession might eventually be challenged in court. After unsuccessfully pressuring the defendant to speak on his own behalf, they decided that a confession through Lewis was better than no confession at all.

The detectives then asked for Rolling's confession:

INTERROGATOR: On August 26, 1990, there were two bodies found in Williamsburg apartments, Gainesville,

Florida, Sonja Larson and the other one being Christina Powell. Was Danny Rolling responsible for these homicides?

LEWIS: Yes, he was.

INTERROGATOR: Is that correct, Danny?

ROLLING: Yes, sir.

The investigators tried to get Rolling to explain his motivation for committing the homicides in such a brutal fashion. They also attempted to determine whether Rolling had singled out his victims in advance:

INTERROGATOR: Bobby, do you know if there was any special reason why Christa's head was taken off?

LEWIS: The best Danny has been able to do is convey the things that he has done. He doesn't even in no way understand why he done these things, except he said there was a strong urge, like a hunger or something driving him—a desire, a possession, a force, to force him to do these things, something he literally couldn't control at the time.

INTERROGATOR: Is that correct, Danny?

ROLLING: Yes.

INTERROGATOR: Had Danny seen Christa Hoyt prior to this night?

LEWIS: I believe so, one or two times possibly. He in none of these cases set out to get these people or just stalk these people intentionally. It was more that he may have seen these people one day ahead of time or something like that, just as he was traveling place to place. He went to a couple of other places where he could do the same thing but wasn't successful. He got run off by the police on a couple of different occasions. It was basically at random. It was, "That's the person I want to get. I'm going to stalk her until I get her.''

INTERROGATOR: Is that correct, Danny?

ROLLING: Yes.

INTERROGATOR: At any of the three Gainesville homicides, did you go there and peek in the windows prior to doing the homicides. Did Danny go to the windows and peek in prior to the homicides?

LEWIS: Do you know that?

INTERROGATOR: Can you answer?

ROLLING: Yes.

INTERROGATOR: You did? OK. At all three crime scenes?

ROLLING: (Inaudible.)

INTERROGATOR: Did you see any of the Gainesville homicide victims undressing or anything on a previous occasion prior to your going in and committing the homicides?

ROLLING: (Inaudible.)

LEWIS: I believe, yes.

INTERROGATOR: Is that correct, Danny?

ROLLING: Yes.

INTERROGATOR: All three homicides?

LEWIS: I don't know. I believe it was just one. If I remember correctly, I believe it was just one.

INTERROGATOR: Which one was that?

LEWIS: I don't know.

INTERROGATOR: Okay. Let's try this. Was it the last one?

LEWIS: I don't think so.

Interrogator: Is that correct, Danny?

Rolling: Umm.

Interrogator: The last one—where the female and the male were, did you peek at that one?

Rolling: Yes.

Interrogator: The night of the other homicides that had been previous to the night of the third homicide crime scene?

Lewis: I don't know.

Interrogator: Did you peek in Tracy Paules's window the night of the homicide?

Lewis: I believe so, yes.

Interrogator: Is that correct, Danny?

Rolling: Yes.

Interrogator: Did you peek into Christa Hoyt's window?

Lewis: Yes.

Interrogator: Is that correct, Danny?

Rolling: Yes.

Interrogator: Did you peek in the windows of Williamsburg and see those girls undressing.

Lewis: No.

Interrogator: Is that correct, Danny?

Rolling: (Inaudible.)

Interrogator: Is that correct, Danny?

Rolling: Yes.

Lewis: At Gatorwood, did Danny know there was a man in that apartment?

Lewis: No.

INTERROGATOR: He had only seen the female?

LEWIS: Correct.

INTERROGATOR: Is that correct, Danny?

ROLLING: Yes.

INTERROGATOR: When did he find out that the man was in the house?

LEWIS: When he walked into the bedroom.

INTERROGATOR: Is that correct, Danny?

ROLLING: Yes.

Most important, the interrogators then tried to get Rolling to reveal to them details of the murders that only the killer would have known:

LEWIS: Tracy Paules heard the commotion in Mr. Taboada's bedroom and opened the door to investigate. She saw the necessity to slam the door, locking it. I kicked it in immediately and was upon her. I taped her hands behind her back and taped her mouth. All she had on was a T-shirt, which I removed, then raped her. I turned her over on her stomach, and I stabbed her once through the back through the heart. She died quickly, eight to ten seconds and it was over. I then removed the tape and dragged her into the hallway between the bathroom and living room. I went into the bathroom, wet a washcloth and washed the blood from her face and then raped her again. I then douched out her vagina with a cleaner. I went through the apartment and took a white muscle shirt from Mr. Taboada's dresser. All the five murders were committed with the same Ka-Bar, which I had bought in Tallahassee at an army–navy store about a month prior.

INTERROGATOR: The answer that you just read about the Gatorwood homicides, is that all true and accurate?

ROLLING: Yes.

INTERROGATOR: Was Tracy taped? Were her hands taped?

LEWIS: I believe she was. He taped her hands behind her back and taped her mouth.

INTERROGATOR: That was before she was stabbed?

LEWIS: That was before she was stabbed.

INTERROGATOR: She was alive when she was raped the first time, before she had been stabbed?

LEWIS: Yes, sir.

INTERROGATOR: Is all that correct, Danny?

ROLLING: Yes.

The detectives were interested in resolving, once and for all, the two-killer theory. Would Rolling implicate Ed Humphrey or any other accomplice, or would he take sole responsibility for the murders?

INTERROGATOR: OK. Did Danny take anyone to these crime scenes with him?

LEWIS: No, he didn't.

INTERROGATOR: Is that correct?

ROLLING: That's correct.

INTERROGATOR: Did Danny take anybody to these crime scenes after the crime was committed?

LEWIS: No, he didn't.

INTERROGATOR: Is that correct, Danny?

ROLLING: That is correct.

INTERROGATOR: Did anyone else at the time of the crimes have knowledge that Danny had done them?

LEWIS: No, they didn't. Nobody had nothing to do with this or no knowledge except Danny his ownself.

INTERROGATOR: That is correct, Danny?

ROLLING: That's correct.

In a plea for forgiveness, Danny Rolling finally chose to speak for himself:

ROLLING: You gentlemen are honorable people. I wish I could be you. But I wouldn't want you to be me. I wouldn't want anybody to be me. People say Danny has no remorse. They don't know Danny. I don't know how I live with myself. If it wasn't for the good Lord, Jesus Christ, I wouldn't be able to live with this man, but he gives me strength and courage. I'm not proud of myself and my life.

INTERROGATOR: If you had something to say to the victims' families, Danny, what would it be? What would Danny say to them?

ROLLING: I would say that the only way for them to go on, and I do, I would say to them that I don't ask them to have pity on me, I cannot be something to have pity on me or anyone else for that matter. But I would say I would ask them if they could find it in their heart to forgive so that the bitterness and the hatred about all of this won't destroy what is left of their lives. I pray for them that God would give them strength and counsel to face every day. I believe somehow, through all of this, that the Lord will give them strength. I can't do anything for them. If I could, I would. I can't. What can I do for them? Tell me.

INTERROGATOR: I have no idea.

ROLLING: I'm trying now.

INTERROGATOR: I know.

INTERROGATOR: I think you're doing the best you can

and that's telling them what happened there that night to their children.

Danny Rolling began to cry.

24

Killer Groupies

Sitting in his barren cell at the Florida State Prison at Starke, waiting month by month for his murder trial to begin, Danny Rolling had more to do than talk with other inmates about his crimes or contemplate his own defense strategy. Unlike others in his cell block, Rolling was flooded with mail. Some letters came from the media, local and national programs inviting him to do an interview by satellite or tape. He would be able to tell his side, ambitious producers claimed. But Rolling wasn't interested in doing interviews, at least not yet. He had nothing special to say.

Rolling also received a large number of letters from total strangers. The letters came in all shapes and sizes, some meticulously word processed, others handwritten with apparent care. Some could be characterized as fan mail, and some of them were love notes sent from women across the country who yearned to meet the man of their dreams, even if he were behind bars, even if he had raped and mutilated innocent young college students. He couldn't be all bad, they must have imagined.

As bizarre as it may seem, it is hardly unusual for vicious serial killers to be deluged by celebrity hounds and lovesick paramours. For example, hundreds of women attempted to visit Los Angeles Night Stalker Richard Rameriz, who was convicted of stealthfully entering over a dozen homes in the dark of night and killing the occupants. The stream of admiring, starstruck visitors became so large and disruptive that prison officials had to put a strict limit on Rameriz's visitation rights. Theodore Bundy, of course, could have had thousands of pen pals had he desired it. And Veronica Crompton became so fascinated with charming and handsome Douglas Clark, the Los Angeles Sunset Strip Killer who raped, murdered, and mutilated at least a half-dozen prostitutes, that she broke off her relationship with Hillside Strangler Kenneth Bianchi. Her affair with Bianchi had grown old and tiresome; Clark was the new kid on the cell block and much more exciting. That relationship didn't last too long, however, as Clark met and later married a freelance journalist who showered him with attention and helped him with his appeals.

Why would someone in her right mind pursue a relationship with a brutal sexual sadist, going so far as to marry him? Actually, there are several reasons why serial killers are pursued by worshiping women—so-called killer groupies. Some of them are attracted to their idol's extraordinarily powerful, controlling, manipulative personality. A Freudian might attempt to trace this attraction to a woman's need to resurrect her relationship with a cruel, domineering father figure. More positively, at least a few killer groupies, like Douglas Clark's wife, strive to prove that their lover is a victim of injustice. Their fight for right may give their otherwise unfulfilling lives a strong sense of purpose. Other groupies wish to break through the killer's vicious facade: "The whole world sees Johnny as a monster. Only I see the kindness in him; he shares that with only me . . . I feel so special." Still other devotees, perhaps out of insecurity, are just comfortable in always knowing where their man is at two o'clock in the morning—even if it's in cellblock 2.

Underlying all of these motivations, however, is the glamour and celebrity status that many killer groupies find exciting. One young teenager from Milwaukee appeared on a national TV talk show to say that she would give "anything" to get an autograph from serial killer Jeffrey Dahmer. It is likely that she also collects the autographs of rock stars. In general, serial killers are more accessible than other celebrities. If a fan wants to get close to a rock idol, she generally doesn't have a chance. But with someone like Night Stalker Richard Ramirez, all she would have to do is write a few love letters and she might get to meet him and perhaps even marry him.

For Danny Rolling, the attention from gushing and adoring females was flattering and a good way to pass the time. But one love connection, his relationship with freelance journalist and true-crime writer Sondra London, became all consuming, much more than just a pleasant prison-cell diversion.

Sondra London, a plumpish but not unattractive fortysomething-year-old with dark hair and a ready smile, was contacted by Rolling, from his prison cell, while she was in the process of editing *Knockin' on Joe,* a book on the writings and poetry of death row inmates. Although she had corresponded with the accused serial killer about participating in her latest literary project and had seen his picture on the tube, she had no idea what would develop out of their first personal encounter. She was immediately swept off her feet, lust at first sight.

"I approached my meeting with Danny thinking I was prepared for anything," wrote London in the preface to her book. "But there was one thing I was not prepared for. I had no idea what a fine-looking man he is today. Instead of the broken and dejected loser I'd seen on TV . . . standing before my hungry eyes was one gorgeous hunk of man."[26]

The relationship grew fast and furiously. The prison walls that divided Danny and Sondra only made their hearts yearn more for each other. Never sharing an in-

---

[26]Joel Achenbach, "Prisoners of Love," *Sun Sentinel,* March 6, 1994, p. 1E.

timate moment alone together, their unrequited passion maintained the excitement and fascination of their love.

Although she long had a weakness for "good-for-nothing men," London never planned to get hooked up with a murderer. She got married at a young age, but that marriage didn't last very long. Later she married a reggae singer, who left her alone most of the time with their baby daughter while he went off, singing on the road. Still, she landed on her feet, managing to support her daughter and herself on what she earned as a technical writer. Feeling unfulfilled and bored with writing computer manuals, however, by the late 1980s she experienced her own midlife crisis; she needed a change.

After reading a book about serial killer Theodore Bundy, London became fascinated with serial murder and contemplated a major career move. She contacted an old high school boyfriend, G. J. Shaefer, who, quite conveniently for her, was serving time in a Florida prison for brutally murdering teenage girls. First, London decided to write about Schaefer, the life and times of a serial murderer, but later considered the notion of expanding her subjects to other brutal men, including the infamous Gainesville student slayer. The rest was history but hardly a Harlequin romance.

On March 11, 1993, in the prison visitors' room, Danny Rolling sat across the table from Steve Dunleavy, reporter for *A Current Affair*, and, as the cameras rolled, professed a message of love, humanity, religion, and wisdom.

To all who had followed his involvement in the case, the accused killer showed a kind and caring side of himself: "Regardless of what people think of Danny Rolling," he said, "there is a soft spot in my heart for people and I care."

When Dunleavy asked him how he felt about the possibility of being executed by the State of Florida, Danny replied, "Sure, put me in the hands of my maker, yeah. 'Cause then, the glory and the peace and the joy—they'll all be waiting for me . . . I have many regrets and I wish to God I could do it all over."

Recalling the incident in which he had shot his father, Rolling said, "I love you, Pop. Believe me, Dad, I didn't mean to hurt you."

He even had some advice for the families of the victims whose lives he was accused of extinguishing in Gainesville: "Don't let hatred just consume 'em, where they can't go on with their lives."

In response to questions about Sondra London, Danny said, "I'm madly in love with her. I find her extremely unique in every way." Then, he got poetic, referring to his girlfriend as "a flower in the breeze."

Dunleavy read from a letter that Rolling had written earlier to his fiancée, in which he had attempted to reassure Sondra that he loved her and, at the same time, to proclaim his own innocence: "Sondra. Dear sweet beautiful Sondra," he wrote. "Oh, please believe me. I would never hurt you. I would cut out my heart first. What has happened was not my fault."

Dunleavy also interviewed Sondra London, who never tried to conceal her affection for the accused murderer. When asked about their relationship, she gushed, "The main thing to know about Danny and why I love Danny is that . . . he loves me. My first husband was a rebel and a musician. My second husband was a rogue and a musician, and I want my third husband to be an outlaw and a musician."

For many spectators to the prolonged and often tedious legal drama of the *State of Florida v. Danny Rolling,* the torrid love affair between Danny Rolling and Sondra London served as an amusing sideshow, making the legal process look like *That's Entertainment.* The press corps, in particular, was entertained, as reporters joked frequently about their "colleague," Ms. London. Not everyone was amused, however, especially the families of the victims, who felt that Rolling had no right to enjoy romance—a right their children would never again have—and that London had no right to profit by writing about her man.

The prosecution flexed its legal muscles to keep the lovebirds apart. When it was learned that Sondra London planned to publish Danny's biography, including his letters and drawings, in a book she called *Rolling Papers,* the prosecution sought to subpoena her correspondence with the accused killer. She resisted the subpoena, citing her First Amendment rights. Next, the state was able to bar her from visiting Rolling in prison, claiming that London had misrepresented her purpose in applying for visitation. She was motivated more by the love of money than of Danny, argued the authorities.

Rolling was not about to remain silent about the state's interference in his love life. On September 26, 1993, he used his robbery sentencing hearing in Ocala to sing the blues. When Circuit Judge Thomas Sawaya asked Rolling if he had anything to say before sentencing, the defendant turned and spoke directly to his beloved who was wearing his engagement ring around her neck: "Sondra, they might keep you from me, but I want you to know that they can't stamp out the love and affection that I have for you in my heart." Rolling then sang his heart out in near perfect a cappella, "Just tell me, baby, what were my words, as all my tears run together, baby, just like rain."[27]

Danny was understandably irate over both the restrictions placed on London's visits and the manner in which their relationship was being judged by reporters. She was portrayed as a gold-digging phoney who was professing her love for the sake of an exclusive book deal. Implicitly, he was portrayed as a fool.

Danny tried to take control by inviting reporter Cathy Belich from WFTV Channel 9 in Orlando to his prison cell on February 14, 1993, ostensibly for an exclusive interview with the suspected Gainesville murderer. Instead, Rolling took the occasion, Valentine's Day, to blast the press for its treatment of his Valentine Sondra and then to slam the door:

ROLLING: Bless your heart. Howdy, miss.

BELICH: Nice to meet you. I'm Cathy.

[27]United Press International, "Accused Killer Rolling Sings at Hearing," September 27, 1993.

ROLLING: Yes, ma'am.

BELICH: Have a seat. I'm going to help you with this. Is that all right?

ROLLING: Thank you.

BELICH: Is that all right?

ROLLING: Yes.

BELICH: So these guys have all told me they promised they won't tell anyone. I was going to ask you how the food is here.

ROLLING: Well. It ain't so bad.

BELICH: No?

ROLLING: Not really. No, it's prison food, though you know there's a big difference between that and McDonald's.

BELICH: And the Cajun food? You don't get Cajun here?

ROLLING: No, I don't get any Cajun food.

BELICH: OK?

ROLLING: Miss Bellick [*sic*]. My lawyer's advised me not to make any, you know, answer any questions. But I have about a three-minute statement prepared. Would you like to listen to that?

BELICH: Sure. Sure. It's Belich. You can go ahead and read it now if you like. I figured there was something you wanted to say.

ROLLING: Yes, ma'am. At this time, I feel it necessary to comment on the blatant statement Mr. James H. Williams (an inmate at Florida State Prison who had said to a reporter that London was exploiting Rolling) has made concerning Sondra London, Bobby Lewis, prison authorities, and myself. I'm compelled to bring this matter into the light because Williams has caused undue pain and problems for those mentioned and on his own tried to muddy the waters and hinder the investigation in progress.

Number one. Miss London and myself have been corresponding for almost a year now. Regarding also of what Williams has said, Miss London is of the highest caliber, sincere and honest, a woman of extraordinary talents. If I were her, I would sue Williams for slander and defamation of character. She did not deserve the things he said or what the *Gainesville Sun* printed about her. It's just not so. I do not know Williams's reason for doing such a thing. It was totally unmerited or called for. I think Williams has left himself subject to be charged with criminal mischief and/or obstruction of justice.

Number two. Sondra London is a colorful and bright woman, intelligent, talented, and it's a shame the way the media has bashed her as of late. She hasn't done anything to deserve that. Sondra is a worthy soul who only tries to bring the very best out of all she does.

Number three. Sondra London did not seek me out. I inquired her services because I had seen some of her work, namely a screenplay under the title of *Red Bone*, about the dramatic story of Bobby Lewis's escape from death row, which would impress anyone. And so I wanted her to do my story.

Sondra London is not, I repeat, not using me, period. No one is using me. I don't care what her previous lawyer Chet Dellinger said about her. Can you imagine that her own lawyer sold her up the river? If I was a client of his, I think I'd find somebody else to represent me for fear that one day Chet Dellinger would have something publicly to say about me.

Over the past 180 days, Sondra and myself have tried to go through proper channels to get her approved to visit me. She was allowed to visit me behind the glass once.

Number five. Any and all parties involved in the investigation under way concerning the Gainesville murders have been and will be dealt with in an honorable fashion. The wheels of justice may turn slow, but they do turn. You don't ask of justice; it asks of you.

Number six. The prison officials here at FSP have not made any deals with me, period. Nor have they made any promises to Bobby Lewis or myself, period. I have not been coerced into making any statements, period.

Number seven. Miss London represents me as editor, agent, and media go-between. From this point on, I shall make no further statements to press unless Sondra London arranges it. If you wish to speak to me, speak to Miss London.

Number eight. Any further statements you wish at that time, please consult my lawyers, Mr. Richard Parker or Johnny Kearns, who are excellent lawyers for the defense and very capable of answering any other questions. I have nothing further to say. Thank you and good day.

BELICH: That's it? You can't answer any questions for me?

ROLLING: No, ma'am, I'm sorry.

BELICH: Is it true that you are talking through Mr. Lewis to the investigating task force?

ROLLING: I can't make any further comments. Good day.

BELICH: Is it true you had anything to do with the murders at all?

ROLLING: Oh. I've still got this on, don't I?

BELICH: Is it true that you had something to do with the murders?

ROLLING: Here you are, miss. God bless you, and ya'll have a good day.

Rolling handed back the clip-on microphone after having had the final word.

25

Old Sparky

Florida has more than earned its reputation as a state where the death penalty is alive and well. Since the restoration of the death penalty in America in 1976, when the United States Supreme Court affirmed that capital punishment was not inherently "cruel and unusual," the Sunshine State has executed more convicted murderers than any state other than Texas.

Florida has earned its inauspicious reputation not just because of the sheer number of times that Florida's "Old Sparky," a seventy-year-old three-legged oak chair, has been revved up, sending two thousand volts of current through the jerking bodies of condemned killers. Florida has also featured some of the most visible and highly publicized executions in recent memory.

On May 25, 1979, John Spinkellink, convicted of the 1973 murder of Joseph Szymankewicz, became the first American since the restoration of capital punishment to be put to death against his will. (In 1977, the state of Utah executed double-murderer Gary Gilmore without delay since he volunteered to die and resisted all attempts by death penalty opponents to file appeals on his behalf.)

One decade and nineteen executions later, Florida performed what many death penalty experts regard as the most infamous execution in American history (with the possible exception of the controversial execution of Julius and Ethel Rosenberg in 1953). On January 24, 1989, serial killer Theodore Bundy was strapped into Old Sparky amidst a flurry of local and national media attention celebrating the event.

In the days leading up to Bundy's scheduled execution, Floridians celebrated an orgy of vengeance. Many bought and wore overpriced T-shirts exhorting the big event with such slogans as Tuesday is Fryday and Roast in Peace; a Florida restaurant sold Bundy Fries; and hundreds rejoiced outside the walls of the Florida State Prison at Starke in anticipation of the execution, complete with firecrackers and sparklers. The festivities and local arrangements were, of course, covered in full by the print and electronic media, which had arrived on the scene just as soon as the other big Florida event—the Super Bowl—had concluded. One supermarket tabloid even paid thousands of dollars to take a photograph of the dead serial killer lying in the funeral home, with burn marks from the electrodes on his shaved head. The tabloid then published a photo of the dead man for all America to see.

Despite the fact that Bundy tried unsuccessfully to the very end to postpone his fate, Bundy folklore—or hypothesis—suggests that he migrated to Florida upon learning that Florida likes to execute its killers. If he had a death wish, then the good people of Florida were ready to grant his. During the 1990 reelection campaign, Governor Bob Martinez exploited his execution of Ted Bundy in his campaign commercials, boasting that he was tough on violent criminals. Over footage of Bundy's evil grin, Martinez's voice-over proclaimed, ''One of the most serious things that I have to address every day is the whole issue of the death penalty. I now have signed some ninety death warrants in the state of Florida. . . . Each one of those committed a heinous crime that I don't even choose to describe. . . . I believe in the death penalty.''

Florida is also a state that has steadfastly maintained its use of electrocution as its only method of capital punishment. While many other states, including Texas, have adopted lethal injection, believed to be more humane and painless than more archaic methods, Florida kept Old Sparky charged and ready.

Then on May 4, 1990, Jesse Tafero was strapped into the chair at the Florida State Prison for the 1976 murder of two police officers at an I-95 rest stop in Broward County. As the executioner flipped the switch, activating the current, flames erupted from the black hood that shrouded Tafero's face and smoke rose up to the ceiling. Despite the malfunction, the execution had to proceed so as mercifully not to let the poor man burn to death. Twice more, without stopping to make repairs, the current was applied to Tafero's body, leaving the death chamber filled with smoke and the fetid odor of charred flesh.

A subsequent investigation revealed the use of an improper sponge had caused the malfunction. But this horrible event was enough to convince Florida's Governor Lawton Chiles to establish a task force to study the question of whether to abandon Old Sparky in favor of a gurney, needle, and poison.[28]

Like all death penalty states, Florida utilizes a two-stage process in prosecuting capital crimes. In the *guilt phase,* a twelve-member jury hears the facts of the case in order to determine guilt or innocence of the defendant, without considering what sanctions might result. The jury weighs the incriminating and exculpatory evidence to determine if the defendant is guilty beyond a reasonable doubt.

Following a conviction, a jury—the same or a different group of citizens—then hears all evidence pertaining to aggravating and mitigating circumstances during the

---

[28]Not only was there a malfunction of the method of execution, but of the process itself. Tafero was posthumously exonerated. Although present during the shooting, he evidently did not pull the trigger.

penalty phase of the trial. Aggravating factors include a defendant with a prior record of violence, a homicide being committed during a rape or burglary, and a crime that is especially heinous, atrocious, or cruel. Mitigating factors, on the other hand, include a defendant who suffers from a mental or emotional disturbance, extreme duress, or an impaired ability to appreciate the criminality of his conduct. Each of these factors must be proven beyond a reasonable doubt, and a death sentence is warranted if the aggravating circumstances outnumber the mitigating conditions.

The two-stage process does tend to prolong the proceedings and therefore increase the costs associated with prosecuting a capital murder case. However, the guilt and penalty phases are separated to prevent juries from making compromise verdicts in weak cases. There was concern among legal experts that in murder trials where the evidence is equivocal juries might improperly compromise by convicting a defendant but with a lighter penalty.

Despite its reputation for being tough on crime, and murder in particular, the state of Florida has an unusual, quirky murder statute. If a defendant is not sentenced to death, then he or she receives a mandatory prison sentence without parole eligibility for 25 years. Oddly, Florida has abolished parole for virtually all offenses *except* murder, whereas many other states around the country have life without any chance of parole for their most heinous criminals.

In 1989, Governor Martinez, a strong death penalty supporter, vetoed a bill that would have abolished parole for first-degree murderers. Although he claimed to be concerned about unclear guidelines when life without parole would be applied, some of his critics speculated that he preferred not to offer juries a reasonable alternative to the death penalty. The fear was that juries might reject the death penalty in favor of a life sentence without parole if given the choice.

By the time Danny Rolling came to trial for the five Gainesville killings, he was already serving five life sentences for robberies, burglaries, and car theft. He would never be free. For this reason, many citizens in and around Gainesville questioned whether it was necessary to move forward with the case against Rolling. The investigation had already cost millions—a cost covered by local, state, and federal funds, and the county was facing millions more to prosecute Rolling for capital murder.

"Here in Florida, we have hundreds of inmates on death row," commented Strope, "but we only execute four or five a year. Capital punishment is not working, it's not efficient. You'd need electric bleachers to take care of them all. Line them all up, have them hold hands, and have the guy at the bottom put his foot in a bucket of water. Then kiss 'em all good-bye."

It is not unusual for death penalty trials to cost upward of a million dollars. In fact, a 1988 *Miami Herald* report calculated that the state of Florida had spent $57.2 million to execute eighteen people, or about $3 million per capital case, six times the cost of keeping these people in prison for their entire lives.[29] Because the stakes are so high and the penalty irreversible, death penalty trials tend to run much longer than noncapital trials, with more witnesses, more expensive lab tests, and costly expert testimony. Generally, the defense is granted fairly wide latitude in preparing and presenting its case in order to minimize the risk of an innocent person being sentenced to die. The bill for lawyers and witnesses runs up fairly quickly.

Some citizens, concerned about the enormous tax burden on the county to prosecute Rolling, suggested also that the defendant be offered a plea bargain. Perhaps the case could be settled quickly and cheaply by offering him a life sentence in exchange for a guilty plea. One Gainesville resident suggested, for example, that the money needed to prosecute Rolling "could more beneficially be spent on children's lunches or better education

---

[29]David Von Drehle, "Capital Punishment in Paralysis," *Miami Herald*, July 10, 1988, p. 1A.

opportunities."[30] The residents could then move beyond this painful episode.

Michael Radelet, professor of sociology at UF and an ardent death penalty opponent, wrote in a *Gainesville Sun* op-ed column,

> If he is guilty Rolling might be persuaded to admit it. In exchange, we could give up our love for the executioner and settle for guaranteed life imprisonment. The victims' families would be assured of Rolling's guilt. They would have an opportunity to speak. They could begin to focus their lives on the difficult process of healing and rebuilding, rather than focusing the next dozen years on appeals, stays and more execution dates—each time reliving the details of their loved one's murder as resurrected by the media.[31]

Serial killers clearly are highlighted by the media as they approach their execution date. Not only was the Bundy execution a major news story both inside and outside of Florida, but the execution of John Wayne Gacy in 1994 by the state of Illinois also made headlines across the country. His execution reenergized the media hype surrounding the man who murdered thirty-three young men and buried the remains in the crawl space beneath his suburban Chicago home. His infamy was greater in death than in life, adding even more salt to the wounds of his victims' families.

The families of Rolling's victims were not focusing on the publicity that the killer might get on his execution date, however, when they argued vehemently against any attempt to curtail the judicial process. Understandably, they wanted justice to be served, regardless of the price tag. "Just because he has a life sentence, big

---

[30]Yvonne Dell, Letter to the editor, *Gainesville Sun*, August 7, 1992.
[31]Michael L. Radelet, "If Jeffrey Dahmer Lived Here," *Gainesville Sun*, August 31, 1992, p. 7A.

deal," cried Tessa Powell, Christina's sister-in-law. "He took a life."[32]

"I cannot believe they would not try someone that could have killed my daughter," complained Gary Hoyt. "I could not live if this does not go to trial."

George Paules, Tracy's dad, put his point of view in no uncertain terms when he said, "We want the son of a bitch to suffer. Execution is not even satisfactory."[33]

The families of the victims demanded that the judicial process run its course, for all the evidence to be heard and debated in court, so they could finally have all their haunting questions answered about what exactly happened to their children and who was responsible.

"We have to know if he's the man," pointed out Ricky Paules, Tracy's mother. "They [the prosecutors] have told us he's the one, but that's not good enough."

As far as the families were concerned, a plea bargain was out of the question. A trial would bring them emotional healing and closure. They could sit in the courtroom, representing their son and daughters, and watch justice being served on behalf of their slain children. If Rolling only got a life sentence through a plea bargain, it would be nothing more severe than the sentence that he already was serving. Without a death sentence, he would, in essence, never have to pay penance for the Gainesville murders—not even a day.

The state had its own special interest in moving forward with a capital trial, whatever the cost and time commitment. "You can never allow cost to be a factor in a death penalty case," said state attorney Len Register. "There are some crimes that are so atrocious. . . . We have every plan to continue with the prosecution." Months later, Register lost his bid for reelection and was replaced by Rod Smith.

The difficulty for the prosecution in considering a plea

---

[32]Mary Shedden, "Victims' Kin Want Trial for Rolling," *Gainesville Sun,* August 12, 1992, p. 1A.

[33]Chris Lavin, "Is the Death Penalty Worth It? Some Question Cost, Time Spent," *Saint Petersburg Times,* August 23, 1992, p. 1B.

bargain was twofold. First, of course, the state attorney would face possible political suicide by exempting the Gainesville killer from the electric chair. It would also jeopardize efforts to seek the death penalty in future murder cases. How could the state settle for a life sentence for Danny Rolling for one of the most heinous crimes in Florida history and then seek death sentences against other defendants who will have been convicted of somewhat less atrocious homicides?

And so the wheels of justice would continue to turn, however slowly and costly. The prosecution and defense teams would prepare for a prolonged and costly battle over Rolling's fate. Through this process, the people of Alachua County and millions across the country would finally learn what exactly happened in late August 1990 to five innocent college students in Gainesville.

26

A Change of Heart

The Alachua County Courthouse is situated in downtown Gainesville, just about two blocks from the center of town. On Tuesday, February 15, 1994, as the trial was set to start on the fourth floor in courtroom 4A, the streets surrounding the red-brick building became lined with television trucks hoisting satellite transmitters. The scene around the courthouse was reminiscent of the terror-filled days in August 1990 when the media couldn't get enough of the Gainesville slayings.

The courtroom wasn't particularly large, although it was the largest in the building. The gallery held a total capacity of 116, which was jam packed for nearly every day of testimony. Seats were in high demand, and so very few were available for the general public. The far left side of the gallery, just behind the *CourtTV* camera, was reserved for the media—all the major papers around the state, the correspondent from the Associated Press, and a reporter from the UF paper, *Independent Florida Alligator*. Also included among the press were a number of freelancers doing magazine pieces or writing books about the case. Sondra London was seated there too.

The families and friends of the victims sat on the opposite side of the room, against the far right wall. This placed them uncomfortably close to Danny Rolling; however, at least they were far away from the jury box. In this way, jurors would be minimally affected by any tears or shouts of anguish from the victims' loved ones, and the families would not be able to peek at the grisly crime photos as they were passed among the jurors.

Forty-seven-year-old Alachua County Circuit Judge Stan Morris was in charge. After practicing private civil and criminal law for many years, he had been elected to the Alachua County bench in 1980 and then appointed circuit court judge in 1986. Since then, he was reelected twice without opposition. Now, he was presiding over what promised to be one of the most sensational trials in Florida's history.

The six-foot-four-inch jurist leaned over the bench, and the trial was finally under way. "Mr. Smith," Judge Morris asked, "is the state ready to proceed?"

"Yes, your honor," responded state attorney Rod Smith. This was the handsome forty-four-year-old former defense lawyer's first major criminal prosecution, and he was eager to make the strongest possible case against Danny Rolling.

The legal proceedings were expected to continue for two and one-half months and cost millions of additional dollars—some 148 witnesses were set to testify—but a guilty decision would for many people be worth every penny. Forty-two months after the hideous murders, the culprit would finally be brought to justice. True to form, he might feign his innocence and concoct a far-fetched tale designed to impress the members of the jury, but it wouldn't be enough. There was the DNA evidence and Rolling's veiled confessions to investigators and fellow inmates. There was his extensive criminal history, his time behind bars, and his bad temper. He had the opportunity and the motivation. All that was left for Rod Smith to do was to spell it out in clear-cut terms that the jury would understand. They would—beyond a reasonable doubt—see Danny Rolling's veneer of civility peeled away layer by layer, revealing the monster that he really was.

But then, in the trial's opening moments, without any warning, the ongoing drama came abruptly to a halt. Danny Rolling was already serving three life sentences for a series of burglaries and robberies. He now calmly announced to the court that he was indeed guilty—as guilty as sin of the five first-degree murders, three sexual batteries, and three armed burglaries of which he was accused.

"Your honor," he said quietly, "I've been running from first one thing and then another all of my life, whether from problems at home or with the law or from myself. But there are some things that you just can't run from, and this being one of them."

Peering over his reading glasses, Judge Morris accepted the defendant's plea. He ruled that Rolling was competent to change his mind about his complicity and that he had done so voluntarily. He would sentence the defendant only after an advisory panel of jurors was appointed and had made its recommendation to him regarding an appropriate penalty. The judge would still have the final say. He could choose to override the jury's recommendation but probably wouldn't. There were only two sentencing options for Danny Rolling: life or death, that is, the electric chair or life in prison without the possibility of parole for twenty-five years.

By admitting to the crimes and waiving his right to a jury trial, Rolling spared the families and friends of his victims the additional burden of a prolonged courtroom presentation of the gory details of the slayings. Rolling's forty-six-year-old public defender, Richard Parker, claimed that it was simply this concern for the families that had motivated his client's change of heart. "He didn't want them to see pictures of what he'd done," explained the bearded and bespectacled public defender, referring to relatives of the victims who were gathered in the courtroom.

* * *

"He didn't get a deal," prosecutor Rod Smith told reporters. "He pleaded guilty because he did it."[34]

Lee Strope offered a slightly different spin on Rolling's surprising admission of guilt: "It wasn't for any gallant reason," he said. "In the grand jury, he was very uncomfortable seeing the pictures. He didn't want to go through another trial. He was embarrassed. He didn't want to look at the families' faces."

But the victims' relatives, though relieved, were much less sympathetic toward the defendant. "I have no pity for the individual. This is a life form gone bad," said Mario Taboada, brother of Manny Taboada.

"He's a liar," said Ricky Paules, reacting bitterly to Rolling's transparent concern for the families' feelings. "I want him as dead as my daughter is," said the irate mother of Tracy Paules. "I don't want him alive."[35]

"Electrocution would be a very kind thing to do to him after what he did to those kids," declared James Cullinane, Christina Powell's uncle who lives in Sarasota. "I don't think anything less than death is justified in this case."[36]

Lee Strope also differed from many of the victims' loved ones concerning whether Danny Rolling should be seated in Florida's Old Sparky. "In my opinion, he should be given five life sentences," Strope said. "Anybody who's ever been to Florida State Prison will tell you it's a hole, a sewer. They'd rather go to the electric chair. You are really doing the killer a favor by electrocuting him. You are not doing him a favor if you keep him alive. Let him suffer. I hope he lives for ninety-five years!"

Whatever its true purpose, Rolling's guilty plea failed to reduce the agony of the victims' loved ones, who

---

[34]United Press International, "Florida Student Slaying Suspect Unexpectedly Pleads Guilty," February 15, 1994.

[35]Arden Moore and Jim Leusner, "Victims' Relatives Want Rolling in the Electric Chair," *Orlando Sentinel,* February 16, 1994, p. A4.

[36]Alicia Caldwell, "Families of Victims Urge Death Penalty," *Saint Petersburg Times,* February 16, 1994, p. 8A.

would still sit through weeks of gut-wrenching testimony and evidence. By erasing the haunting doubts in their minds as to whether the right man had actually been caught, however, Danny's confession was a welcome relief. Prior to Rolling's admission of guilt, the two-killer theory remained to be torn apart, and Ed Humphrey was still very much on the hook as a possible monster. Danny Rolling had, for years, professed his own innocence. But after his guilty plea in court, it was now abundantly clear to almost everyone that he was really the culprit and that he had acted alone, with malice aforethought but without an accomplice.

Ed Humphrey, on the other hand, who was once the perfect suspect, was now seen instead as the perfect patsy, a misunderstood and disoriented young man whose behavior just happened to get more and more bizarre precisely during the period of time when the five grisly student murders had occurred. Off his medication, Humphrey had looked every bit the part of a deranged maniac capable of committing even these hideous atrocities; yet he turned out to be a tragic figure who was simply in the wrong place at the wrong time.

On February 16, the morning after Rolling's shocking confession in court, Judge Morris began the proceedings by questioning forty-seven prospective jurors for the sentencing hearing. With all of the pretrial publicity, it would be no easy task to find a dozen impartial residents of Alachua County. The defense had unsuccessfully attempted a change of venue, but Judge Morris ruled that media saturation does necessarily create bias in the jurors' ability to evaluate the case on its merits.

Morris determined, in short order, that six of the prospective jurors would not be able to serve, and they were excused. After Morris completed his interviews, state attorney Rod Smith and defense attorney Rick Parker had their turns to question the candidates.

Then, for two weeks, both sides—defense and prosecution—worked through the arduous process of finding an acceptable jury of twelve regulars plus four alternates. The defense claimed that the potential jurors could not return an impartial recommendation, because they were aware of details of the murders and of Rolling's past that were entirely inadmissible. But Judge Morris disagreed. He overruled, ordering that the questioning of jurors continue until a suitable panel could be convened.

By early March, sooner than most observers had predicted, a jury was empaneled to hear testimony. The question before them was clear: whether Danny Rolling should die because he viciously murdered five college students or should be allowed to live because his mind was deeply warped by a dreadful childhood. To support a recommendation to execute Rolling, the prosecution would present a series of aggravating circumstances surrounding the murders: their premeditated and cold-blooded character, the pain and suffering of the victims including sexual battery, and the killer's fifteen-year criminal history covering five states.

In urging the jury to recommend a life sentence rather than the death penalty, the defense would counter with evidence indicating that Rolling himself was a victim of sorts—a victim of childhood abuse and brutality, a mentally ill loser who had long suffered with depression and poor self-esteem.

27

State of Florida v. Danny Rolling

On Monday, March 7, in his opening argument, state attorney Rod Smith described the killings in depth. During the days that followed, witnesses confirmed and provided additional details regarding Rolling's evil deeds.

Rod Smith's opening statement apprised the members of the jury of the aggravating circumstances surrounding the murders. Smith urged the jury to listen closely to the evidence that he would present over the course of the penalty hearing. He said, ''We feel that at the end of this evidence, you will find, as I have shown you, that as to Sonja Larson, the aggravation is massive. As to Christina Powell, the aggravation is massive. As to Christa Hoyt, the aggravation is massive. As to Manuel Taboada, the aggravation is massive. As to Tracy Paules, the aggravation is massive. It weighs so heavily in favor of the death penalty that he has earned, but it will be your duty to go through that weighing process and to make that recommendation to His Honor for a sentencing recommendation.''

As the trial unfolded, and witness after witness added details, the sequence of events became clear. On July 18, 1990, more than a month before the murders in Gainesville, Danny Rolling had strolled into an army–

navy store, near the bus station in Tallahassee, Florida. Calling himself Michael Kennedy, he looked over the inventory and purchased a Marine-issue Ka-Bar knife. He chose this particular weapon because it was so sharp, because it was so effective in performing precise surgery, because it was part of his plan for having the time of his life.

Then, on July 22, Rolling checked out of his Travel Lodge motel room and left the Tallahassee area. He took a bus directly to the picturesque city of Sarasota, on the west coast of Florida. During the month he remained there, again calling himself Michael Kennedy, he visited the shops and restaurants around Saint Armand's Circle and, at night, frequented the area's bars and lounges. But along with playing tourist and picking up women, he also purchased a 9-millimeter automatic pistol to add to his collection of weapons. Then, still thinking about murder, he made the short trip over to the city of his dreams.

On August 18, Danny Rolling arrived in Gainesville and immediately checked into the University Inn, located only a few blocks from the campus of UF. That evening, he invited a prostitute to his hotel room in order to play out his fantasies—at least some of them—with a willing participant. It may also have been a "dress rehearsal" for his sadistic crimes to occur in the days ahead.

Rolling told the woman to take off her clothes and then lie on her back on the bed with her feet raised. He then grabbed her ankles and pulled her body to the edge of the bed, spreading her legs open so they dangled over the side. Taking a scalpel from a cigar box under the bed, he ran the sharp instrument lightly up and down the prostitute's arms, legs, and torso. After a few minutes, Rolling ordered her to turn over, with her feet on the floor, her hands on the bed, and her buttocks in the air. He sat cross-legged on the floor between her legs, placing mirrors in position so that he could examine her vaginal area. With his free hand, he masturbated.

The inn made a convenient command center for Rolling's operations over the next few days. He could easily make frequent covert recon visits around the area, becoming familiar with the nearby apartment complexes in which students resided, sneaking up behind buildings and spying on possible targets. Five days after coming to town, his intelligence missions completed, Danny vacated his motel room and moved into the woods.

The WalMart store in the southwest area of town had almost everything Rolling would need for his big adventure. Among other things, he purchased a tent and a mattress for his campsite. On the same trip, he also stole some items that had nothing to do with camping: a screwdriver, a large roll of duct tape, and a pair of tight-fitting athletic gloves. He now had his weapons and his tools and was prepared to have the time of his life.

On August 23, Rolling took all of his equipment into the hot and muggy Gainesville woods and set up his campsite. As soon as he had pitched his tent, he took out his cassette recorder and continued taping a message to his family that he had started earlier in the month while he was traveling through Sarasota.

First, Danny professed his love:

Contrary to popular belief I don't know what people think anymore. All I know is I'm just one man alone in this world, facing the whole world by himself. But I'm sending this to the three people I love the most. I'll always love you. I love my mother. I love my father. And I love my brother. No matter what anybody thinks about this man, Danny Harold Rolling, I want these three people that I'm talking to right now to know that this is not the road that I really wanted. This is not what I wanted. But it is the road that is before me now, and I will walk it like a man. And you know, Dad, you know, I love you, Pop. And I'm so sorry, Dad. It rips my heart out to think what happened between you and I. I'm sorry, Pop. If it means anything, I'm so very sorry. And I suffer a lot behind this. I hurt, hurt in my heart, and it never goes away, Pop. I wish it was me instead of you. I wished it had happened to me instead of you. This isn't easy. Nothing's ever been easy for me.

He tells his mother that this is his final message to the family:

Mom, I want you to go on. What I'm trying to say is that after this tape you're not going to hear anything else from me. Just—just forget about me. Well, I won't say that because you can't forget your own. I'm just saying I want you to go on and live your life. I don't want you to have sleepless nights because of me. Do this for me, Mom. You deserve a hell of a lot more than the pain that I've brought you. And I regret it with all my heart. But you know, if you want to make things easier on me, Mom, please, I'm asking you, go on. I love you.

Then Danny proceeds to sing "every song I ever wrote," including a frightening, if prophetic, number titled "Mystery Rider" in which he talks about himself. For a moment, he changes his mind, saying to his family "I don't know if I want to play that one or not." Then he can be heard quite clearly singing about a "Grim Reaper": a killer gone insane.

Then Rolling advised his brother as to the most effective method for hunting down and killing a deer, how to make sure you have hit its vital organs to ensure death:

Kevin, you better get a daggum deer for me with that bow I got you now. Yeah, just go a couple of times and see if you don't get lucky with it. Take it out in the backyard and practice with it when you ain't got nothing else to do before deer season comes up this October. And give it a shot. Just make sure that you put on some camouflage, good

*camouflage, because you know when you're going
bow hunting you got to have camouflage. I tell you
something else too. Aim for the lungs. Straight
through the rib cage. Either there or the heart, but
the best thing to do is hit the lungs. It's the best
shot for a deer. Straight through the lungs. He
don't go very far. Don't chase after him when you
hit him, when you stick him, when that arrow hits
him. What you got to do is you've got to just watch
which way he goes, and when he goes out, when
he's out of sight, listen. You'll hear him banging
into trees and stuff, and then finally you'll hear
him either fall down or you'll hear him stop running. He'll stay right there until he bleeds to death
if you don't go and chase him. So what you need
to do after you stick him is just sit right down there
for about thirty minutes to an hour. That just depends upon how you feel about it. That is, if you're
ever going to do any deer hunting. I never could
get you interested in it when you and I was able
to go. I don't know, that just didn't interest you.
Well, Brother, I'm hanging in there. Yeah. I'm
hanging in there. I'll say that much for myself for
the moment. I plan on going the distance. I'll give
it my best shot.*

Finally, Danny Rolling signed off with what prosecutor Rod Smith suggested "surely will be forever remembered as one of the most ominous phrases ever
uttered in Gainesville." Rolling said, "Well, I'm going
to sign off for a little bit. I've got something I've got to
do." He turned off the tape recorder and left his campsite in the woods.

According to Smith, "what he had to go do was to
commence the slaughter he had planned of students in
this community." Of course, Smith was only speculating
about what that "something" was. Whether or not it
referred to murder, the impact of Smith's interpretation
and delivery was indeed powerful.

From August 23, with his plan for murder still uppermost in his mind, Rolling went in and out of the woods on reconnaissance missions. He roamed the area, hiding in the darkness, creeping down out of sight as he searched apartment complexes and duplexes around the southwest section of town for appropriate targets.

His early efforts were thwarted at every turn. He stood on a woman's balcony and stared through her window as she washed dishes in the kitchen. He had completely stripped to make certain that he didn't get blood on his clothes. But just as he was about to attack, a downstairs neighbor spotted Rolling and chased him away. In a second episode, Rolling stood on a trash can and watched two women through a window. As he was set to make his move, a suspicious security guard approached out of nowhere and forced him to abort his mission.[37]

But Danny Rolling was no quitter. He was a very persistent guy who simply would not be denied the thrill of his life. At three o'clock in the morning, wearing black ninja clothing, his athletic gloves, and a ski mask to conceal his face, the drifter from Shreveport approached the rear of building 11, apartment 113 at the sprawling Williamsburg complex, where numerous students from UF resided. By this hour, most of the laughter and noise coming from adjacent apartment units had subsided and the hush of darkness had settled over the entire complex. Being careful not to be seen, Danny moved stealthfully to the back door and carefully pried it open with his black-handled screwdriver. Then, in the dead of night, he entered the darkened apartment.

Rolling immediately found a pretty young woman sleeping peacefully on the first floor. Her slight build and brown hair were reminiscent of his ex-wife, the mother of his daughter, the woman who used to love but then betrayed him. He stood over Christina Powell for a few moments, preparing for his assault. Everything was going according to plan, and he would soon have

[37]Donya Currie, ''Rolling Nearly Killed Others, Inmate Says,'' *Gainesville Sun*, March 15, 1994, p. 1A.

his fun. But, first, he had to check out the rest of the apartment. There could be no witnesses.

Rolling walked gingerly up the stairs and, and without making a sound, turned into the top-floor bedroom, where Sonya Larson lay fast asleep on her bed. He stood hunched over the woman with brown hair, his military knife clutched tightly in his gloved fist. His large frame was obscured in the darkness as he stopped for a moment to consider which of his two victims he would rape and which he would eliminate. Then, without further hesitation, he viciously plunged his knife into the sleeping woman. Before she could cry out for help or scream, he had already covered her mouth with duct tape.

Larson awoke with a start to realize she was under deadly attack, but it was too late. She squirmed and struggled in a valiant attempt to guard herself with her arms and hands and to fend off her attacker. But Larson's defensive efforts were in vain as Rolling stabbed her again and again and then watched with some satisfaction as she drew her last breath of life.

His preparation now completed, the masked intruder crept back downstairs for his big thrill. Christina Powell was still asleep, totally unaware of what had happened to her roommate or what was about to happen to her. Taking advantage of the situation, Rolling took out his roll of duct tape and swiftly bound his second victim's hands behind her back and covered her mouth. Christina was now utterly at his mercy. The roommate silenced, his next victim subdued and restrained, Rolling could take his time; he could do anything to Powell that he damn well pleased.

In a sadistic urge to maximize her pain, suffering, and terror, Rolling explained to his young victim that he intended to rape and then kill her. He took his knife and ripped off the frightened woman's bra and other clothing, forcing her to have oral sex on him, and then he raped her. When she cried out in agony, Rolling responded callously, "Take the pain, bitch, take the pain." The more his victim suffered, the better he liked it. It made him feel superior, a sensation he hadn't had for months. After a period of time, Rolling had satiated his immediate desire for sex. So he turned Powell over on her back and repeatedly stabbed her until she stopped moving and he was sure she was dead.

Now it was almost time to make his getaway, but first he had to clean up and prepare the scene to shock those who would later discover it. So as not to leave incriminating evidence, Rolling took the tape off Christina Powell's hands and mouth and put it in his pocket. He went back upstairs to Sonja Larson's body and ripped the tape from her face. Then he positioned her body in a provocative pose. He went downstairs again to where he had raped Christina Powell and posed her body as well. Taking a bottle of liquid detergent and paper towels from the kitchen, he cleaned her genital area, hoping to reduce the possibility of leaving evidence that might implicate him in the hideous crimes.

But Rolling stayed awhile longer, eating an apple and a banana from the refrigerator as he enjoyed the bloody scene of human destruction and misery he had created. As he munched on his midnight snack, he contemplated his only regret: he should have killed the girl downstairs and raped the one upstairs instead. She had a better body, he thought. When he finally tired of it all, he left.

Even prior to killing Christina Powell and Sonja Larson, Rolling was busy making plans for his second foray. Indeed, he had already chosen his next victim. While prowling in the southwest area of town, Rolling had earlier discovered a small duplex that looked like an easy mark. On the night that he murdered the two young women at the Williamsburg apartments, he had also gone back to the duplex. Peering through a sliding glass door at the rear of the building, Rolling secretly watched as a lovely young coed in an apartment unit emerged from the shower and toweled off. He had no idea who this girl was but was attracted to Christa Hoyt's slim figure and brown hair. She looked astoundingly like his ex-wife.

At nine o'clock on the evening of August 25, Rolling

returned to the rear of Christa Hoyt's small duplex. She was out playing racquetball with a friend.

He wore the black outfit, the gloves, and the dark ski mask; he carried the same gun and military knife that he had taken on his earlier escapade. Making sure not to be observed, he skillfully pried open Hoyt's sliding glass door with his screwdriver and entered her rear bedroom.

Rolling walked through the empty apartment, making certain that it was completely vacant. He wanted no surprises. He then stood in a small alcove by the front door and waited patiently for his intended victim to return.

It was almost 10 P.M. when Christa Hoyt arrived. She parked her car in an adjacent lot and walked up to the front door, completely unaware of the monster lurking inside her apartment. Rolling watched as the unsuspecting young woman turned the key in the door and entered.

Almost immediately, even as she was closing the door behind her, Christa sensed that something was wrong, but it was already too late. Danny was on her from behind, easily choking her to the ground with his overpowering strength as she struggled to free herself from his grip.

After subduing his victim, Rolling took out the roll of duct tape, tore off a piece, and secured her hands behind her back. He cut off another piece of tape and covered her mouth. Next, he dragged her back to the bedroom, flung her on the bed, and sliced off her clothes with his large knife.

Rolling sexually toyed with Christa until he discovered that she was having her period. He removed her tampon and threw it in the corner of the room. And then he raped her. When he was finished, Rolling made sure that he would never be identified. He turned the brutalized young woman on her back and gave her the news she most dreaded to hear: he told her that she was about to die, that he was going to murder her in cold blood, that he would now stab her to death. Then, true to his word, he took his military knife and slashed her through the heart.

Just as he had done in the earlier murders, Rolling posed Christa Hoyt's body and cleaned up before leaving her apartment. He then snuck back into the woods.

Upon returning to his campsite, Rolling was startled to discover that he had lost his wallet. If he had left it at the murder scene, he was in big trouble. The police would surely find it and trace it back to him. He really had no choice but to take a chance and return to Christa Hoyt's duplex before someone discovered the body and it was too late!

Still under the cover of darkness, Rolling put on his mask and gloves and made his way back to Christa Hoyt's apartment. But his wallet was nowhere to be found, and everything was just as he had left it with one exception. Rigor mortis had set in, and Danny was able to manipulate his victim's body, like a mannequin, in ways that were impossible to do immediately after he had stabbed her to death.

Just to assure that his risky return was not a total waste of time, Rolling decided to leave a message for those who would later discover the corpse of Christa Hoyt. According to Bobby Lewis, the inmate in whom he often confided, Danny wanted to terrorize the residents of Gainesville and to become a superstar among serial killers. He may also have discovered that his victim worked for the ASO from her hat on the bureau and, like his father, was regarded as the enemy.[38] A final source of motivation for his extreme sadism may have been the similar appearance of Christa Hoyt to his ex-wife.[39]

Rolling moved a bookcase from the living room to a wall in the back bedroom that faced the front door. Using skills he had learned from years of hunting deer, he decapitated his victim with his big knife and carefully

[38]Currie, ''Rolling Nearly Killed Others,'' p. 4A.
[39]Jaime Abdo, ''Deliberation of Confessed Killer's Fate Draws Near,'' *Florida Independent Alligator,* March 21, 1994, p. 1.

cleaned the blood from her head. He then placed the severed head on the top shelf of the bookcase so that it would be the first thing that anybody saw when they opened the door. Before finally leaving for the second time, Rolling then positioned Hoyt's headless body at the edge of the bed in a sexually provocative pose.

As much fun as this may have been for the killer, Rolling was still left with the problem of finding his lost wallet. Careful not to be detected by curious neighbors, he let himself out of the sliding back door and headed for a nearby phone booth. It was almost one in the morning, and there were very few passersby on the streets.

Using the alias Michael Kennedy, Rolling called the police emergency number 911 to report that his wallet was missing. He then returned to his campsite for a good night's rest.

The next evening, Danny continued roaming around Southwest Gainesville. Dressed in black, he slipped unseen behind apartments in the Gatorwood complex, where he crouched down out of sight and did his "peeping Tom" routine. It didn't take long to select another victim. Inside one of the ground-floor Gatorwood apartments on Archer Road, there was a pretty young woman with brown hair and an attractive figure. He watched in the darkness near the woods for a while as she could be seen walking from room to room and resting in her bedroom. Then, at about 3 A.M., he made his move.

Just as before, Rolling had his knife, his gun, and his black screwdriver. He broke into the tiny two-bedroom apartment through a sliding glass door on the side and immediately checked its rooms for possible witnesses.

Tracy's roommate and dear friend from home, Manuel Taboada, was sleeping in the adjoining bedroom. A football player in high school, Manny's two-hundred-pound muscular torso covered much of the waterbed he rested on.

The masked intruder walked into the young man's bedroom. He stood over Manny for a moment and then plunged his knife with full force through the sleeping man's abdomen. This was enough to impair his victim but not quite enough to kill him. Manny somehow managed to awaken and sit up. He held Rolling; he fought Rolling; he cursed Rolling; in fact, he almost subdued the killer in a bloody battle of brawn against brawn. Surprised by his victim's brute force and incredible determination to survive, Danny was forced to slash and stab Manny a number of times before he finally succumbed.

Meanwhile, Manny's roommate, Tracy Paules, hearing the ruckus, had rushed out of her bedroom across the hall to see what was going on. Immediately, she observed the masked intruder, covered with his victim's blood, standing over Manny's eviscerated remains. In a terrified but futile attempt to flee, she ran back into her own room, slamming the door behind her. But Rolling was quick to recover. He chased the petite young woman across the hall and easily kicked down her door.

Tracy had just talked to her friend on the phone who told her about the brutal murders of fellow students. She turned to Rolling and asked, "You're the one, aren't you?"

Danny replied matter-of-factly, almost with pride, "Yeah, I'm the one." He then taped his victim's mouth and secured her hands behind her back. Careful not to be observed, he closed the drapes of the bedroom window and, with a small piece of duct tape, shut them tightly together so that no one could possibly peer inside.

Then he threw Paules on the bed and ripped off her T-shirt. While sexually playing with her, he explained that he intended first to rape her and then to stab her to death, as he had done his previous victims. Gagged and bound, the horrified young woman was absolutely defenseless, her muffled cries for help and mercy being totally ineffective.

He raped Tracy in an act of anal sodomy and then, when he was finished, stabbed her repeatedly until he was certain she was dead. All the while, he delighted in hearing her muted screams through the tape covering her mouth. He reveled in the fact that he had caused a young, beautiful woman to suffer excruciating pain and anxiety. He was in charge now, and he liked it.

Afterward, Rolling dragged Tracy's lifeless body from the bed into the hallway, where he placed her on the floor with her legs apart in a sexually provocative pose. Just as he had done at the first murder site, he attempted to destroy any physical evidence by cleaning his victim's corpse with liquid dishwashing detergent. It gave her body a brilliant but eerie sheen.

It was just before daybreak as Rolling finally fled the apartment. His killing spree accomplished, he now looked for a safe place to dispose of the tools and weapons he had employed in carrying out the five murders. Not far from his tent in the woods, he buried his knife and bloodied gloves.

Following Rod Smith's powerful opening remarks, the prosecution paraded before the jury a number of witnesses, including lab technicians who analyzed the crime scene evidence, police investigators who discovered the bodies, as well as friends who had had contact with the victims prior to the murders. The state's burden was not to prove that Rolling had committed the crimes—he had already pleaded guilty. Instead, the job of the prosecution was to demonstrate through its witnesses and exhibits just how vicious the crimes were. Some of the most horrific details were inadmissible, however. The jury was not permitted to hear about Hoyt's decapitation or other postmortem mutilation. By law, any act occurring after death could not be regarded as an aggravating circumstance, regardless of how aggravating it may be to the victims' loved ones.

This ground rule imposed on the proceedings was not necessarily a loss for the prosecution. The state had enough evidence of pain and suffering on behalf of the victims to justify the most extreme penalty; introducing photos of a headless body might only have convinced the jury that Rolling was out of his mind during the commission of the crimes, making him less—not more—eligible for the death penalty.

28

The Making of a Sadist

Serial murder is usually a crime of sexual control. The killer is typically driven by an excessive need to be powerful and dominant, which he expresses in sadistic treatment of his victims. He plays a cruel game with his victims' lives. He tortures, sodomizes, rapes, strangles, and stabs. The more excruciating their pain, the better the killer feels about himself. The more his victims suffer, the greater the thrill, the excitement, the sense of superiority.

Inmates who got to know Danny Rolling nicknamed him Psycho or Psych Man, because of his bizarre and irrational behavior behind bars. They told investigators that he often made cryptic references to the part he played in the Gainesville murders.

Rolling's conversations with fellow inmates suggested that his motivation for murder contained a need to prove that he was superior in every way to his victims. According to inmate Paul Fuqua, Rolling "would slice women up . . . because they thought they were too pretty for anybody and he couldn't stand that, so he made it where they wasn't so pretty." Another inmate told police that Psych Man killed women he believed engaged in premarital intercourse; at two of the crime scenes,

Rolling left his victims' birth control pills on display. He confided in another inmate that he killed out of resentment toward his father, his ex-wife, and the prison system. In fact, he set out to murder eight people—the number of years he had spent behind bars.

In Rolling's sentencing trial, a mental health expert for the defense confirmed what Danny had confided to fellow prisoners. Dr. Harry Krop testified that Rolling's killing spree was motivated by a desire to get even, to make other people suffer in the way that he had suffered as a child and as a prisoner. Danny told Dr. Krop that the most horrifying death would be committed by someone who came in the dead of night with a knife and told the victims they were going to die.[40]

Dr. Krop referred to the defendant as "a seriously disturbed, emotionally disturbed individual." Testifying for the defense, the clinical psychologist characterized Rolling as suffering from "a borderline personality disorder" resulting from his volatile childhood. This is a disorder that is marked by a pattern of instability in mood, relationships, and self-image. In response to a stressful situation, the borderline type may become "pseudopsychotic" for a short period of time. The behavior of borderline types often includes impulsivity, intense anger, and chronic feelings of boredom. They often feel a profound sense of abandonment and rejection and may be extremely manipulative with other people.

The roots of the sadistic need are often found in a lifetime of rejection and abuse. Many serial killers were treated brutally as children, being sexually abused or molested, abandoned by their parents, shunned by peers, or rejected by members of the opposite sex. After experiencing years of frustration and disappointment, they develop a profound sense of powerlessness that later motivates their relationships with other people. They only

---

[40]Mary Shedden, "Rolling's Disorders 'Severe,' " *Gainesville Sun*, March 16, 1994, p.1; Chuck Murphy, Laura Griffin, and Jim Ross, "Police Reports Detail Crimes of the Man Called 'Psycho,' " *Saint Petersburg Times*, March 8, 1994, p. 5B.

feel superior to the extent that they make others feel inferior.

Danny's mother, Claudia Rolling, had written an Ocala judge in 1990 that much of her son's problems were because of abuse by his father, James Harold Rolling. She claimed that her husband, a retired police lieutenant who had been on the local police force for twenty-three years, also had mental problems. By the time of Danny's murder trial in 1994, Claudia was severely ill with liver cancer and couldn't make the trip from her Shreveport home. Instead, in a videotaped interview recorded in May 1992 and shown to the jurors during the trial, she held Danny's father responsible for having created a monster.

According to Claudia, even before he was born, Danny Rolling was already a loser. He was rejected by his authoritarian father, who was a decorated Korean War veteran but who also had a serious temper and wandered in and out of his stormy marriage. In 1954, just after their wedding, the couple moved into a tiny garage apartment in Columbus, Georgia. Claudia's pregnancy, discovered only a couple of weeks later, added to the burden of responsibility that James felt had been unfairly placed on his shoulders. He didn't want a child. He wasn't prepared for one. He blamed Claudia for the pregnancy and often made her feel that he was ashamed of it—and her. He rarely left the apartment to go anywhere with his wife when she wore maternity clothes. While she was carrying Danny, James once became so enraged that he attempted to choke her. In a fit of anger, he shoved Claudia down and held her to the floor before finally releasing her from his grip.

Even before she gave birth, Claudia already felt compelled to escape her rocky relationship with her husband. When things got to be intolerable, she ran to her home in Shreveport, but James followed her there and persuaded her to return, at least for a period of time.

After Danny was born, life in the Rolling household only deteriorated. James, an extremely possessive man, wouldn't allow his wife to develop friendships. Almost nobody ever came to the door of their modest home in the southwest section of the city. And the angry outbursts became more and more frequent and intense. James once slammed Claudia across the face, splitting her lip. He shoved and pushed her. He was unreasonably jealous. There were times when he refused even to let Claudia use the phone, especially when one of her relatives called to find out how she was doing.

Danny's brother, Kevin, was born a year later, but nothing else changed very much. James was fired from a job and was despondent. He became verbally abusive to the boys, always putting them down and making them feel stupid. When Danny was a baby and just learning to crawl, James couldn't stand the fact that his son continued to drag himself across the floor. He would shove Danny with his foot in order to move him along. As the children grew, James even refused to eat dinner at the same table with them—they made him too nervous, he said. Hugging was not allowed in the house, not so long as father James was around. Danny later recalled having received "an ass whipping" from his father "for any trouble."

There were also the threatening gestures with a knife or a gun. During an argument, James would take out his police-issue revolver and wave it in the air, shouting, "I'm going to get you." Or he would flip open the blade of his knife and threaten to "cut somebody open like that."

Her patience depleted, Claudia fled again in a panic, but James convinced her to come back to him. The cycle of frustration and aggression continued, repeating itself again and again over many years. And as Danny and Kevin grew into teenagers, the punishments administered by their father became even more severe. Gripping a cigar between his teeth, James whipped his younger son with a belt so hard that the boy wet his pants. He oftentimes got Danny by the throat and held him against a wall so he couldn't move. He hit his boys in the face or shoved them to the ground. When he worked as a Shreveport police officer, he handcuffed them to a kitchen chair in order to teach them a lesson. Every report card brought another beating; any minor infraction of family rules meant being treated as an utter failure, being reprimanded in a harsh and threatening way, getting kicked out of the house, or—for getting drunk— even spending time in a juvenile detention center. As a lieutenant in the local police force, James had the clout to administer punishment to his boys that fit not any crime, but his own sadistic needs. James would get out of control, and Claudia was powerless to stop him.

According to Claudia, the effects of a brutal home life on Danny's development were obvious from an early age. He became a nervous and sickly child, who repeated the third grade, placing him in a position to be ridiculed by his peers and in the same class with his younger brother, Kevin. He had frequent nightmares about monsters and about the world being blown apart. He was constantly trying to get his father's approval but with little success. To any of Danny's accomplishments, James would respond, "It's all right, son, *but . . .*" Then his father would proceed to find as many negatives as he possibly could, listing them for his son who was so eager to please and so damaged by the criticism he inevitably received.

By adolescence, Danny's self-esteem had become nonexistent. He grew up believing that he was a complete failure, and every setback now seemed to confirm what he had long suspected about himself. In the area of sexuality, Rolling's difficulties became translated into a voyeuristic compulsion. As a teenager, he had recurrent sexual fantasies and urges and was obsessed with peeping at women through windows. He frequently masturbated as he watched. Several times a week, he peeped at women or watched families having dinner.[41]

Danny's moods changed abruptly. He ran hot and cold—one minute happy, polite, and laughing, the next

[41]Shedden, "Rolling's Disorders 'Severe,' " pp. 1A, 4A.

mean and suicidal. According to Claudia, who herself had suffered a nervous breakdown under the pressures of family life, Danny was "trying to get rid of that person that his daddy made him believe he was."

29

Everything Is Relative/ Relatives Are Everything

Psychologists and psychiatrists often reconstruct the troubled childhood of a killer by relying on the accuracy of memories, many of which are quite selective and perhaps misleading. Eager to be seen as a victim, the killer has a vested interest in persuading the court that he has suffered abuse. To save himself from being executed as a cold-blooded monster, he has a strong incentive to lie.

In addition, a killer's friends and family, testifying on his behalf, may tend to recall only those incidents in early childhood that support a victimization defense. It isn't necessarily that they fabricate their testimony; in fact, they may be totally unaware that their memories are biased and distorted. But whatever the source of their false information, the result may be to create sympathy for the defendant in the minds of jurors and, in the process, unfairly stigmatize one or both of his parents. For Danny Rolling, being regarded as a sick man with a troubled past rather than as a monster might have been considered mitigating circumstances that would allow him to escape Florida's electric chair. This is exactly the strategy that Rolling's defense team had in mind.

Rolling's mother recalled severe abuse administered by an uncaring father. Danny's first cousin Chuck Strozier concurred. He told the court that Danny had tried in vain to show his father that he loved him. James simply wouldn't accept his son's love. In addition, a neighbor and close friend of Claudia Rolling, Bernadine Holder, testified that Danny once came running to her house across the street, screaming that his father was going to kill him. When she went back to the Rolling house to talk with James, Holder caught him in the carport, pacing back and forth and holding a .38-caliber handgun. "He told me he was going to kill [Danny] if he got in his way," Holder said. "I was afraid he was going to take that gun and kill one of my children or one of the neighbor children."

James Rolling, speaking with Dr. Krop before the trial, had much to say in his own defense, however. He accused his wife and her family of conspiring against him to explain Danny's violent disposition, of using him as a scapegoat. He denied ever abusing his wife or his son. "I've never laid a hand on him, I never whipped him," James said.[42]

Some people who witnessed Danny grow up weren't so sure that he had experienced abuse at the hands of his father. Jeanette Caughey, Danny's aunt from Phenix City, Alabama, could remember nothing at all unsavory about Rolling's childhood. She described Danny as a good kid who was never in serious trouble and his mother and father as "loving and kind parents." She suggested that Rolling only "went off the deep end" after his divorce.

Similarly, Danny's ex-wife, O'Mather Ann Halko, testified that she never witnessed abuse or, for that matter, any problems between Rolling and his father. She claimed that Danny's parents were very supportive of their marriage, providing them with both furniture and groceries in time of need. She said that she never saw James hit her ex-husband, nor did Danny ever tell her

---

[42]Shedden, "Rolling's Disorders 'Severe,' " p. 4A.

about being abused by his father while he was growing up. In a soft-spoken voice, Halko instead contended that she never saw James denigrate his son.

Whatever the actual extent of abuse, it should be emphasized that a horrible childhood, by itself, is simply not enough to explain why some people become serial killers when they reach adulthood. If all it took were a bad childhood, we would surely have hundreds of thousands—perhaps millions—of Danny Rollings on the loose. Indeed, almost every convict will give you a sad story of childhood neglect, abandonment, and abuse. Many such stories are undoubtedly true, but so are the sad stories about the childhood of many "normal" people who have gone on to rise above personal adversity.

Terrible experiences early in life definitely help to create emotionally needy adults, yet only a relatively few of them will turn to murder, let alone serial killing, no matter how needy they become. In fact, some children who have suffered considerably as they grow up are somehow able to learn positive lessons from their experiences: they actually compensate in a socially acceptable way, develop a burning need for achievement, try even harder, and become highly successful adults. Instead of becoming murderers, they turn out to be corporate executives, attorneys, or even police investigators.

While incarcerated at Starke, Rolling once told Lee Strope, "My dad was a cop for twenty years. Look how I turned out." In response, the police detective could only think to himself, *My dad was a prisoner and look how I turned out!*

It is interesting, in this regard, to note that the typical serial killer—just like thirty-six-year-old Danny Rolling—is a middle-aged man. Unlike those who kill a single victim in a fit of rage, in the heat of passion, or even for the love of money, they usually do not begin to commit their string of murders until they are in their late twenties or thirties. Some are even older—forty or fifty—when they get started.

What has happened to these killers after leaving high school? How have they made important changes in their lives? By focusing so much on early childhood, we may have overlooked a critical factor in the development of serial killers: how they make the transition into adulthood. Are they able to find legitimate opportunities to achieve success and, more important, to satisfy their strong need for power and control in nonviolent ways? Do they continue to be mistreated by the important people in their lives? Or have they developed alternative support systems capable of giving them the encouragement and love they so much desire? Do they have friends and relatives to get them through tough times? Or are they essentially on their own, just as they were as children? According to criminologists Rob Sampson and John Laub, authors of *Crime in the Making: Pathways and Turningpoints through Life,* bonding in work or marriage as an adult may be as critical as bonding to Mom and Dad as a child.

By the time Danny Rolling approached adulthood, he had learned a bitter lesson, namely, that he could count on no one, not even himself. When he was seventeen and at the end of his sophomore year, he left Woodlawn High School to join the air force. In the military, he received his general equivalency diploma, but he also became a user of LSD, as well as marijuana, quaaludes, and alcohol. His service record was quickly blemished by a series of disciplinary infractions, including possessing illicit drugs, wrecking a bicycle, and failing to obey orders. Within a period of less than two years, owing to lack of maturity and an inability to adjust to military life, he was discharged and back in Shreveport.

For a period of time, Danny then held a job driving a truck for the Louisiana Paper Company. All the while, children in the neighborhood referred to him as "Rambo," because he often dressed in camouflage fatigues as he jogged down the street, shadowboxing and carrying a heavy log across his shoulders. Years earlier, when church members rescued Rolling from the street in a drunken stupor, they also convinced him to join King's Temple United Pentecostal Church in his hometown. It wasn't long before he sang in the choir, drove the church bus, spoke in tongues, and attended services. At Easter, he even put on a rabbit's costume and played the part of the Easter Bunny for youngsters in the church.

But the most important thing that happened to twenty-year-old Danny Rolling while he was a churchgoer was that he established a close relationship with another member of the congregation—petite and dark-haired O'Mather Ann Halko, who also was twenty years of age at the time. Within a few months, Halko and Rolling were married. Six months later, O'Mather gave birth to their daughter, Kylie.

Just like his stint in the military, Danny's marriage to soft-spoken O'Mather Halko was as short-lived as it was stormy, lasting little more than two years. During this time, Danny attended a part-time program to learn how to become an automobile mechanic. He also held a job with the water department but often didn't make it to work. Instead, he stayed in bed and smoked marijuana. Or he snuck out at night to peek in windows. When his temper went out of control, he put a shotgun to his wife's head and threatened to kill her. Then O'Mather left him for another man, whom she quickly married. Rolling did not see her or their daughter for some fifteen years. During this entire period, he made only one child-support payment of one hundred dollars. At the time of the trial, Kylie was eighteen years old. She only recently discovered the shocking truth that her biological father was Danny Rolling.

Danny took the divorce very hard; by all accounts, it was a turning point in his life. When the sheriff came to his door to deliver the separation papers, he screamed in pain and disbelief. Running in circles through the house, like a raving lunatic, he repeatedly shouted, "No, no, no. She's my wife. This can't happen. We can fix it. No, no, no!"

Then he became even more depressed, going off by himself to sulk, feeling that he had "snapped." He often refused to get out of bed in the morning and forgot to eat his meals. Moving back in with his parents for a time didn't work either. According to Claudia Rolling, her son and her husband were constantly at one another's throats, until Danny could take no more of it.

Early one morning in May 1979, before his mother and father had awakened, Danny packed his bags and headed for Montgomery, Alabama—his first stop in what would turn out to be a career in and out of prison. While in Montgomery, using his father's service revolver, he robbed a Winn-Dixie supermarket. Then he drove ninety miles to Columbus, Georgia, where he was caught robbing a Winn-Dixie again with his father's .38, for which he was convicted and sent to Georgia State Prison in Reidsville. In 1982, after serving his sentence in Georgia, he was transferred to an Alabama prison to serve time for the armed robbery he had committed earlier in Montgomery.

In June 1984, Danny Rolling was released from custody. He then returned back to his parents' home and took one menial position after another. Having failed to hold a job for any length of time, he left town again, this time hitchhiking to the state of Mississippi. Once more, Danny couldn't find a job he could keep. Once more, he was convicted for robbing a grocery store of less than three hundred dollars—this time a Kroger supermarket in the town of Clinton—and was sentenced to do time. As a gesture of his desire to change his ways and go straight, Rolling shaved off his eyebrows and his hair. Behind bars, he worked out with weights on a regular basis and became skillful in the martial arts. Also, while working in the prison bakery, Rolling had an accident that caused him to slice the ends of two fingertips on his left hand. Eyewitnesses to his subsequent crimes would remember the man with the missing fingertips.

In 1988, after serving three years of his fifteen-year sentence for armed robbery, he again returned to Shreveport on parole. This time, although his ability to maintain employment hadn't improved very much, he was at least able to scrape together enough money from working several minimum-wage jobs to buy a used car and pay the insurance. The one bright spot in his otherwise dreary life occurred when he met Lillian ''Bunnie''

Mills, a part-time country-and-western singer and song-writer.

From childhood, Danny had played the guitar and written country music. Beginning years earlier with his membership in the church choir, he had always used his talent for music to sustain himself during particularly hard times and to impress the girls.

It didn't take much for Bunnie to recognize that Danny had potential as an aspiring musician. Over Sunday dinner at the Rolling home, Bunnie listened attentively to Danny's repertoire of songs and was impressed enough to encourage him to promote himself. From that time on, she befriended the Rolling family and dated Danny Rolling for almost two years.

Danny appreciated his relationship with Bunnie. He bought her a necklace and a guitar. On many evenings, they played their guitars and sang country and gospel songs together. But from the outset, Mills recognized that Danny had serious problems with self-esteem and that he was unstable at times. She sensed that Rolling kept "searching for something. He never felt he was accepted by society."[43]

Unfortunately, even Bunnie's concern and moral support couldn't lift Danny Rolling out of the doldrums for very long. In November 1989, after holding a job as a cook for five months at Pancho's Mexican Restaurant, he was fired. Danny threatened to kill the manager but finally left the premises without further incident. He cooked for a time at Western Sizzlin' and clerked at a convenience store. He took part-time work as a telephone solicitor and a mechanic but never lasted very long at any job. For several months, Danny was doing well working for a local electrical contractor, but business worsened and he was laid off. For most of the time, he remained unemployed.

It was May 1990 when the hostility between Danny

---

[43]Jim Leusner and Lynne Bumpus-Hooper, "Grandmother: 'He Was Just Like the Clouds In The Sky' " *Orlando Sentinel,* May 23, 1993, p. A14.

and his father came to an irreversible head. In what might easily have been a trivial incident, Danny propped his foot up on a bench in the utility room of the family house merely to tie his shoe. But James was irate about it—he had already argued with his "good-for-nothing son" earlier that day about putting up the car windows during a rainstorm, and he was now at the end of his rope. He had told Danny many times not to put his shoes on the furniture but to no avail.

Just as he had always done, James snarled at his son, demanding that he remove his foot—or else. He grabbed his service revolver and waved it in the air. But this time Danny refused to back off. He glared menacingly at his father and said, "I got my foot on the bench, old man. What are you going to do about it?"

Furious that his son would dare to defy him, James chased Danny out of the house and into the backyard, firing a number of rounds into the air. When his father went back inside, Danny fetched a handgun he had hidden in the shed and tried to enter the house. Finding the back door locked, he kicked it in and yelled, "Old man, you want to shoot it out?"

Danny finally had the upper hand. In an instant, he had twice pulled the trigger. His father lay bleeding on the ground, shot in the face and the stomach. James lived but was permanently blinded in one eye.

Danny went on the run. The Shreveport Police issued a warrant for his arrest on an attempted murder charge, but Rolling had already fled the state. He went first to stay with some rock musicians in Kansas City, where he hid from the law and acquired the tools he would later use in his crime spree. On June 2, 1990, he broke into the residence of an older couple whose son Michael J. Kennedy was a Marine Corps veteran who had died in 1975. Inside the house, Rolling stole the couple's two .22-caliber handguns and their dead son's identification card.

Investigators later tracked calls that Danny had made to his friends and relatives in Louisiana from a pay phone located near the Kennedy home. Detectives also interviewed the manager of a convenience store and employees at a motel in Kansas City who identified the man they met as Danny Rolling. Shortly afterward, Bunny Mills received a phone call from Danny, who claimed to be in a midwestern state and to be in fear for his life concerning possible reprisals from his father. There was no way that Danny could return to Shreveport.

Michael J. Kennedy—otherwise known as Danny Rolling—checked into a Tallahassee motel on July 17, 1990, where he stayed for six days. Then he began to think again about his ex-wife, who, in his mind, had betrayed him. He reflected on what he remembered as a horrid childhood spent under the thumb of his domineering father and on all the years he had received cruel treatment behind bars. Psych Man was ready to fight back—ready for revenge.

30

Gemini

In her videotaped testimony, Claudia Rolling had suggested that Danny might have been a multiple personality. In July 1988, they were sitting at the dinner table when her son abruptly changed into someone she hardly knew.

"His voice was deeper, harsh, and I don't remember what he said," she recalled. "But his face got real hard, almost no emotion there at all—just kind of a deadpan expression. And if I didn't know Danny so well, I probably wouldn't have known it was him."

Claudia's observations of her son's behavior were reminiscent of remarks made about Danny by his fiancée while she visited him in prison. According to Sondra London:

Danny has multiple personalities. The first personality of Danny that I fell in love with was little Danny—little Danny never grew up past the age of eleven. There is a personality in Danny that goes by an alias—Jesse James. This person is more of a psychopath. I don't really have a warm relationship with this personality. There is another

*personality beyond the psychopath that is even
darker. And I have never met the murderer.*[44]

Many serial killers seem to possess powerful psychological facilitators for overcoming or neutralizing whatever pangs of guilt that might otherwise plague them. They are able to compartmentalize their attitudes toward people by conceiving of at least two categories of human beings: those whom they care about and treat with decency and those with whom they have no relationship and therefore can victimize with total disregard for their feelings.

For example, Hillside Strangler Kenneth Bianchi clearly divided the world into two camps: those whom he cared about and everyone else. The group toward whom he had no feelings included the twelve young women that he brutally tortured and murdered. Ken's inner circle consisted of his mother, wife, and son, as well as his cousin Angelo Buono with whom he teamed up for killing. "The Ken I knew couldn't ever have hurt anybody or killed anybody," recalled Kelli Boyd, his common-law wife and mother of his child. "He wasn't the kind of person who could have killed somebody."[45]

In the same way, serial killer John Wayne Gacy, who was recently executed by the state of Illinois for killing thirty-three young men and boys, also had a relatively normal life otherwise. He and his wife lived in a middle-class suburb of Chicago, where he often gave barbeques for the neighbors and played a clown at children's parties. Gacy was once voted Jaycee Man of the Year and was active in local politics. But on weekends, when his wife was away visiting, he had parties consisting of sex, torture, and murder.

According to psychiatrist Robert Jay Lifton, author of *Nazi Doctors*, the physicians who performed ghoulish

---

[44]Interview with Steve Dunleavy on *A Current Affair*, "The Ghoul of Gainesville," March 11, 1994.

[45]Public Broadcasting System, "The Mind of a Murderer," *Frontline*, Number 206, March 1984.

experiments at Auschwitz and other concentration camps compartmentalized their activities, attitudes, and emotions. Through what he calls "doubling," Lifton suggests that any possible feelings of guilt were minimized because the camp doctors developed two separate and distinct selves—one for doing the dirty work of experimenting with and exterminating inmates and the other for living the rest of their lives outside of the camp. In this way, no matter how sadistic they were on the job, they were still able to see themselves as gentle husbands, caring fathers, and honorable physicians.

The compartmentalization that allows for killing without guilt is an extension of a phenomenon used by many normal people who do not suffer with multiple personalities. Instead, they play a number of different roles in which their everyday behavior varies from setting to setting. An executive might be a heartless "son of a bitch" to all his employees at work but be a loving and devoted family man at home. Similarly, many serial killers have jobs and families, do volunteer work, and kill part-time with a great deal of selectivity.

Rolling's ability to compartmentalize was extraordinary. Even in the days immediately following his Gainesville murder spree, he had a normal, even warm and compassionate, relationship with a woman he befriended in Tampa. During the Labor Day weekend, while riding a bike through Tampa's Lowry Park, Rolling noticed a young woman on a bench who was quietly sketching drawings in chalk. He stopped and said, "You look like you could use a friend." After giving her one hundred dollars cash to do his portrait, they went to an arcade, where he won a teddy bear for her. They then went to her duplex, had Chinese food together, and watched *Good Morning, Vietnam* on her VCR. Danny spent the night sleeping on her couch.

Rolling acknowledged that there was a dark side to his criminal activities as well as his personality, and he attempted psychologically to disassociate himself from it. He confessed to Gainesville psychologist Elizabeth McMahon during extensive interviews that "Danny robs,'' but it was his ''alter ego named Gemini'' who murdered the five college students.

Gemini is a ''spirit,'' he told Dr. McMahon, a spirit that appeared initially while he was serving time in a Mississippi prison. ''It does not talk to me in terms of words,'' Danny said. ''I can feel it. I can sense its presence. I know when it's here. It loves the dark, not the light.''

The defense strategy was to treat Rolling's story about his alter ego as a symptom of extreme mental illness. On March 16, 1994, while on the stand, Dr. McMahon suggested that the defendant had created an alter ego in order to cope with the maliciousness of his crimes, to attribute to Gemini what he couldn't accept about himself.

The origin of Gemini as a symptom of long-term mental illness was thrown into question, however, when State Attorney Rod Smith cross-examined Dr. McMahon. In attempting to portray Rolling as more methodical than mad, Smith pointed out that just hours before beginning his killing spree in Gainesville, the defendant had gone to Litchfields–Butler Plaza Cinema to watch a newly released horror movie, *The Exorcist III*. In this film, the spirit of Gemini was portrayed as a dead serial murderer who possesses a prisoner and compels him to kill. Like the Gainesville murders, the movie contained scenes of stabbing deaths, decapitation, and disembowelment. Also in the film, a bird was shown perched on a windowsill and then suddenly dying. Rolling had told Dr. McMahon that, years earlier, while serving time in Mississippi, he saw a dead bird and that he took it as a spiritual sign. In addition, Danny sometimes referred to his alter ego as ''Ynnad''—the reverse spelling of his name. In the same way, names of characters in *The Exorcist III* were recited backward.

There were simply too many similarities between the movie and Rolling's story to be coincidental. Danny was a moody, changeable sort all right, but his claims to a

Dr. Jekyll and Mr. Hyde "schizophrenia" now seemed self-serving and contrived.[46]

Dr. Daniel Sprehe, a psychiatrist for the prosecution who had practiced in the state of Florida for twenty-three years and had frequently served as an expert witness in murder cases, only added credibility to the idea that Rolling had invented the details of his "multiple personality." Instead, the psychiatrist focused on the role of the horror movie Danny had seen hours before committing his first Gainesville slaughter.

Referring to the remarkable similarity between the defendant's self-appraisal and depictions in the film, Dr. Sprehe testified on March 21:

> *I think it's significant that these ideas were introduced to his mind or to his awareness around the time frame of the crimes, and it's more than just coincidental that he never mentioned all of these things to a lot of other people before the time of his crimes. He had been examined by various psychiatrists in connection with other things at various points in his life, yet this had never come up. It had never come up in talking with his family, et cetera. These things . . . were in the movie. The bird at the window, the dead bird; the reverse spelling that went on. The Gemini character, the name of the evil presence, evil spirit. And then certain ways in which the victims were arranged also were quite similar to what was mentioned in the movie.*

Dr. Sidney Merin, who would later testify for the prosecution, saw the same "uncanny parallels" between the plot of *The Exorcist III* and Danny's statements about his Gemini side. "What this movie did was give him a way of doing things," Merin said. "It gave him

---

[46]Jaime Abdo, " 'Exorcist III' May Have Inspired Alter Ego," *Independent Florida Alligator*, March 17, 1994, p. 1.

a way of explaining a lot of things . . . that fit his personality.''

Merin argued that Rolling had a character disorder rather than a mental illness caused by an abusive childhood, that he was a sociopath or an antisocial personality type who has ''a problem with guilt.'' A sociopath lacks a conscience, feels no remorse, and cares exclusively for his own pleasures in life. Other people are seen merely as tools to fulfil his own needs and desires, no matter how perverse or reprehensible.

''Rolling has what I would refer to, personally, as a Swiss cheese sort of conscience,'' Merin would testify. ''Sometimes it holds and he drives children to church, but the rest of the time it just goes through the holes.''

With Dr. Sprehe still on the witness stand, prosecutor Smith turned his attention to the issue of whether or not the defendant was mentally ill.

Q: Doctor, do you have an opinion, within a medical degree of certainty, as to whether or not Danny Harold Rolling suffers from a mental illness?

A: Yes, I have a opinion.

Q: Sir, what is that opinion?

A: Well, my opinion is that he has a personality disorder and that that's not usually thought of by psychiatrists as real mental illness; it's a personality diagnosis. He does have, however, also a paraphilia, which is a voyeurism; however, that's a rather minor part of this case, in my opinion, in that that's a sexual perversion. It doesn't drive anybody or force anybody to do anything. It's a preference for sexual gratification, and it can be exercised as a preference or not exercised, as the person who has the perversion would want to, depending on whether or not they think it's safe, et cetera. And then it does appear that, at least by history, he has a history of some multiple substance abuse including alcohol, though that didn't really play much of a role in this case.

Q: Within the types of personality disorders, do you have an opinion as to what type of personality disorder you think most accurately depicts Danny Harold Rolling?

A: Yes, I do have an opinion.

Q: And what is that opinion, sir?

A: In my opinion he has an antisocial personality disorder.

Q: Doctor, if a person has an antisocial personality disorder, is that person able to choose between and discern between wrong and right conduct?

A: Oh, sure.

Q: Do you have an opinion as to whether or not Danny Harold Rolling on the nights in August 1990, about which we are now concerned, was able to conform his conduct to the requirements of the law?

A: Yes, I have a opinion.

Q: Sir, what is the opinion you have as to his ability to conform his conduct to the requirements of the law, and please tell the jury that upon which you base that opinion?

A: OK. It's my opinion that he was at all times able to conform his conduct to the requirements of the law. And my main reasoning for this is that he at no time showed any signs of an illness that would cause someone to be under any kind of driven compulsion. There was considerable planning, there was a real scenario that was thought out, there was assembling of equipment, there was stalking and casing of the victims, you might say. By casing, I mean seeing if this was a good safe time to go in after the victims. And then there was evidence throughout his admitted behavior with the victims that indicated that he was operating as a real cool sort of person who knew what was going on all the time. He could do such things as eat an apple and a banana while he's surveying the scene and thinking it all over. So there was no evidence whatsoever of any kind of huge rage reaction or anything. He was cool, operating in an almost military operation type of manner throughout all of this.

Q: Doctor, do you have an opinion as to whether or not during those nights in August 1990, about which we are concerned, Danny Rolling was under the influence of an extreme emotional or mental disturbance?

A: Yes, I have an opinion.

Q: Doctor, would you give us your opinion as to whether he was under the influence of an extreme emotional disturbance and tell this jury that upon which you base that opinion?

A: Well, individuals with a personality disorder, especially an antisocial personality disorder, are never out of control of themselves. They always know what is right and what is wrong. They may not be willing to do what is right or refrain from what is wrong. But willingness doesn't have anything to do with it. There's ample evidence by his own statements and by the physical evidence that he was operating very aware, very rationally aware, of what was going down at the time.

Q: Doctor, taking you now to scene 2 in particular— that being the scene of the death of Christa Hoyt—I don't want you to detail anything from the photographs in terms of what happened, but what I would like you to say is did his actions upon returning to search for his wallet impact your opinion in any manner?

A: Yes.

Q: Would you tell this jury how that would impact your opinion?

A: Well, those are the actions of someone who knows that he has left a damaging piece of evidence behind and that he's got to do something about it, and it takes an enormous amount of coolness to be able to go back and look for that. And then also later to call and ask if it was lost under the name that was under the identity that was in the wallet. This is a person who is doing a lot of covering up or attempting to cover up. And that goes to the issue of whether or not he knew exactly that he was committing a crime.

Q: Doctor, are you familiar with the terms *histrionic, narcissistic, dependent,* and *obsessive-compulsive* as they relate to that which is contained in the diagnostic and statistical manual of mental disorders?

A: Yes. Those are all labels for other types of personality disorders, and though he showed a few traits in each of those categories, he didn't show enough in each of those categories to make those categories his diagnosis. Frequently, in any personality disorder, you'll see some overflow of traits in other personality categories. But he has a really strong cluster of traits in the antisocial personality disorder.

Q: Doctor, do we choose the personality that we have or even the personality disorder that some of us may have?

A: No.

Q: Within that personality and within that personality disorder, are we capable of making choices?

A: Oh, yes. Yes.

Q: Sir, do you have an opinion as to whether or not he had any conditions that prevented him on the nights of August 1990, about which we are concerned here, from making choices to stop, refrain from, or not commit these acts? Did he have that ability?

A: Yes. He had that ability to make choices at all times.

Q: Upon your review of these materials, do you find that Danny Harold Rolling came from a family that you would typify as dysfunctional?

A: Yes. I think the family was dysfunctional as best I could piece together; there's some difference of opinion among various witnesses, but in my mind, it does sound dysfunctional.

Q: Do persons from a dysfunctional family have the ability to conform to the requirements of the law?

A: Yes. Many of us are from dysfunctional families and turn out just fine in life and never break the law in any major way.

Q: Are persons who have a personality disorder, either an antisocial behavior disorder or a personality disorder of the type called borderline personality disorder, able to conform their conduct to the law?

A: Yes.

Q: If they do not conform their conduct to the basis of the law, are they able to understand that their conduct is criminal?

A: Yes.

Q: Is it your opinion that Danny Rolling understood the criminality of his conduct in August 1990 and had the ability to conform his conduct to the law if he had wanted to?

A: Yes.

31

The Jury Speaks

On Wednesday, March 23, 1994, the fourth-floor court-room was crammed to its 116-person capacity with law-yers and their assistants, reporters, family and friends of the victims, as well as investigators who had spent years working on the case against Rolling. Wearing a blue blazer and polka-dot tie, the defendant sat quietly, as he had done through most of the proceedings, with his hands clasped in front of him.

In the morning session, closing arguments were made by both the prosecution and defense teams. Family and friends of the victims wept in agony as prosecutor Rod Smith recounted for the last time the gruesome details of Rolling's crimes in Gainesville. Jurors were visibly shaken as Smith again displayed the crime scene pho-tographs, showing the bloodied, dismembered, and posed bodies of the murder victims. He described Danny Rolling as a "predator." "Everything he did was de-signed with one purpose in mind: to rape and murder," said Smith.

Even the defendant showed flashes of revulsion, pleading with his attorneys to let him leave the court-room. "I've got to get out of here," Rolling said as the state attorney waved the hideous photos in the faces of the jurors. Danny's face grew flushed; he closed his eyes and held his head. He was escorted back to his cell, but only after the state had finished making its case.

In his closing remarks, assistant public defender Johnny Kearns emphasized that Rolling's abusive childhood and the resulting mental illness he suffered should be considered mitigating circumstances supporting a life sentence.

"I don't have any pictures, I don't have any videos . . . ," Kearns said. "You had an opportunity to see the reaction, what happened in Gainesville in August 1990. It was horrible. My question to you now is: Can you imagine what was going on in Danny Rolling's mind?"

The public defender also reminded members of the jury that a recommendation of a life sentence for Rolling guarantees that he will serve life without hope of ever being released. "It is the absence of hope," Kearns argued, "which equals the despair that is the punishment."[47]

Judge Morris spent the afternoon delivering his charge to the jury. Morris explained as simply as possible to the panel of laypersons the legal issues related to their task. He instructed them on law pertaining to aggravating and mitigating circumstances and asked them to deliberate and then return with a recommendation: life or death for Danny Harold Rolling.

On the very next morning, Thursday, March 24, 1994, the jury was finished. After nearly three weeks of hearing evidence and testimony and then deliberating overnight, the jury of nine women and three men locked hands and prayed for Danny Rolling's victims. They had seen the gruesome crime scene photographs and had listened to expert witnesses recount the horrid details of the crimes. They had heard all the stories about the defendant's troubled childhood and had heard his confession. Indeed, they had heard all they needed to hear. They had spent more than four hours during the previous

---

[47]Mary Shedden, "Jurors Still Out," *Gainesville Sun,* March 24, 1994, pp. 1A, 4A.

day huddled around a large table in the Alachua County Courthouse, deliberating the fate of Danny Rolling. Now, it was finally time to announce their unanimous recommendation to Judge Morris.

Morris had made it clear from the outset of the penalty-phase trial that he would take the jurors' recommendation very seriously. Gray showing through his brown hair, he now turned to the jury.

"Your advice as to what sentence should be imposed for this defendant is entitled by law and will be given great weight by this court," the judge said. "It determines what sentence will be imposed in this case. It is only under rare circumstances that this court could impose a sentence other than what you recommend."

Jurors responded unanimously with a message of death for the defendant. Five times they said that Rolling should die in Florida's electric chair.

Danny listened with apprehension from his chair in the defendant's box as he heard each juror cast the vote that would determine his fate. Hearing the recommendation, he nodded somberly and clenched his teeth. He then shook hands with his lawyers and was led back to his cell in Florida State Prison, where the state's electric chair is located.

Throughout the thirteen days of testimony, the presence of the families of the victims in the courtroom had been a constant reminder of the pain and suffering that Danny Rolling's murder spree had inflicted. As the death sentence was announced and the names of the victims were again read, those who were closest to Tracy Paules, Christa Hoyt, Manny Taboada, Christina Powell, and Sonja Larson—their loved ones—wept openly. At a press conference a few minutes later, each mother held a white rose. Family members and friends urged people never to forget Rolling's victims.

As the families of the five murdered college students looked on, victim/witness advocate Laura Knudson then read the following statement on their behalf:

As the families of Sonja, Christi, Christa, Manny, and Tracy, we are pleased with the recommenda-

tion of the jury to sentence the killer of our loved ones to death. We are respectful of the burden the jury faced in making this recommendation. Though not their job, we are respectful of the discretion shown with the crime scene photographs, the concern for the privacy of our children.

As jurors, you have come to know our children in death and in the terror they faced at the hands of this killer. Our hope for you is that you will heal from this exposure and maybe someday know the beauty of our children in life. We also hope you will feel the depth of our gratitude for your service these last weeks.

As the judge weighs the aggravating and mitigating factors and considers the jury's recommendation, we know we will be visited by our grief as we have been for three years and seven months. The absence, the silence of Sonja, Christi, Christa, Manny, and Tracy, is felt even more starkly than before. Now we know of their desperate suffering. But we can hold on a little longer for the judge's decision. We wish him Godspeed in his deliberation.

We extend our thanks to the city of Gainesville and Alachua County for your warm hospitality; to the media for your respect for our privacy and discreet coverage; to the courthouse personnel, particularly the bailiffs for your graciousness; to the prosecution team for doing such an excellent job; and to all the task force members who were with us since the beginning, especially Ed Dix, Steve Kramig, Martin Snook, and LeGran Hewitt. They have worked so hard and for so long. It is because of your work that our nightmares have an end point—we now know the last moments of our children's lives. We now know their killer.

This is a shallow victory, though. Nothing will bring back Sonja, Christi, Christa, Manny, and Tracy. A sentence of death simply means that we will not live in fear that this killer will kill again.

We continue to be haunted with the fear that people will remember this killer, even glorify him for the slaughter of our children. We challenge you to do otherwise. We challenge you to remember Sonja Larson, Christi Powell, Christa Hoyt, Manny Toboada, and Tracy Paules—not the man who killed them.

To all the other survivors of violent crime who have cried with us these last years, to those who will follow us, God bless you. And to our precious children: We love you and we desperately miss you.

On Tuesday, March 29, 1994, attorneys for the prosecution and defense were given a final opportunity to present last-minute evidence in order to influence Judge Morris's sentencing decision. He already had the recommendation of the jury. Now he would hear from the killer.

Many spectators in the packed courtroom expected Rolling to sing. He had sung in the courtroom when he was sentenced for committing armed robbery in Ocala; he sang when he was sentenced for bank robbery in Gainesville.

At this hearing, however, Danny Rolling only apologized. In a two-minute statement to Judge Morris, which many spectators characterized as stilted, unnatural, and detached, Rolling said:

There is much I'd like to say, Your Honor, about our world and my beliefs and the destiny of man. However, I feel whatever I might have to say at this moment is overshadowed by the suffering I've caused.

I regret with all my heart what my hand has done. I have taken what I cannot return. If only I could bend back the hands on that ageless clock and change the past. Ah, but alas, I am not the keeper of time, only a small part of history and

*the legacy of mankind's fall from grace. I'm sorry,
Your Honor.*

The victims' loved ones never had the opportunity to
testify in court about their children and the impact that
their deaths had had on them. Before the end of the
hearing, however, prosecutor Rod Smith handed Judge
Morris a small stack of written statements from the family and friends of the victims to be filed into the court
record.

Christina Powell's brother and sister-in-law wrote,
"One of our most difficult tasks was having to tell our
daughter that Christi was gone, but we would one day
see her in heaven. Our daughter is now six and she only
remembers Christi from the photographs we have. . . .
We are only able to endure her murder knowing that she
is no longer in pain and we will one day be with her . . .
but it's the way she left that hurts us the most."

Servando Careaga, a close friend of Manuel Taboada,
wrote that he and his wife recently named their newborn
child after Manny. He said, "I look forward to telling
my son about who he was named after. Even though he
is gone now, Manny will always be a positive influence
in my life and that of my family's. Because for as long
as I live, Manny's memory will never die. Nobody will
ever be able to kill that. . . . If every individual in this
world would know a Manny Taboada the world would
be a better place."

Christa Hoyt's mother said, "My daughter, Christa
Leigh Hoyt, wrote me a letter when she was graduating
from high school in June of 1989 and told me that I was
the wind beneath her wings. She said I had taught her
to be a leader, fighter and a winner and that anything
she wanted to achieve in life she could. . . . Danny Rolling is a robber of life, an author of pain, a corrupter of
justice and innocence, a begetter of death, and a sworn
enemy of the human race."

Tracy Paules's mother wrote, "To me, her mom, it
means that my daughter was terrorized and suffered a
great deal and I, too, was not there to protect her. I yearn

to hold her in my arms, that small body I know so well, and to tell her how much I love her, how much I cry for her, how much I miss her and most of all to hear her say, 'I love you, Mom.' ''

Writing that she can no longer sing in the church choir because of the pain that she feels, Sonja Larson's mother referred to her daughter's plans to become a teacher: "Sonja loved children. Having been an honor student throughout her school years, she could have chosen any career. . . . People say something good will come of these horrible murders. For me personally, there can never be anything good to come from the senseless death of Sonja, not in my lifetime.''

32

Judgment Day

Wednesday, April 20, 1994, was judgment day for the defendant. Almost a month after the penalty trial had ended, Danny Rolling, wearing a white shirt and dark tie, was led into court to receive his sentence from Judge Stan Morris. The atmosphere in the packed fourth-floor courtroom was electric as the gallery, comprised of dozens of family, friends, and supporters of the five slain students, fully anticipated that the judge would affirm the unanimous recommendation from the jury for the death penalty. Rolling appeared as resigned to his fate as the families were eager for it.

Rolling shuffled his feet nervously as Judge Morris gazed firmly down upon him. In a forty-minute session, the judge read a detailed twenty-seven-page sentencing order in which he explained that the state had proven the presence of aggravating circumstances, including the fact that the murders were premeditated and heinous. As the final sentence was given, Rolling sat impassively and listened.

"The defendant's own words show that he had planned the murders in advance and that these activities were directed toward their commission," Judge Morris read from his prepared statement. "Although the court cannot determine the defendant's motive, the defendant's words clearly demonstrate his intent and prior planning."

After reviewing the facts of the case in excruciating detail, Morris then said:

> *The court has very carefully considered and weighted the aggravating and mitigating circumstances as they relate to each conviction of first-degree murder as set forth in Counts I through V of the Indictment, being ever mindful that a human life is at stake in this balance. The Court finds, as did the jury, that the aggravating circumstances outweigh the mitigating circumstances as to each of the first-degree murders in this case. Accordingly, it is ordered and adjudged that the Defendant, Danny Harold Rolling, is hereby sentenced to death for the murder of the victim Sonja Larson, as charged in Count I of the Indictment.*
>
> *It is further ordered and adjudged that the Defendant, Danny Harold Rolling, is hereby sentenced to death for the murder of the victim Christina Powell, as charged in Count II of the Indictment.*
>
> *It is further ordered and adjudged that the Defendant, Danny Harold Rolling, is hereby sentenced to death for the murder of the victim Christa Hoyt, as charged in Count III of the Indictment.*
>
> *It is further ordered and adjudged that the Defendant, Danny Harold Rolling, is hereby sentenced to death for the murder of the victim Tracy Paules, as charged in Count IV of the Indictment.*
>
> *It is further ordered and adjudged that the Defendant, Danny Harold Rolling, is hereby sentenced to death for the murder of the victim Manuel Taboada, as charged in Count V of the Indictment.*

The Defendant is hereby committed to the Department of Correction of the State of Florida for execution of this sentence as provided by law.
May God have mercy on his soul.

33

Surviving Murder

Despite the outcome of Rolling's sentencing trial, the families and friends of the five murdered college students continued to struggle with their tragedy. For the most part, they had sat quietly at Rolling's trial, listening from the back of the courtroom to weeks of testimony about the brutality of the crimes and about the defendant's troubled past. After the trial concluded, however, several of the victims' loved ones could no longer hold back their frustration and anger.

After sentencing, as the condemned man was being escorted out of the courtroom for the last time, Mario Toboada, Manny's brother, stood up and yelled at Rolling, "Five years. You're going down in five years, you understand?" waving all five fingers on his left hand as his mother tugged on his right arm to restrain him.

While being helped out of the courtroom by a bailiff, Taboada shouted again that the families would have "the last say." "Justice is beyond these walls," he said. "We will prevail. Our children's names will be remembered over him."[48]

---

[48]Jon Glass and Derek Willis, " 'You're Going Down in Five Years,' " *Independent Florida Alligator*, April 21, 1994, p. 1.

Although everyone shared Taboada's anger and thirst for vengeance, Jim Larson, Sonja's half-brother, was the most threatening in his words. Seeing Rolling's fiancée and sole supporter across the courtroom, Larson approached London and screamed, "From this moment on, if you make one red cent off my sister, we're going to come after you. We'll both go down. I have nothing to lose. I'll kill you!"

Clearly, family members, including Mario Toboada, were very much concerned about the celebrity status accorded Danny Rolling by the media. At an impromptu press conference, Christa Hoyt's mother, Ann Garren, directed her criticism at reporters. "It sells your newspapers. It sells your magazines," she said.

"It's sensationalism," Diana Hoyt, Christa's stepmother, added.

Sonya Larson's mother, Ada, talking to another group from the press corps, argued that people focus too much on Rolling's horrible life and on his evil alter ego, "Gemini." "Our children are dead," she said. "Giving the reason for the killings a name doesn't excuse what happened."

Diana Hoyt told reporters that she was furious with people like Rolling's fiancée, Sondra London, because she wants to make money off of his hideous crimes. Along with several other parents, Hoyt has sought to keep London and Rolling from legally being able to profit from the murders. In addition, Christa's stepmother has attempted to give her point of view to the media, agreeing to be on national television shows when she discovers that Sondra London is scheduled to appear.

"How would you feel about it if your daughter was the one killed?" she asked rhetorically. "I am Sondra London's shadow."[49]

Following their informal press conference, the families went to lunch together at a local restaurant. Laurie

---

[49]Mary Shedden, "Rolling's Fame Has Victims' Families Irate," *Gainesville Sun*, March 19, 1994, p. 7A.

Paules Lahey, Tracy Paules's sister, said that the victims' loved ones would continue to see one another, even though the trial had ended.

"I used to be selfish—my grief was just for Tracy," Lahey said. "I've fallen in love with these people. They are part of my family."[50]

For the classmates of Sonja, Christina, Christa, Tracy, and Manny, the Gainesville murders will continue to linger in their thoughts and memories. They have all graduated by now, but August 1990 will remain as a dark and painful chapter in their college yearbook.

The students who were on campus at the time of the Gainesville massacre left behind a memorial of sorts for future generations of students to ponder. Amidst the graffiti along a concrete wall on Gainesville's Thirty-fourth Street, they painted the names of the five slain students as a special tribute to their memory—as a place where students and townsfolk can go to pay their respect and lay flowers. On the campus itself, five trees—one for each victim—grow in a memorial garden next to the library, with a small plaque that reads, "In memory of the five students whose lives were needlessly lost, August 1990."

For many students currently enrolled at UF, the memory of the brutal murders has all but faded. They were still in high school when Danny Rolling committed his acts of butchery and caused pandemonium to sweep the campus. Like almost everybody else, they watched news reports on television and read newspaper accounts. But for most of them, the crimes seem like ancient history. What they see now is what they believe; and they see a relaxed and peaceful community, where they can make friends, party, and study in safety. "I'm from Ohio," remarked freshman Susie Krueger. "I didn't even know about the murders until I got here."[51]

---

[50]Derek Willis, "Families Want Change, Not Sorrow," *Independent Florida Alligator*, April 21, 1994, p. 3.

[51]Arden Moore, "Gainesville Recover, but It Will Never Forget," *Fort Lauderdale Sun-Sentinel*, August 27, 1995, p. 1A.

Even the faculty have somehow managed to put the horrible episode behind them. "It's not something I think about until someone raises the issue," noted UF criminologist Ron Akers. "Then I think back to those students killed in that gruesome way and feel that twinge again."[52]

August 1995, the fifth anniversary of the brutal slayings in Gainesville, was more a time for public celebration than mourning. The UF Gators football team looked like a strong contender for the national championship. At the same time, *Money* magazine released its latest rankings of the most livable American cities. At the very top of the list stood Gainesville, Florida, specially cited for its low crime rate.

Yet even today, the fear in Gainesville has not totally dissipated. Indeed, the legacy of Danny Rolling extends beyond the families of his victims, whose lives obviously have been permanently altered by his sinister acts, to encapsulate the culture of the entire community.

"The pain and memories these heinous acts inflicted on our community will never go away," Lombardi said. "The loss of these five wonderful young people will always be a part of our institutional and individual memories. It will remain a constant reminder of the fragility of life."[53]

To this day, every violent crime in Gainesville is measured against Rolling's brutality; each and every murder that touches the town is a gruesome reminder of a past that many would prefer to forget but cannot. In June 1991, for example, when Eleanor Anne Grace, twenty, of Fort Myers, and Carla Marie McKishnie, twenty-two, of Brandon, two coeds at UF were found strangled to death in a condominium complex in southwest Gainesville, residents naturally tried to connect these murders with the five students brutally slain in August 1990.

[52]Arden Moore, "Gainesville Recover, but it Will Never Forget," *Fort Lauderdale Sun-Sentinel*, August 27, 1995, p. 1A.

[53]Tom Leithauser, "Doubts Vanish and Relief Flows Through Gainesville," *Orlando Sentinel*, February 16, 1994, A4.

Then a local carpet cleaner was arrested. Police suggested that he had been in the women's apartment to clean the rugs when he became uncontrollably enraged by something they had said to him. The new murders were vicious, but they were definitely not the work of *the* Gainesville student killer. Alan Robert Davis later received two life sentences for the double murder.

Edward Lewis Humphrey is one individual who will probably never to able to put the Gainesville murders completely behind him. His erratic behavior, violent outbursts, and unseemly appearance made him the perfect suspect. His public rantings and ravings helped to convict him in the eyes of the community and to make him the focal point of the task force from the beginning of its investigation.[54]

Even when DNA evidence failed to link Humphrey to the crime scenes, Humphrey was not exonerated. Instead, he continued to be regarded in many circles as some kind of dangerous freak of nature and possibly as one member of a diabolical killing team. Until Danny Rolling confessed that he had single-handedly committed the murders, Ed remained under a lingering cloud of suspicion.

Not that everyone considered Ed a monster. He always had the support of his family, in particular, his grandmother, who died only a few days before he was to be released from prison, but also his mother and his brother, George.

Right after getting out of prison, Humphrey went to live in Orlando with George, who was extremely concerned about his younger brother's personal safety. There were many people out there who still considered Ed a killer and who would be more than happy to snuff out his life. As a precautionary measure, he gave Ed a cellular phone to carry around in case he was ever attacked and had to dial 911 for help. But Ed would have none of it, never carrying the phone, although he also rarely left the house without his brother by his side.

Humphrey then went to Indiatlantic to live with his mother. He tried in vain to get some kind of job, invariably confronting people who remembered seeing his image on TV or reading about him in the newspaper and were simply scared to death of him. The last thing they wanted was to work along side someone who might turn out to be a deranged monster, a sadist, a crazed killer.

When the police caught him having a few drinks with some friends, it really looked like Ed was headed back to prison. Drinking was a violation of the terms of his probation, and he could easily have been locked away for another fourteen months, the remainder of his sentence. Instead, in a judicial decision that would turn out to be extremely helpful, he was asked to donate sixty-two hours of community service at the local branch of the Central Brevard Humane Society.

By his twenty-first birthday, Ed Humphrey had gotten his act together enough finally to pick up the pieces of his young life and to move emotionally beyond the Gainesville tragedy. Humphrey's facial scars were considerably more subtle and unobtrusive after plastic surgery, and an effective diet had left him some fifty pounds lighter. No longer being controlled by mental illness, he once again smiled easily, looked decent, and made sense when he spoke. He even began to date.

In fact, Ed's psychological condition improved so much that he was able to return to school and pursue a degree. While living with his mother in Indiatlantic, he attended Brevard Community College, where he was an outstanding student and a model citizen. At the same time, he continued to work part-time at the humane society; they liked him so much while he served out the terms of his probation that they asked him to stay on in a paid position afterward. His fellow workers there cheered when they learned that Danny Rolling had pleaded guilty.

Of course, strangers on the street still point and whisper when they encounter Ed. And friends who haven't been told his history are shocked when they find out who he is.

Twenty-four-year-old Kelly McClory hadn't a clue. She joined the kennel staff of the humane society several months after Humphrey and knew him only as a good friend and hard worker. They went bowling, played pool, and enjoyed one another's company. Then, thinking that Kelly already knew about his days as a suspect in the Gainesville murders, Humphrey let it slip.

"My mouth dropped open when he told me," Kelly later told a reporter from the *Orlando Sentinel*. "It was like, Oh, wow. That's who you are?! It was kind of funny really that it hadn't clicked before. . . . But it didn't change the way I felt about him," said Kelly. "I am still his friend, and I think what happened to him is wrong. I told him: 'Your real friends will stand by you.' "[55]

Lamenting his treatment at the hands of the media and investigators, Ed Humphrey emphasizes how much he has suffered. He accepts responsibility for having not taken his medication that summer but believes that he was arrested for assaulting his grandmother only so that investigators would have an excuse to keep him behind bars as a suspect in the slayings.

"The main thing is, I'm just like anybody else," he asserts. "I've got feelings, too, and that stuff really hurt me. You know I'll never, ever get over it completely. No way. And I'll never be able to forget it. . . . But that's pretty much how I feel."[56]

Lee Strope never attended Rolling's sentencing trial. Once the killer was in custody and on his way to conviction, he felt that his job was done. In the meantime, he moved on with his wife and children to another city and another horrible homicide.

After transferring to the Clearwater FDLE office in

---

[55]Santich, "Nearly Three Years After the Gainesville Killings."
[56]*Ibid.*

1992, he immediately was assigned to investigate the background of a forty-five-year-old man who was charged with committing a triple murder there. Oba Chandler was accused of having killed a thirty-six-year-old woman and her two teenage daughters who were on vacation from their dairy farm in Ohio. According to the charge, Chandler had lured the unsuspecting family onto his boat for a sunset cruise in Tampa Bay. Once they were far away from shore, it was alleged, Chandler bound his victims' hands and feet, taped their mouths, and then raped them. He then tied them to concrete blocks with rope around their necks and pushed them overboard.

Strope's assignment took him north to Ohio and west to California. He drove the lengths of I-75 and I-10, checking for similar crimes that might have been committed by the same defendant. Although Lee came up empty-handed, Chandler was convicted and sentenced to death for the Tampa Bay drownings.

With the Chandler case completed and Danny Rolling sentenced to die, Agent Strope can now contemplate what he brought away from the Gainesville slaughter, which he helped resolve. Relaxing with a cup of coffee, Strope reflected on the significance of the Gainesville student murder investigation to his own life:

> In spite of its problems, the task force in Gainesville was a mix of some of the most dedicated, devoted, and brightest investigators that Florida has to offer. They are all a tribute to their profession.
>
> But I also learned that there is an unfortunate but inevitable link between politics, egos, and all sorts of nonessential elements in a case of this magnitude. Ideally, cases such as this one could be more quickly solved if it weren't for all the hidden agendas of participants who care much more about their own career paths than about solving this homicide. I have learned that investigators should, at all costs, avoid tunnel vision—

not to focus too quickly on a suspect without conducting a thorough investigation.

In the Gainesville case, if you read the first 600 reports in the file as well as Ed Humphrey's admissions, you would think he was guilty. Many of the task force members refused to think otherwise until the DNA test results came in.

I remember the meeting in which Steve Platt announced that the DNA found at the crime scenes was not that of Ed Humphrey. It was astonishing to think that Ed was not the donor of the semen and, more important, that the real killer was still possibly on the loose. In this case, not only did DNA help put away the guilty party, but it also protected the innocent.

From the time that Danny Rolling went to the grand jury, I felt that he would never be able to go through a trial. His discomfort was obvious. I don't believe for one minute that he pled guilty to spare the feelings of the victims' families. He didn't have the courage to face what he had done because he was a coward. He didn't have any more compassion for the parents than he did for the victims.

We spent many hours during the Gainesville investigation researching and identifying individuals who could have committed the crimes. I was shocked to realize that in the Southeast alone, we found hundreds of individuals who could very well have been the Gainesville killer.

Above all, I learned to appreciate my family more and to enjoy every day, knowing that death and misfortune can come into any of our lives with little or no warning. Before the student murders, I was fairly complacent about safety. But the nights that we spent with windows and doors open are gone. I've learned to be a little more aware of how vulnerable my family is. No one is totally safe.

I have tried hard to put the years I spent on the

Gainesville case behind me. In spite of my supposed rough exterior, I was very much affected by "man's inhumanity to man." I've seen a lot of pain and suffering in my life. I'll probably never be able to erase the memory of my time working the Gainesville murders, but I'll sure as hell continue to try.[57]

---

[57]Personal letter from Lee Strope, January 9, 1995.

Appendix I

A Time Line

August 26, 1990	University of Florida students Sonja Larson, eighteen, and Christina Powell, seventeen, are found murdered in their Williamsburg Village apartment. Larson and Powell had been killed during the early morning of August 24.
August 27, 1990	Santa Fe Community College student Christa Hoyt, eighteen, is found in her apartment at 3533 Southwest Twenty-fourth Street. Hoyt had been murdered on the evening of August 25.
August 28, 1990	University of Florida students Tracy Paules and Manuel Taboada, both twenty-three, are found murdered in the Gatorwood apartment complex. Paules and Taboada were killed early in the morning of August 27.

August 30, 1990   University of Florida freshman Edward Humphrey, eighteen, of Indialantic, is identified as a top suspect. He is also accused of beating his seventy-nine-year-old grandmother, Elna Hlavaty.

September 17, 1990   A DNA comparison of Humphrey's blood with the semen from the crime scenes is negative.

October 10, 1990   Humphrey is convicted of assaulting his grandmother and is sentenced to twenty-two months at the state prison hospital at Chattahoochee.

January 11, 1991   Danny Rolling, a thirty-six-year-old Louisiana drifter in custody since September, becomes the prime suspect when a preliminary test of his blood matches semen found at the crime scenes.

February 8, 1991   Rolling is charged with robbery of a Tampa grocery store in September 1990. He also faces charges in three burglaries committed about the same time in Tampa.

July 10, 1991   A federal grand jury in Tallahassee indicts Rolling on charges of robbing a Gainesville bank on August 27, 1990

September 18, 1991   Rolling is sentenced to life in prison as a habitual offender for an Ocala Winn-Dixie robbery. Humphrey is released from custody after serving thirteen and one half months of his twenty-two month sentence for assaulting his grandmother.

October 18, 1991	Rolling is sentenced to three life terms plus 170 years for robbery, assault, and burglary charges related to the Tampa crimes in September 1990.
November 15, 1991	An Alachua County grand jury indicts Rolling on first-degree murder, burglary, and sexual assault charges in conjunction with slayings of five college students in Gainesville.
May 21, 1992	Rolling is sentenced to life in prison for bank robbery. He is later resentenced to thirty-two years.
June 1, 1992	Rolling attempts to hang himself with a bed sheet in his cell at Florida State Prison.
June 7, 1992	Rolling enters a not guilty plea to charges associated with the Gainesville slayings.
February 15, 1994	On the first day of trial, Rolling changes his plea to guilty. A penalty hearing must still be held before a jury to determine whether Rolling will be sentenced to death or to life in prison.
March 7, 1994	Following jury selection, opening arguments are heard in Rolling's penalty hearing.
March 24, 1994	After four hours of deliberation, the jury unanimously recommends the death penalty.
April 20, 1994	Judge Stan Morris formally sentences Rolling to die in the electric chair.

Appendix II

Rolling's Statement

While at Florida State Prison at Starke, Danny Rolling dictated this letter to fellow inmate Bobby Lewis, describing how he had committed the Gainesville student murders:

> *No. 1 Time 3:00 P.M. Entered the 3rd story apartment of Sonja Larson + Christina Powell through the back door at top of the staires, the door was unlocked. Christina Powell was asleep on the couch in the livingroom—I stood over her for a moment then crept up the staircase into Sonja Larson second floor bedroom. She was stabbed several times. the first blow landed in the area of her upper left chest near the collor bone at the same instant I pressed a double strip of maskin tape over her mouth to muffle her cries. She fought I stabbed her again. She tried to fend the blows with her arms one blow pierced her right upper breast but only nicked it she continued to struggle I stabbed her again I'm not sure how many times are where. Except the last blow was inflicted to the inside of her left thigh. The whole thing lasted maby 3 seconds and she died. Then I crept back*

down staires and stood over Christina Powell she had not heard anything and was still asleep on the couch. I then pressed a double strip of maskin tape over her mouth she put up little resistance. and raped her. then led her to the middle of the living room. made her lay down on her stomach and stabbed her in the back one time through the heart or upper right lung. then I went back upstaires and removed the tape from Ms. Larson. she had on panties printed with little animals on them. I think it was teddy bears I'm not sure but I removed them, spread her legs. I had no sex with her—I only looked. then I descended the staircase pulled the knife from the back of Ms Christina Powell—removed the tape from her mouth and hands—then douced out her vagina with a clenser they had in the kitchen, turned her over on her back and cut off her nipples, and moved to the kitchen where I ate a apple and banana and left taking Ms Powells nipples with me in a sandwich bag which was thrown away next day.

No. II Time about 10:00 P.M. entered the rear double glass sliding door of Ms Christina Hoyt's duplex apartment using a large screwdriver once inside I moved a book case shelf from behind the frount door in the corner in the living room to the bedroom in order to be able to suprize Ms Hoyt upon her arriving home. this did occur at about 11 or 11:30 P.M. I observed her walking across the grass towards her apartment carring a tennis racket and balls she was dressed in shorts, t-shirt, tennis shoes. She entered the apartment. sensed she wasn't alone. to late. I was upon her and a brief struggle began. she was taken to the floor her hands taped behind her back. her mouth taped masking tape was used. then she was led to the bedroom and placed on the water bed. her tennis were removed along with the rest of her clothing except her socks. I think they were left own. I began to play with her and discovered she was on her period. I pulled out the kotex and threw it own the floor. then raped her. then turned her over on her stomach and stabbed her one time in the heart threw the back—she died quickley. A matter of 8 to 10 seconds and it was over. Then I removed the tape from her hands + mouth when I turned her over on her back. split her from pelvis to breast bone—cut off her nipples, placed them own her gutts one above the other. then I left later I discovered I had lot my wallet. I went back to Ms Hoyt's apartment about an hour before sunrise and searched for it. but did not find it. then I cut off Ms Hoyt's head and placed it on the shelf I had moved from the front room I used a book or something to prop up the head so it would sit up right facing the hallway. then I sat up the body of Ms Hoyt's on the edge of her waterbed. propered her elbows on her knees her hands resting on the inside of her thighs as I did so a stream of blood poured from her left brest and pooled at her feet I then left. later that day I telephoned the police station and ask if a wallet had been found with Micheal Kennedy's I.D. in it. it should be own police tape.

No III Time about 3:00 P.M. entered Tracy Paules and Manuel Tabouda's domicile at the Gator Appartments I used the same heavy duty screwdriver to pry my way through the double glass sliding doors. once inside I entered Mr. Taboada's room He was asleep on his back—I stabbed him first in the solar plex upward into the heart he fought I stabbed him 8 or 9 times more. The struggle lasted perhaps 40 to 60 seconds and it was over. Ms Tracy Paules heard the commotion in Mr Taboada's bedroom and open her door to investigate she saw me and slamled the door locking it. I kicked it in immediately and was upon her. I taped her hands behind her back taped her mouth all she had own was a T-shirt which I removed then raped her turned her over on her stomach *and stabbed her once in the back through the heart she died quickley 8 to 10 seconds and it was over. I then removed the tape and dragged her into the hallway between the bathroom + livingroom went to the bathroom. wet a wash cloth and wiped the blood from her face and raped her again. I then douched out her vagina with a cleanser I found in the apartment and left taking a black mussle shirt from Mr Taboada's dresser.*

All 5 murders were committed with same weapon a standard combat issue KA-BAR which I had bought in tallahassee at an army navy store about a month prior. I know where the knife is— after the trial I will take the authorties to it.

I have read that some of the victims in Gainesville slayings had there faces slashed and were sodomized. This is verry odd because I did neather. I did not sodomize or slash there faces if I did not, who else did???

Appendix III

Claudia Rolling's Testimony

Claudia Rolling, Danny's mother, was too ill to come to Gainesville to appear on the witness stand during the trial. The court, however, permitted the defense team to introduce her videotaped deposition, taken on May 8, 1992, as testimony before the judge. Johnny Kearns conducted the direct examination.

MR. KEARNS: Would you please state your name?

A: Claudia Rolling.

Q: In what city do you live?

A: Shreveport, Louisiana.

Q: And do you have a trade or occupation, ma'am?

A: Well, I did. I did work for Shreveport Housing Authority .

Q: And how long did you work for them?

A: Almost four years.

Q: And are you currently employed with them?

A: No, I can't work any longer.

Q: Is there a reason why you cannot work any longer?

A: My illness.

Q: And want is your present physical condition?

A: It's not good. I have cancer of the liver.

Q: What type of treatment are you receiving?

A: Right now radium.

Q: May I ask your educational background, please?

A: High school, some nursing school.

Q: And how long have you lived in Shreveport, Louisiana?

A: All my life.

Q: Are you currently married?

A: Yes.

Q: And to whom are you married?

A: James Harold Rolling.

Q: And how long have you been married?

A: Thirty-seven years.

Q: Do you have any children?

A: Yes.

Q: And can you give me their names and ages please?

A: Danny Harold Rolling, he's born May 26. And Kevin James Rolling, he was born—I can't think—August 15, 1955.

Q: By stipulation, it is agreed that the Danny Harold Rolling named as the accused in Case Number 91-3832 CF-A in Alachua County, Florida, is the same Danny Harold Rolling named by Mrs. Claudia Rolling as her son.

Q: Where were you when you and James Rolling married?

A: We were married in Columbus, Georgia.

Q: How old were you when you were married?

A: I was nineteen.

Q: And do you remember what year you were married?

A: 1953.

Q: How long after your marriage did you become pregnant with your oldest son, Danny Harold?

A: Probably a couple of weeks.

Q: How did your husband feel about the fact of your being pregnant?

A: He wasn't too happy about it.

Q: Did he ever express this dissatisfaction with you?

A: Yes. I had a friend that had just had a baby, and he told me that I did this just because she had one. And also my mother and dad came to visit us and he also told my mother, he said, "This is not my fault, don't blame me."

Q: Where were you living when you got married, when you were pregnant?

A: In Columbus, Georgia. I don't remember the address. It was a little garage apartment.

Q: While you were pregnant with Danny, did your husband ever strike you while you were carrying Danny?

A: Not exactly strike. This is very hard for me to remember. He choked me one time.

Q: How badly did he choke you?

A: Well, I survived. It left some red marks, but they disappeared within the day.

Q: Did you pass out?

A: Almost.

Q: Did he ever physically strike you?

A: Yes. But he—he did not have the habit of using a fist or anything like that. He would more, hold me down. It was almost as if he was afraid I would just disappear or something.

Q: Did he leave any impressions on you when he was holding you down?

A: Yes.

Q: Where would those impressions be?

A: Oh, on my arms or wherever he would have a hold. And the marks were very easy to come by because I bruise easy.

Q: How was your husband's behavior while you were pregnant with Danny? How would you characterize his behavior?

A: I sometimes felt like he was ashamed of me because we never went anywhere. One time, we did go downtown to a movie. But I felt like he was a little bit ashamed of me. That might have been just me, but that's the way I felt.

Q: During the time that you were pregnant with Danny did you ever leave your husband?

A: Yes.

Q: And what were the reasons or grounds for why you left your husband?

A: He was very demanding. He had started sleeping with a knife under his pillow.

Q: Was that the same pillow that you were sleeping on also?

A: Yes.

Q: Was there a reason why he had the knife under his pillow?

A: I never asked. But he he played pool a lot and I was by myself a lot, and my mother and dad came down to visit like I had told you and they left. It just got to the point where I couldn't stand any more, so I came to Shreveport. Danny was born here in Shreveport.

Q: When you left Columbus, Georgia, you were still carrying Danny?

A: Yes.

Q: Prior to Danny's birth, did you see your husband after?

A: Yes. He came back to, he came to Shreveport.

Q: And where was Danny born?

A: He was born in Shreveport, Willis-Knighton Hospital.

Q: And after Danny's birth, where did you live?

A: We stayed in Shreveport .

Q: And who did you live with?

A: We moved to an apartment. A garage apartment, and we didn't live with anybody.

Q: After Danny's birth, when he is a toddler or small infant, did his father ever handle him in an abusive manner or inappropriate manner?

A: James always acted like even though he was a baby, that he should have all the answers and know exactly how to act and he would be very verbally abusive to him. I don't recall that he ever really hit him until Danny was a toddler and he never really crawled. He sat on his little backside and put one leg underneath and pushed with the other leg, and James didn't like that. To him I think it looked crippling or something, and with my husband, everything has to be perfect. So he took his foot. Danny was in the hallway; we had moved to another apartment and it had a long hallway. And he took his foot and just kind of shoved him down the hall.

Q: How far?

A: Well, he was on his little heinie. He just kind of bounced down and it scared him and I just went and got him.

Q: How soon after you had Danny did you become pregnant with your second child?

A: There's about thirteen months' difference in their age. From May 26 to August 15, so that would be about—about three months, something like that. Two or three months.

Q: How did your husband feel about your second pregnancy?

A: He never reacted one way or the other. It was almost as if he was resigned to it. Kevin was sort of an afterthought.

Q: While Danny was still a young child, did you ever leave the Shreveport area?

A: Yes.

Q: And where do you go?

A: We went to Columbus, Georgia, but this is also after Kevin was born.

Q: And why was it that you moved away from Shreveport to go to Columbus, Georgia?

A: Because James and I separated. I don't know if you wanted this long story. We had gone fishing and I had deep burns on my legs, and I was sitting in the living room and he asked me for a cup of coffee. And he had been really demanding all that morning. I had turned the TV on so I wouldn't have to just sit, and he kept turning it. Anyway, to make a long story short, in my mind I said, I'll throw this coffee on you, that will stop you, but I had better sense than to do that. I changed my mind before I even got to the table. I set the coffee on the table, he shoved it aside, and he hit me and busted my lip.

Q: How old were the boys at this time?

A: They was preschool, about three and four. And as soon as he left, I went to my mother's . . . with the boys.

Q: And then how did you get from Shreveport, then to Columbus?

A: We stayed separated for about five or six months. And he kept begging and he kept saying, "I'll change. This won't happen again. We'll buy us a home, we'll do all this good stuff. But let's go to Columbus." And I said, I thought, well maybe in Columbus it will be better. So that's why we moved there.

Q: At any time did you ever consider getting a divorce?

A: Yes. I filed for separation. That was during this time.

Q: Did you ever follow through?

A: I never followed through.

Q: Was there any reason why you would?

A: I always thought that marriage was forever. And I'd always been the kind of person that thinks, I still do, that if there's a problem, there's got to be a solution somewhere, but I just never found it with him.

Q: How long did you stay in Columbus?

A: Four years.

Q: And while you were in Columbus, Georgia, did you ever return to Shreveport?

A: Yes.

Q: And why did you return to Shreveport?

A: I was working for a division of May Situations and we were getting ready for, I may get off track here. We were getting ready for a storewide warehouse sale and I had been working long, long hours, and a store manager finally gave me a half a day off. I went back to sign my leave slip, and as I went down the corridor in the furniture department, the old man that worked in the warehouse just grabbed hold of my hand. He was really old, he was like everybody's daddy, but at that same time, James got off the elevator because I had called him and told him, I lucked out, I got a half a day off so he was coming to get me and he saw Mr. Allen take my hand, and he dragged me to the elevator, just about threw me in the car, took me home, and there was a gun in the house.

Q: Did he physically strike you at this time?

A: It was shoving and saying that he wasn't going to have a red light hanging in his front door; accusing me of having anything to do with that old man was ridiculous. No. He just shoved and pushed; he didn't hit that I can recall, but I went on in the house and he stayed outside, the best I can remember.

Q: How old were the boys at this point?

A: Four and five.

Q: Did you leave Columbus right after this?

A: Yes. Shortly after.

Q: Where did you go after that?

A: I came to Shreveport.

Q: And where did you stay in Shreveport?

A: I stayed with my mother and daddy like a good little girl.

Q: And how long did you stay in Shreveport that time?

A: I can't remember.

Q: Let me ask, where did the boys stay? Did they go with you to Shreveport?

A: They stayed with me always.

Q: What would it be like when your husband would come home for supper? What were the dining arrangements like at your home?

A: Well, I always fed the boys first.

Q: Was there a reason for that?

A: Yes. Because he made them so nervous that they would invariably drop something, knock something over, something to give him an excuse to let down on them.

Q: How would he make them nervous?

A: One thing, we were all at the table and he told the boys, he said, don't worry about it. And I knew what he meant, and I just assumed that the boys did. So I was eating and I happened to look up and their little faces were turning blue. They were holding their breath. I told them, I said, "breathe, you can breathe at the table." Danny didn't hold his utensils to suit his dad. He held his spoon and fork and everything like this. And James would take it out of his hand and say you hold it like a pencil and he had Danny so nervous until he could hardly hold a fork to eat. And he questioned about what went on during the day. And if anything, if they said anything at all that would give him an opening, then he would begin to tell them that, you know, that's bad, you've done a bad thing. And just generally verbal abuse.

Q: How long did you have these dinner arrangements where they would eat first before your husband?

A: When I started feeding them first? Until they left home.

Q: How was discipline administered in the house?

A: Well, I disciplined the boys because it was just me and them. And he would discipline them when he came home.

Q: What form of discipline did he use?

A: Sometimes he whipped them with a belt. I don't ever remember a switch or anything like that. He had a way of he'd make a fist and in the top of their head, he'd do this [indicating] really hard and you could just see them [indicating], you know, try to hold themselves in.

Q: Did he ever strike the boys excessively?

A: Yes.

Q: Can you give an account of that?

A: I don't remember what it was about. But they were in the hallway and Kevin was about fourteen years old, and he whipped him with a belt until Kevin wet his pants. And that's got to be pretty hard for a fourteen year-old boy to wet his pants. For just a whipping.

Q: Mrs. Rolling, we were talking about how discipline was administered in the home. How frequent—how frequently were the boys, particularly Danny, received a whipping?

A: Well, if it was a verbal whipping, it was every day.

Q: How about physical?

A: Often. Probably about twice a week, something like that.

Q: Would this be Danny?

A: Danny and Kevin. Kevin never got a whole lot though.

Q: Who got whipped more?

A: The worst that he ever got was the one in the hallway. Danny always carried the brunt of the whippings. There was a lot of shoving, and he'd get him by the throat and hold him against the wall.

Q: By he who do you mean this would be?

A: James to Danny, to Danny.

Q: Around the throat?

A: Yeah. He'd just hold him against the wall that way. He did that a lot with all of us, just you know, you're held and you can't move.

Q: Did James ever strike you?

A: Yes.

Q: Did he ever strike you in front of the boys?

A: I'm sure they saw it. Our house is very small. We still live in the same house, and four people couldn't live in a house and never see anything. So I'm sure, well, I know that they saw him push me down a lot.

Q: How did the boys react to this type of?

A: As they got older, they did try to help me. But you've got to understand they were terrified of their dad. They were terrified of him. But they used to beg me to leave. And stay, stay, don't leave and come back.

Q: How did you manage to cope with all of this?

A: To be perfectly honest with you, I don't know. I think I did a lot of hiding. It was sort of like I would say, don't look and it's not real or go away and it will stop and disappear, just like an ostrich that puts its head in the sand.

Q: Did your family members visit you often at your home?

A: Well, as often as they could. There was always some member of my family that was not allowed in the house.

Q: Who would not allow them in the house?

A: Oh. James.

Q: How about friends? Did you have close friends?

A: Not like couples. No. I had friends. And he had

friends on the—on the police department I'm pretty sure. But we did not have a couple, like you go eat and do things with, we didn't have that.

Q: You just mentioned police force. Where was your husband employed?

A: Shreveport Police Department.

Q: Do you know if Danny ever had to repeat a grade?

A: Yes.

Q: What grade did he have to repeat?

A: The third grade.

Q: The third grade. What was the reason for repeating the third grade?

A: Danny was sick almost that whole year. I wish I had those pictures to show you. He was like a skeleton. He had gotten so in this and it was his tonsils. And Dr. Strain said we can't take them out until we build him up and he was out, oh, a lot that year. And he had a very special teacher, Miss Wisham and she would come by the house in the mornings and leave his work and then pick them up, so that he wouldn't miss out on so much, but he missed out on too much and she called me in for a consultation. And she said we could pass Danny on the grades he has, but it would not be good for him because he really hasn't accomplished that much that year. So she suggested holding him back, and we did.

Q: Did she ever suggest any counseling for Danny?

A: Uh-huh.

Q: What was the basis for her suggesting counseling for him?

A: Because of Danny's personality and the talents that he had and his difficulty in just regular school, things like math, reading, that kind of thing. She suggested that we get counseling for him and also channel his talents where they needed to be so that when he was grown, he could have some sort of livelihood.

Q: Was anything ever mentioned about any type of nervous condition?

A: Miss Wisham did mention that he was extremely nervous, but I already knew that.

Q: How did your husband react to Danny staying back in the third grade?

A: Just as he suspected, this no-account kid of his failed again.

Q: Did he ever express that to Danny?

A: Yeah. I don't remember the exact words, but what it came out was you failed and you got to do the third grade again. You'll be in the same grade with your baby brother; you're a failure. You didn't study, you didn't do your work, you know, that kind of thing.

Q: While Danny was in his preteen years, did his father ever give him any praise or encouragement?

A: The kind of praise that James gave was the boys would do something, and this, this was from the time they were able to talk. They'd do some little special project and bring it to him, wanting to get this praise from this man that they still just loved to death, and he would look at it whatever it was and he'd say, well, it's OK, but . . . and then he'd list all the negatives. You should have done this, you didn't do this right, you left that out and it should have been put in, it's messy. So the only praise they got was, it's all right, but. . . .

Q: You have Danny as your older son and Kevin as the younger son?

A: Yeah.

Q: Did they react differently to their father?

A: Yes.

Q: In what ways?

A: It almost seemed as if Danny did everything to draw attention to himself, and I was trying to go over in my mind last night and remember what they were really like as little boys, because I worked a lot and that means you miss a lot. But he would do things to draw attention to himself in front of his dad. It was almost as if you won't hug me, so hit me. Something there, recognize me in some way. Kevin didn't. Kevin learned early stay out of his way. So he would—he would go somewhere where his daddy wasn't.

Q: Did the children ever have bouts with nightmares or episodes of nightmares when they were small?

A: Yeah.

Q: How about Danny?

A: Uh-huh.

Q: Approximately when would the nightmares have started with Danny?

A: I don't know. Probably three, four, something like that.

Q: How long were these nightmares?

A: I think he still has them. He would dream about monsters, and that was when he was a little kid. Then he would dream about terrible things happening.

Q: How frequently would these occur?

A: Pretty often. About probably once or twice a week, something like that.

Q: Did you ever consider taking him to see a psychologist or psychiatrist?

A: Yes. Everything I ever did in our marriage I got permission. And when I would ask James, he'd say no, there's nothing wrong with him, he's just mean.

Q: Who was responsible for taking care of the lawns at your house?

A: Well, they were responsible along with their dad, and it was an all-day project. About the only thing they were allowed to stop for would be a drink of water.

Q: What was their job?

A: All of it, but their biggest job was edging.

Q: What did they use to edge?

A: A butcher knife.

Q: Was there anything unusual that would have occurred or that you can recall an incident?

A: Yes. They had worked all day in the yard. I had slipped them, well, I won't say slipped them, but I had taken them maybe a cookie. I would make Koolaid and stuff like that. All day in the yard. July and August is hard on a grown person, let alone the two kids. Well, he—he decided to shut it off and he was picking up these tools and he started yelling. I already had the boys in the house, and I was going to feed them. He came simpering in, wanting to know what they'd done with his pliers. And they said nothing. "Dad, we haven't had them." So he told me what did I do with them. I said, "I haven't been out there. Haven't bothered your pliers." So he got flashlights and we went in the yard. And we covered every inch of the yard, looking for a pair of pliers, and I was behind James and I saw something move in his back pocket. I said, "James, stand still a minute." It was his pliers that had hung up on a cord inside the pocket. They were just hanging there.

Q: Where did Danny go to high school?

A: Woodlawn.

Q: When he was in high school, did he ever have any afterschool jobs?

A: Uh-huh. One time.

Q: And where was that at?

A: It was at the Dairy Queen, right up the street from us.

Q: How long did he have a job for?

A: He only had the job about a week.

Q: Why did he only have the job for about a week?

A: Because his daddy made him quit.

Q: How did he make him quit the job?

A: He told him, "Tell them you're done." You can't work anymore.

Q: How did Danny react to that?

A: Very bad. He wanted the job so bad. And he just busted out of the house into the backyard. I think that's the way it happened. Usually when these things occurred, I just got so completely nervous it's hard for me to remember exactly how it happened, but he busted out of the house and went in the backyard. And James went behind him. Because you don't turn from James like that. You stay and you listen. Do whatever he has to say until he releases you and says, "OK, I'm done." And they had a fight in the backyard.

Q: What do you mean by fight?

A: I mean they had a fight. Danny never raised his hand to his daddy in his whole life that I can remember. He may have after he came home one time, but—I heard him in the backyard. And you could hear the blows, and it was James hitting Danny. And he had him against a utility room, a house that we have in the backyard, it was an old one we had. And he drew back to hit Danny and Danny moved and James's hand went through the plate glass. And I don't know if Danny just ran in the house or if James made him come in, but he was covered in blood.

Q: Who was?

A: Danny. He was just literally—his clothes, everything. It was in his hair, everywhere. And I said, "Danny, my God." He said, "It's OK, Mom. It's OK." I said, "Go in and clean up." And James came in after that and he was bleeding from his hand. He had cut it pretty bad. And he said I'm going to have to have stitches. I kept waiting for Danny to come out of the bathroom because I heard the water running and I waited a pretty good while and James had already left. I think he went to get stitches in his hand. And I still heard the water running in the bathroom, so I knocked on the door and I didn't get any answer. And I opened it. And Danny wasn't there. The bathroom window was open. And with one of my lipsticks on the mirror he had written, "I tried, I just can't make it." And there was a drive-in movie not too far from the house that was within walking distance. He had taken a razor blade with him, and he sat there all night and tried to take his life, but he just couldn't do it.

Q: Did he tell you this?

A: Uh-huh.

Q: Did he ever tell you at any other time about any attempts at trying to take his life, about thinking to take his life when he was a child?

A: Yeah. He—he was always trying to get rid of that person that his daddy made him believe he was. He had no self-esteem. No self-worth. I could say, "Danny, I love you," and he'd look at me and say, "You love me, Mom?" And I'd say, "Of course I love you." And it was like, he would say, "Why? What is there here for anybody to love?" And he still does that.

Q: Did you hug a lot in your family?

A: Yeah. Only when James was gone, when the boys grown up a good size, he told me that women don't hug their children when they get up that big, and you don't kiss them. Or you know anything like that, that it looks bad. And he never liked for me to hug my dad. So he made me feel very guilty about it, so I just went and left. And then we hugged up a storm.

Q: You made mention of the fact of Danny bringing home a bad grade. What was it like at the house during report card day?

A: It was a day that we dreaded for a whole month.

Q: What would happen?

A: Because they were going to get a whipping if there was anything on that report card below a C. They were going to get a whipping. And he would go over every grade, every grade.

Q: Did Danny have grades that were satisfactory to his father?

A: No. Hardly ever. Hardly ever, because, after the third grade, Danny just kind of went down, he was really good in school. Up till then he made straight A's. But after being held back in the third grade, he just sort of gave up.

Q: So you're implying that he would get a beating during report card day?

A: Every report card day. Danny always had a D or a F on his report card after the third grade. And he just sort of took it like, I'm going to get it, so get it over with.

Q: At any time when Danny was a teenager did his father actually put him out of the house?

A: Yes.

Q: And what happened then?

A: We were going to church, and Danny had on blue jeans, and I really didn't want him to wear blue jeans to church so I was—I was talking to him and said "Son, you've got dress pants. Go get your dress pants on." And he really didn't want to wear them. I thought well, you know, think Lord can see him in blue jeans just like a pair of dress pants. I said, "OK, we'll go. Just like you are." And when we got back, all of his clothes had been thrown out into the carport.

Q: Who put them there?

A: His dad. And he was pushed out, too. My mother and dad didn't live too far from us, and I told him, I said, "Go there. And I'll come pick you up." My sister was with me. Artie Mae. And her daughter-in-law lived in an apartment complex, and she was in pretty good with the manager there, so she helped me get an apartment and I moved out.

Q: Is this another time that you separated from James?

A: Yeah.

Q: And how long were you gone then?

A: About two months, I think. Kevin—was going into of the navy, and I was depending a whole lot on the boys helping me survive in this apartment. I worked and I made a pretty good salary, but I knew that I'd have to get things like insurance and that kind of thing. Well, I couldn't tell Kevin, no, you can't go in the navy. I just couldn't do that. So knowing that he was going to do that and Danny knew that he was going to do that, we just couldn't handle it, so I moved back.

Q: You've talked about being accosted by your husband and the boys also being struck. Did your husband ever push any weapons in front of you or exhibit any weapons in front of you or threaten you?

A: Yes, uh-huh. I didn't—didn't really take it as a threat at the time. I do now. Because he—he did this and it was like in a joking manner. And he'd take the gun and just wave it and say, "I'm going to get you," that kind of thing. Or the knife. He had a way of—he had a knife that he could flip the blade out. Now it wasn't one of those things where it's a little button, but he somehow could flip that knife out with just one hand and he'd slide the knife down so that all of it, just the tip end of it, would show, and he'd say, "I can cut somebody open like that." Or something to that degree. And he did that one night. I really never took him serious. I probably should have. James did that one time in front of a friend of mine. And I just ignored it like I usually do, and when he walked out of the kitchen, she was just practically in shock. She said, "I can't believe that you just sit there and let him do that." But it was part of what he was.

Q: Now, you said that your husband was a police officer. Did he have a pair of handcuffs?

A: Yeah.

Q: Did he ever handcuff Danny at any time?

A: Yes.

Q: What happened in the incident with the handcuffing of Danny?

A: There was an old man that lived down Mansfield Road. He took up a lot of time with kids and he took up especially a lot of time with Danny, and one afternoon Danny had walked down Mansfield Road. The old man gave Danny a beer and Danny was fourteen, fifteen, something like that. And he drank it. Made him feel like a big grown man, I'm sure. Well, he came home, and the minute he walked in the door you could smell the beer, and his daddy jumped him before he could get even through the living room. And he shoved and pushed and fought all the way to the bedroom and got Danny hemmed up between the bunk beds they slept on. And it was shoving and pushing and that kind of thing, and he finally got a really good grip on Danny and he pulled him out and he pulled him all the way to the kitchen and he threw him down on the kitchen chair pretty much like the one you're sitting in, and he handcuffed him to it and he called the police.

Q: What happened then?

A: He put him in juvenile hall.

Q: How long did he stay there?

A: About three weeks, I guess, two or three weeks—something like that.

Q: Did you ever go see him in there?

A: James wouldn't let me.

Q: Did anyone go see him?

A: Only James.

Q: Did Danny ever tell you how he felt about that?

A: He felt betrayed. What he did certainly didn't require that kind of treatment. I told James, I said, "You know, if I was you, I would make him go to bed, and I would have told him we'll talk about this tomorrow." I mean, I didn't feel like he did anything that deserved being handcuffed and put in juvenile hall. He had committed no crime. But Danny felt that I betrayed him too because I didn't go see him.

Q: Did Danny ever graduate from high school?

A: He did. But not from the school itself. He graduated in the service.

Q: When did he leave school?

A: When he was seventeen. No. He was sixteen going on seventeen. If I remember right, it was in his senior— I think it was in his senior year.

Q: Do you remember what branch of the service he went in?

A: Yeah. He went in the air force.

Q: You say he was seventeen?

A: Seventeen.

Q: So this was probably around 1971?

A: Uh-huh.

Q: And how long did he stay in the service for?

A: It wasn't a year. He had made rank, and something happened and they took the rank away from him. But it was less than a year.

Q: Did you ever talk to any of the military people about him?

A: Yes. His commanding officer called, and I talked to him and he said that Danny was not mature and that there was no way in this world that he could handle military life. Any military life. He just didn't have the nervous system for it or the maturity.

Q: And then he was discharged from the military?

A: Yes.

Q: Do you know what type of discharge it was?

A: It was a general discharge with honorable conditions.

Q: How old was he when he got out of the military?

A: Almost nineteen. See, when he went in at seventeen, he was working on being eighteen, so it had to be almost nineteen because he got married. Well, that's the best I can do.

Q: Since you brought up marriage, did Danny ever get married?

A: Yes.

Q: And how was he when he did get married?

A: Okay. He was nineteen.

Q: And to whom did he get married?

A: O'Mather Halko.

Q: And do you know how Danny met O'Mather?

A: Yeah. He met her in church.

Q: Was Danny an active member of the church at that time?

A: Yes, he was.

Q: Which church would that have been?

A: United Pentecost church.

Q: And how long had he belonged to the church?

A: Just a matter of weeks really there. Was a man that picked him up. He was walking along the street, and there was a man that picked him up and took him to church with him, and this man told me later that he just had a feeling that Danny needed somebody and he happened to be there, so I prayed all night long and Danny became a member of the church.

Q: And that's the same church that he met O'Mather?

A: Uh-huh.

Q: Did Danny participate in church activity?

A: Yes. He drove the church bus for a while, you know, that goes and picks up those that are handicapped and what have you. I know he played the Easter Bunny one year, and he wanted to be in the choir.

Q: Did he sing?

A: He sang beautifully. And he did sing in the choir for a short spell, but what he actually wanted to do was to write. Music for the church and the choir director told him that his music had no value. And that—that really upset him.

Q: Did any of the church people say he had any special gifts or talents?

A: Yeah. They all knew that he could write music and sing and he was almost an artist. He can draw anything, and I'm sure the members were aware of that but I think what they really admired most in Danny was his kindness to the older people in the church and the little children. He liked to help them.

Q: Do you know what the expression to speak in tongues means?

A: Yes. He did that.

Q: What do you mean he did that?

A: I think it was the very night that he was saved he spoke and sang in tongues.

Q: Who told you that?

A: He did. And the minister to the church.

Q: How long were Danny and O'Mather married?

A: About two years.

Q: Did they have any children?

A: They had Kiley, a little girl.

Q: How did Danny feel about the child?

A: He worshiped her.

Q: There was a separation or a divorce?

A: It was about two years, yeah, they divorced.

Q: How did Danny take the divorce?

A: He took it very hard. The sheriff came to our door, and he had separation papers, and somehow we all three wound up at the door to let this person in. He tried to hand Danny the papers, and Danny got a glance at what they were, and he started screaming and running around and around the house. I don't know how many times he ran around the house. And he would say, "No, no, no, she's my wife. This can't happen. We can fix it. No, no, no." We finally caught him and got him calmed down. And his daddy told him, he said, "You have to take the papers. And you have to sign them." So he did.

Q: During the time that they were married, was there any confrontation between Danny and his father that might have occurred in front of O'Mather?

A: Yes.

Q: What would that have been?

A: Their marriage got real shaky, and they were having trouble all the time. And Danny worked for the water department. And O'Mather called our house one day and she said, "You've got to come over because Danny won't get up and go to work." When things got bad, Danny would go to marijuana. And he had been smoking marijuana, and we went to the house and James didn't even stop. He went straight to the bedroom where Danny was, he jumped right on and straddled him, and he grabbed his hair and held his head back and put a knife to his throat.

Q: How was Danny dressed?

A: He was nude.

Q: Did Danny ever say anything bad about O'Mather even after the divorce?

A: Never. Never to this day. He'll tell you that she's nothing but a good woman and a good mother. Because he loves her still.

Q: At any time up to this point, did you ever think that Danny might benefit from seeing a psychiatrist or a psychologist?

A: I felt like that for a long time.

Q: Did anyone in the family ever take him to a psychiatrist up to this point?

A: Oh. A friend took him to Shreveport Health Center,

and he did have one session with one of the ladies there.

Q: Did he ever go back?

A: No.

Q: Was he depressed after the divorce?

A: Very.

Q: How did he show it?

A: That's kind of hard to say because Danny had moods, but he would get very quiet, he could get angry if things didn't seem to go exactly like he wanted it. He'd go off by himself. He slept a lot. Right after that time when O'Mather left. I had forgotten about that. But it was like, well, that was an escape. He could be asleep and everything was OK.

Q: After the marriage did he ever leave Shreveport?

A: Yes.

Q: Do you remember how he came to leave Shreveport?

A: Well, he had moved in with us, and like always with him, his dad struck a sour note from day one and I think it just built up until he couldn't stand it any more, so he left early one morning before I got up.

Q: When is the next time you heard from him?

A: The next time I hear is he's in jail.

Q: Where was he?

A: Columbus, Georgia.

Q: And what was he charged with there?

A: Armed robbery.

Q: Did you ever go out to see him when he was in Georgia?

A: Yes.

Q: What did he look like when you saw him?

A: He looked like somebody that had become a little boy. I had gotten a letter from Danny, and I didn't know if James was going to let me go see him or not. He made me wait like a week before he said, "Let's go." But at the time I got a letter from Danny and it said, "Dear Mommy and Daddy." And there was two pages of I love you. That's all. Just I love you.

Q: Did you actually physically see him during this time?

A: Yes.

Q: How did he act or behave when you saw him?

A: Well, when we first went to the jail, the jailor made me talk to Danny through a little bitty hole. And you'd have to put your ear and listen and then put your mouth and talk and let him listen and it just—I couldn't stand that, so Danny's lawyer got a room, one of the interrogation rooms I imagine, and he had them bring Danny in. Danny was wearing just shorts. No shoes, nothing. And he come in the room like a little kid. He went straight past me, which kind of shocked me to begin with, he went straight to his dad, and he begged him, he said, "Say you love me. Tell me you love me. Please tell me you love me." And his lawyer—I looked over and his lawyer had tears coming down. And his daddy was just looking at him, and he said, "Please tell me you love me." And he finally said, "I love you." So, sort of offhanded, like I'll say it and that will shut you up. I went out to Danny and took him in my arms to kind of let him know that someone did love him.

Q: Did he ever tell you why he became involved in this robbery?

A: He thought that somebody would blow him away. It was another way of getting rid of that no-account Danny. I had money laying around the house all the time. He never took a penny. He or Kevin, neither one. Was just you don't touch that. They never stole anything that I know of. But to Danny, I knew this and I'm not a good shot or anything like that. And by the way, the gun was empty that he had. He had his daddy's .38, and it was empty there. Was no bullets in it. Of course the person at the convenience store didn't know that. But from what I understand, he just went outside and kind of waited.

Q: OK. I believe he gets out of prison around 1982?

A: Something like that. I can't remember those dates at all.

Q: Did he come home after he was released from the prison?

A: Yes.

Q: OK. And he stayed here in Shreveport?

A: Yes. He stayed with us.

Q: Was there any talk about taking him to community mental health?

A: I don't think so. I can't remember. I talked to him quite a bit about it all the time. But he only said, "Mom, there's nothing wrong with me." So I just let it go.

Q: How was Danny—how was Danny's work history when he came back from prison?

A: His work history was always really broken up. He couldn't hold a job for very long.

Q: Did he ever leave Shreveport again?

A: Yes.

Q: And where did he go, do you know?

A: Mississippi.

Q: And what happened in Mississippi to him?

A: The same thing. We got that call. Armed robbery.

Q: Did you go to see him in Mississippi?

A: Uh-huh.

Q: How did he look in Mississippi?

A: He had gotten very thin and he didn't look good at all, but that was due to stress, and everything he was going through right then, I'm sure, because when Danny gets under a lot of stress, it's hard for him to eat. But we visited him more than once in Mississippi, and the second time we went he looked so much better; he had gained a lot of weight. It seemed that he was doing real good in that area. He had learned to cope with whatever went on.

Q: I believe he comes back from Mississippi in 1988?

A: Something like that, yeah.

Q: Did he try to find work when he came back?

A: Uh-huh.

Q: How-how much success did he have with work then?

A: He didn't have a whole lot of success. He wrote a song, and the title of the song is "I Need a Job." And he had been trying to get a job at a Bush distributing company that's up the street from us—I think it's Bush, one of, one of those companies—as a forklift operator. And he was there almost every day talking to them, pleading with them, then he got real discouraged because they would show a lot of interest, but they, you know, they didn't call him back. We was sitting out in the front yard one night and he wrote a song called "I Need a Job." And I do wish you could hear it because it's a darling song and he said, "You know what I'm going to do, Mom?" I said, "What?" He said, "I'm going to take my guitar and when they open in the morning, I'm going to walk up and down in front of that and I'm going to sing my song." And I said, "You do that, Danny, then maybe they'll hire you."

Q: Did he seem depressed about not being able to get a job?

A: Yes. He was very depressed. And he felt, well, he even told me, he said, "I'm not worth anything. I can't even get a job."

Q: How did he act around the house?

A: Well, it was just Danny and I, and he was fine. When his dad was there he didn't stay around long. He did get a job, not now, we're talking about the very last time he came home aren't we?

Q: Yes, ma'am.

A: OK. He did get a job. I guess y'all have to excuse me. I get confused, but my nephew had a car. And he told Danny that he could have a car for five hundred dollars, and Danny saved his money and bought the car so he did have transportation then, and he had worked at Pancho's and Western Sizzler. I can't remember where else. But he worked long enough to buy him a car and get insurance.

Q: Do you know a person named Bunnie Mills?

A: Yes.

Q: Who is Bunnie Mills?

A: She's a lady that's into country-western music. My husband knew her. And he told Danny, he said, "This lady might be able to help you with your music." Well that just floored Danny that his daddy would try to help him do anything in the world so he was just elated and said, well, "When can we meet her?" James said any time. I said, "well, I'd like the meet her too." So we invited her over for Sunday dinner, and she came and she just took to Danny immediately. And she listened to some of his music, and she said that it was very good and it was really worth trying to promote. And she just became a real good family friend.

Q: Do you know whether or not Bunnie at any time ever tried to take Danny to see a psychiatrist or psychologist?

A: She's the one that took him the time he went. Uh-huh. And she did try to get him back to go again. She tried real hard. She did get him to LSU I think. LSU Medical Center.

Q: Mrs. Rolling, at any time, to your knowledge, did Danny's father ever threaten him with a weapon?

A: Well, what we did when I told you about the knife, and then he had used a gun.

Q: Approximately how many times?

A: I have no idea. I worked. My neighbor told me, well, my neighbor one time, in particular, Danny ran to her house, and she came across the street and talked James out of the gun.

Q: Does your husband have a gun or did he have a gun in the house?

A: Yeah. But he still had his .38, but he has an—it's a little—it's a .32. Is there such a thing as a .32? I think that's what it is. He has a shotgun. I think he has another gun, but I'm not sure.

Q: When was the last time that you saw Danny in your house?

A: The night of the shooting.

Q: Why don't you explain that then, OK?

A: OK. I've told it so many times. I came home from work, and the work that I was doing was teaching the elderly and the handicapped how to do things like that there. Were some items I needed so I told James I was going to Cloth World which is up the street from us, I don't know if Danny was in the house at that time or not. He might have been in the back, but I went to Cloth

World and I didn't realize it was as late as it was, and there was a young black boy cleaning up. I was sifting through patterns and he was cleaning that area, so I asked him what time it was, and he said it was, something like five or ten minutes until nine o'clock, so I left.

And when I got home, well, I put all my stuff on the table, and I think I was checking it out or something, I can't remember, but Danny came through the kitchen, and we have a utility room that's attached to a kitchen and I have a bench there, and Danny is so tall—he's six feet four inches—he can't just stoop over like you or I could, and tied his shoe so he always put his foot on the bench and either buckled or tied it.

James came in the kitchen and he started yelling at him. He said "I told you, don't put your foot on that bench." And just before that, I said, "Danny, are you going out again?" And he turned to me, he said "Are you going to bitch at me too?" And I said, "No, I'm not." And that was before the shooting thing. But I knew something really bad had gone on in that house earlier, I could feel it. Danny's never told me and neither has James. They had had a real hard argument because I could tell. Danny put his foot back on the bench, and he looked at his dad, and he said, "I got my foot on the bench, old man. What are you going to do about it?" And he said, "I'll tell you what I'm going to do about it." So James went to the back of the house, and Danny just nonchalantly tied his shoes. He wasn't expecting anything and he was going out the door, and James ran through the kitchen and he had a gun. And he ran out the door, and I heard five shots. Was it five? Five shots, I think. Three shots. There was three inside, five outside. And I just—I heard those three shots and I thought, All right, he's dead.

Q: Who did you think was dead?

A: Danny. He had no gun. And James ran out with a gun, so it had to be Danny. And a neighbor saw this.

And James came back in the house, and he said, "Call the police." I said, "Why? You've killed him. Why call the police?" And about that time Danny busted in the back door because James had locked the door when he came in, and I thought that was sort of strange, but he locked the door when he came in and Danny busted the door in. And he came in in a crouch and with God as my witness I did not see a gun in his hand. I'm not saying he didn't have one, but I didn't see it. He crouched down at the table and James was in front of our refrigerator and waving this gun around; and Danny said "You want to shoot somebody, you want to kill somebody, kill me, but don't hurt my mom." Because when James chased Danny out of the house and fired those three shots, I heard him say, "I'll just get rid of all of you." That's probably not verbatim, but it's as close as I can remember.

So I believe that's why Danny came back. He thought that James was going to kill me. Well, I heard after Danny crouched and said that, James turned like this [indicating], and I covered my eyes and I heard a shot. And I thought, OK. Now he's dead. And then I heard another shot and I said, "I better get out of here." So I went through the living room down the hallway to our bedroom. And I bolted myself in the bedroom and I went to a window. I had to pull the table away from this window and I unlocked the window and I raised it or started to raise it and I listened and it was totally quiet. The only thing I could smell was this smoke. But I couldn't hear a sound anywhere. And I said, "OK, they're both dead. You've got to go check it out."

So I undid the door, and I went down the hallway and I went in the kitchen, and the way James was lying, I couldn't see him. So I thought, well, they went outside then or something. So I went around the table and that's when I saw James because he was lying halfway in the kitchen and halfway in the utility room, and he was conscious and he had a bullet in his head. And he told me, he said, "Call the police."

Q: And did you call the police?

A: Yeah, I did. There was blood on the telephone. That was kind of hard for me to figure out how blood got on that phone and he's down there, but I figured it out later. He called work before he ever fell where he fell. I know that's what he did. And he told that he was having problems at home and couldn't come to work. And it had to be that because I hadn't touched anything. I didn't have any blood on me.

Q: How was Danny acting, say, approximately a month or two weeks before this incident?

A: He was trying to get everything together to move out of the house. Kevin, my younger son, was going to buy a house, and he was doing it strictly to get Danny out of our house. Because he felt like I did, something terrible was going to happen. They were; I knew it; I felt it. And James—James would say things like "He's getting out of here one way or the other. I'd as soon shoot him as look at him." He had been saying things like that for two months.

And not only had I heard this, but Kevin had heard it, and the few neighbors that came over had heard him say it. My sister heard him say it.

Q: How did Danny treat you?

A: First and foremost, I'm his mother, and in Danny's eyes, I'm the greatest lady that ever lived, capital L. He always tried to protect me from anything that he thought was not for a lady's ears. He tried to protect me from hurt. Because he knew I was always going to be there for him. But Kevin was the same way. They both treated me the same way. And still do.

Q: How would you describe Danny's level of maturity?

A: I really don't think that Danny ever got much past fifteen. I know that right now he's allowed to call me, and his conversation is more mature, but every once in a while he'll revert back to that little fifteen-year-old that I know so well. But I don't think he ever really got much older than that.

Q: In the course of your marriage, Mrs. Rolling, approximately how many times did you and your husband separate?

A: Oh, mercy. I used to have a joke about that. People would ask us how long we'd been married and I'd say off and on this many years. Fifteen, twenty. I don't really know. But a lot.

Q: OK. Mrs. Rolling, have you ever heard the term *multiple personality?*

A: Yes.

Q: Do you remember discussing that type of situation with law enforcement before?

A: Yes, I do remember.

Q: Did you ever suspect that Danny had some problems?

A: Yeah, I did. We were at the kitchen table. Danny and I and Kevin, we spent a lot of time together because it was so likely it was just the three of us, that this was the last time that Danny came home. We were talking, and I can't remember what we was talking about, I can't remember what was said that might have triggered this but I looked up, and Danny looked totally different to me. His whole manner was different, it was hard, and his voice took on a voice that I didn't really recognize. It was coarse and deep, and Danny has a very to, be a man and to be as large as Danny is, he has a very light sound to his voice. And it didn't last very long. I just was sort of shocked. I was trying to figure this out. He just kind of flipped back, and he—his face even softened, and his voice went back like it should. And I said, "Danny. What? What happened?" And he didn't know exactly what happened. I think he surmised what happened. And he told me that he had a person and he had even had a name, but I can't remember the name.

Q: Did he say where this person was?

A: It was part of him. And I thought he was kidding me at first. I said, "Ah, Danny." He said, "No, Mom." He said, "I do," and I wish I could remember the name, but I can't remember the name. It was a horrible name. It was not something that I'd want to ever remember, I guess.

Q: Is there a history of mental illness or mental disorder in the family?

A: Yes.

Q: Can you please explain that?

A: I'll have to go back only as far as I know because the family really never wanted me to know anything about their past history or anything: My husband's granddad killed his grandmother. He cut her throat from ear to ear. Well, when my husband was a little boy, he saw that. She was sitting at the table and she was soaking her feet in a big pan of water, and James remembers looking down in that, what and it being all bloody that. Was the first incident. The family tried to say that he'd been drugged. I was told by a family member that he was not drugged, that he had always done strange things. He has an uncle who laid down on the couch, put a shotgun in his mouth and pulled the trigger and blew his head off. He had another uncle that died in a mental institute. He has a brother that lives in California that is the only way he functions is on medication.

Q: During the time that you were married, did you socialize much with other couples or other people?

A: We had no friends that we socialized with.

Q: Did James Harold ever bring other police officers and their [wives] to your house?

A: One couple, Shelton and his wife, they came to our house once, and we went to their house once, but that was all.

Q: When would that have been?

A: Oh, years ago, years and years ago. Danny was just a baby.

Q: Did you ever attend any social functions with the police department or picnics?

A: I never knew they had them. He kept me completely separate.

MR. KEARNS: With that I don't think I have any more questions. Thank you very much, Mrs. Rolling.

Note: A few months after the trial, Claudia Rolling died of cancer.